Peter G. Cooksley ARHistS was a training officer in the RAF/ROC, and is the author of over twenty books on aviation including Sutton Publishing's *VCs of the First World War: The Air VCs*. He was one-time vice-president of Cross & Cockade Society International – the Society of First World War Aviation Historians and is an associate member of the Royal Historical Society. Peter lives in Surrey.

ROYAL FLYING CORPS HANDBOOK

1914–1918

PETER G. COOKSLEY

SUTTON PUBLISHING LIMITED

First published in the United Kingdom in 2000 by
Sutton Publishing Limited, an imprint of NPI Media Group Limited
Cirencester Road · Chalford · Stroud · Gloucestershire · GL6 8PE

This paperback edition first published in 2007

British Library Cataloguing in Publication Data
A catalogue record for this book is available from the British Library.

ISBN 978-0-7509-4772-5

Typeset in 10/13 pt Sabon.
Typesetting and origination by
Sutton Publishing.
Printed in England.

CONTENTS

'They are the knighthood of this war, without fear and without reproach: they recall the legendary days of chivalry, not merely by the daring of their exploits but by the nobility of their spirit.'

David Lloyd George

ACKNOWLEDGEMENTS

For the benefit of opinions, the advantage of recollections, the loan of photographs, the discovery of sources and the courtesy of encouragement in the preparation of this book, the author wishes to state his indebtedness to the following persons: Mrs I.W. Austin, D. Barton, Keith Chambers, Dr June Cunbrae-Stewart, Peter Cooper AMRAeS, T.F. Deery, Norman Gillam, Peter Lamb, G.S. Leslie, R.G. Moulton, Bruce Robertson, John Selby CEng, MIEE, Dr Robert Suchett-Kaye, Kenneth Slocombe, Trevor Smale and (bearing in mind the words of an Imperial War Museum spokesman in 1998: 'The number of First World War veterans who are still alive is now very small') special gratitude is due to C. Webster (formerly AM 275947) who lent photographs from his album as well as putting his recollections at my disposal, as did the pair – one from each service! – who did likewise but wished to remain anonymous. A number of those who gave assistance are members of Cross & Cockade International – the Society of First World War aero-historians.

INTRODUCTION

In 1917 Lord Hugh Cecil wrote about the RFC: 'The Flying Corps is the greatest of the novelties of the war. And it appeals to people in several ways. Its military importance is great and increasing; it unites in a singular degree the interest of a sport with the deeper and stronger interest of war; the gallantry of its flying officers touches sympathy and thrills imagination; and the development of its mechanical and scientific apparatus inspires wonder and almost astounds belief.'

It is now over ninety years since the short-lived Royal Flying Corps ceased to exist, but it was forged and tempered in the holocaust of the greatest conflict mankind had witnessed up to that time – the First World War. In its brief existence it laid the firm foundations on which the Royal Air Force was built – ready to claim hard-won victory in the Battle of Britain only a little over twenty years later. Today, the admiration expressed by Lord Cecil in 1917 is still commanded by the pilots of the RFC's successor, the RAF.

It has been said that if an author steals from a single book, he is guilty of plagiarism, but if from many works, he has conducted research. Many men, most of them now dead, have contributed much to this volume, but the written record is not always enough: it must be studied, weighed and assessed in the light of knowledge gained by interview and consultation with survivors of the period and an understanding of the morals, attitudes and social structure that coloured their upbringing. For most people the famous battles of history are little more than dates and dry facts on a page, and the recollections of members of the RFC and RNAS would doubtless have soon faded too and been lost for ever were it not for organisations such as Cross & Cockade International and Over the Front which have kept the memories green. Their work, and that of the various specialised museums, allows modern students of the period to recapture the atmosphere and spirit of the early flying services. These gallant airmen went aloft armed with a service rifle and just five rounds of ammunition before the introduction of Lewis guns, and chivalry flourished between the pilots of both sides. One famous example was Lieutenant Pilcher who, having clearly run out of ammunition, was allowed to make good his escape from a dog-fight by his German adversary; subsequently the Englishman deliberately 'got in the way', as he later described it, when he saw his gallant foe in danger. Such conduct was confined largely to the early days of the war and was perhaps not universal but it was still present in 1918 when a Fokker D.VII was brought down intact (the first thus secured, according to the squadron responsible) and Lieutenant L.E. Bickel remembered his colleagues 'entertaining the pilot to lunch before handing him over to Intelligence'. Something of this spirit even survived until 1940 when Air Chief Marshal Sir Arthur Longmore, then C-in-C RAF Middle East Command, sent a letter of sympathy to the Italians on hearing of the death of General Italo Balbo, shot down in a 'friendly fire' incident.

Culture was not sacrificed either. In Salonica in 1916 Captain Murlis-Green, flying a BE12 of 17 Squadron, would drop carefully padded cases of gramophone records for his 'enemy' who would reciprocate with consignments of fresh green vegetables. The friendship between the two was reflected in Murlis-Green's fury when the courteous German pilot was killed after being lured to attack a captive balloon. But it would paint an inaccurate picture of the period to suggest that such displays of gentlemanly conduct were common – in fact, they were only remarked on at the time because of their rarity. Generally speaking, the air war reflected the horrors of the ground war.

As the few survivors of the RFC gradually vanish for ever from the scene, I have seized this final chance to present an accurate picture of the RFC, so that what you hold in your hands is a unique and unrepeatable document, in both social and military terms. It is a comprehensive overview, describing the aircraft, uniforms, tactics and feats of arms, but neither human interest nor the lighter side are forgotten. Since the Royal Flying Corps formed the basis on which the RAF was formed, the book also looks at its influence beyond 1918.

All this may be summed up by an incident remembered by Sergeant A.E. Jessop of 615 Squadron, RAF, in the Second World War, when he still wore the badge of 56 Squadron, RFC, with which he had served in the First. An inspecting officer strode down the line of men and paused in front of the sergeant, barking 'What's that in your cap?'

'Royal Flying Corps, sir,' replied Jessop, stiffening a little more as he spoke.

'Redundant service' came the reply as the officer moved on down the line, but his lack of an order to replace the offending badge was a silent acknowledgement of the service's enduring pride in its history and the debt it owed to its predecessors.

Peter G. Cooksley
London, 1999

THE FOUNDATIONS ARE LAID

The existence of the Royal Flying Corps was brief, less than six years to be exact, but during the period when it flourished it fought in the greatest war mankind had ever experienced, and it proved to be the precursor of what is arguably the finest and most efficient independent air arm in the world. This in turn became the pattern for the air forces of every nation that has emerged since. However, the birth-pangs of the Royal Flying Corps were protracted and painful. Only a year before it was formed, the Chief of the Imperial General Staff, Field Marshal Sir William Gustavus Nicholson, whose experience of warfare extended back to the Afghan War of 1878, had declared: 'Aviation is a useless and expensive fad advocated by a few individuals whose ideas are unworthy of attention,' although Orville Wright believed that he and his brother were 'introducing into the world an invention which would make further wars practically impossible'.

It is not too fanciful to trace the beginnings of the RFC back to 1862 when Lieutenant Edward Grover RE began trials to investigate the military potential of balloons, basing his tests on a paper written by Captain T.H. Cooper of the 56th Regiment of Foot in 1809. However, it was not until 1878 that the War Office introduced the British Army to military aviation with the establishment at Woolwich of the so-called Balloon Equipment Store, at the same time allocating the sum of £150 for maintenance and equipment. Captains H.P. Lee RE and J.L.B. Templar of the Middlesex Militia (and subsequently KRRC), assisted by Sergeant-Major Greener, were appointed to oversee development work. Templar was a burly, genial man who was already an experienced aeronaut and owner of the coal-gas balloon *Crusader*, the first such vessel to be used by the Army. In the same year *Crusader* was joined by the 10,000cu.ft hydrogen *Pioneer*, specially constructed from varnished cambric at a cost of £71 – almost half of the original budget – before making its first ascent on 23 August 1878.

This sudden interest in lighter-than-air vehicles was in part due to the influence of Captain F. Beaumont RE and Lieutenant G.E. Grover RE,

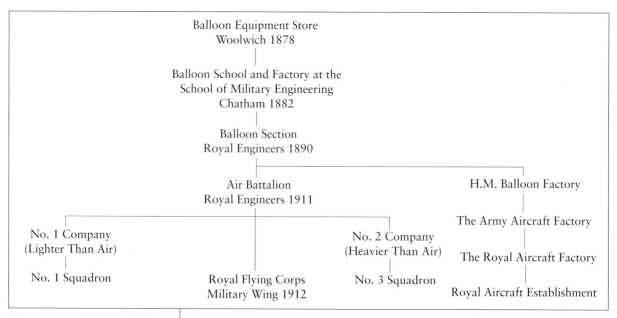

The emergence of the Royal Flying Corps. (Author)

both of the Ordnance Select Committee. They had been attached to the Federal Army Balloon Corps during the American Civil War and subsequently made experimental ascents from Aldershot and Woolwich with equipment borrowed from the dentist and balloon pioneer Henry Coxwell.

In 1879 *Crusader* appeared at Dover during the Easter Volunteer Review and at Brighton twelve months later, when a programme of balloon training was begun at Aldershot. In the same year there was a balloon detachment at the summer Army manoeuvres. A year later, on 24 June, the Army manoeuvres saw the first use of a man-carrying balloon, and in October the complete unit, now termed the School of Ballooning, was moved to Chatham, becoming part of the School of Military Engineering. Captain Templar took charge of a small balloon factory in old huts belonging to St Mary's Barracks. A derelict ball-court was reroofed and used as an erecting shop and old beer barrels held the granulated zinc and sulphuric acid necessary for the production of hydrogen. Rough and ready measures were adopted to save expense and later investigations resulted in the varnished cambric envelopes being replaced with those made of 'goldbeater's skin' (taken from the lower intestine of an ox), which proved lighter, more impervious and stronger, and was used for the new 10,000cu.ft *Heron*, completed at the end of 1883. During this year, Templar was joined by Lieutenant John Capper RE, then serving with the 11th Field Company at Chatham, and in the search for new coverings the pair set about the construction of the experimental silk-covered and linseed oil-treated 5,600cu.ft *Sapper* in the search for new coverings.

With plans for Bechuanaland to become a British protectorate in 1885, the Army dispatched an expeditionary force which arrived in Cape Town on 19 December 1884. This force included an aerial section equipped with three balloons under the command of Captain H. Elsdale, assisted by Lieutenant Trollope, and although their use was confined to limited

A British war balloon with its attendant horse team. (Author's collection [380/16])

observation duties, it is interesting to note that the force commander, General Sir Charles Warren, made a number of ascents in the balloon *Heron*. In addition to the balloons themselves, the section would have needed to take all the necessary equipment, consisting of a horse-drawn, limbered winch-wagon, a single GS wagon and three tube-carts each carrying forty-four heavy steel gas cylinders. Each cylinder was 8in long and 5⅛in diameter and contained hydrogen gas stored at 1,500lb/psi pressure in peacetime but increased to 1,800lb/psi on active service. The following year, on 15 February, another balloon section was posted overseas, this time to the eastern Sudan. It was commanded by (now) Major Templar, assisted by Lieutenant Mackenzie who achieved something of a record by remaining aloft for seven hours at an altitude of 750ft, while the balloon was towed along by the mobile winch in the centre of a marching column en route from Suakin to Torfrik. As a result of such operations, it was concluded that such lighter-than-air craft were reasonably successful as observation posts, although their full potential had not been realised owing to inadequate transport facilities. In 1888 Captain Elsdale, now returned to England, was succeeded by a friend of Major Templar, Major C.M. Watson, who promptly took steps to create a self-contained Balloon Section, requesting (unsuccessfully) that it should have its own horses and drivers since borrowing these from other units had been a frequent source of irritation. But within a few years this was achieved, reflecting the official realisation that there was a future for the new arm of the Army, although this was not supported by the niggardly grant for 1888 of £1,600, a reduction of £400 on that allocated two years earlier. Nevertheless it was not altogether surprising that the year 1889 was marked by the announcement that a detachment from the Balloon Section, acknowledged as the most interesting and novel branch of the Army and staffed by enthusiasts, should visit Aldershot during that year's manoeuvres. Coupled with a favourable report on balloons for military work from General Sir Evelyn Wood, the GOC Aldershot Division, who had gained a Victoria Cross during the Indian Mutiny, this ensured that the Balloon Section was established on a regular basis in the following year. It was decided to move the section and the gas-producing establishment to Aldershot in 1891, the workshops and shed being occupied in the following year. The gas plant was set up adjacent to the RE's Stanhope Lines, near the Basingstoke Canal, and the name 'Balloon Factory' came into use locally after the founding of the necessary workshops at South Farnborough in 1894 (although the name was not officially adopted until three years later). Three officers and thirty-three other ranks made up Superintendent Templar's staff, forming in effect the nucleus of the future RFC, and the Army store now contained a total of '32 fully equipped balloons ready at an hour's notice to go on active service'.

When the 'Great Boer War' broke out in October 1899, the Army still had only a single balloon section and depot stationed at Aldershot, but nevertheless a detachment of the Royal Engineers, including an aerial section, was among the British troops sent to Africa. This section, commanded by Captain Jones, made aerial observations before the Battle of Magersfontein in December, and the subsequent heavy losses among the troops on the ground could probably have been avoided if Lieutenant-General Lord Methuen had made proper use of the balloon observer's report (although it probably saved lives later in the battle). However, there was partial redress for this blunder when information gathered by a captive Army balloon was intelligently used during the siege of Ladysmith between November 1899 and February 1900. This balloon was also used to survey the terrain across which troops were to advance on Pretoria in May and to provide reconnaissance information for the town's subsequent capture by Lord Roberts' troops in June. As a result of these operations, the strength of the balloon detachment was increased to twenty-one NCOs and men. By this time supporting equipment had improved and the gas wagons, increased in number to six, now carried thirty-five 9ft long, 8in diameter spun steel tubes each, enabling a balloon to be filled in twenty minutes.

As the new century dawned, technical innovations were introduced, some of which were later to be adopted for the Flying Corps. One of the most important was the transmission and receipt of wireless messages to balloons in flight, first achieved successfully in May 1904. Handling and controlling unpowered lighter-than-air vessels soon became established procedures, knowledge of which was to prove valuable for the Caquot-type balloons used during the First World War for observation, to support defensive balloon aprons and to act as aerial barrages flown from ships such as the sloop *Penstemon* in 1917.

Early ground-to-air wireless experiments being conducted by the Army at Aldershot at a distance of 30 miles. (Author's collection [156/19])

MAN-LIFTING KITES

Intended for observation, these kites could be operated in wind speeds of up to 50mph (much too strong for balloons), and were adopted by the Army in 1906. The idea of such kites was traceable back to 1894 when a team of kites capable of lifting a man to an altitude of 100ft was devised by Major B.F.S. Baden-Powell of the Scots Guards, brother of the founder of the Boy Scout movement. However, it was the kite-teams devised by S.F. Cody that were used by the balloon companies. These were capable of lifting an observer to an altitude of 1,500ft (over 3,000ft on one occasion). They consisted of a pilot kite below which were three to seven lifting kites, according to the wind strength; suspended beneath the lifting kites was a carrier kite, below which was the observer's basket. The first man to be lifted by this system was a sapper who went aloft over Pirbright Camp.

June 1894 saw the establishment of the Army's Balloon School. S.F. Cody was appointed Chief Instructor, Kiting, and during 1906 secret investigations were launched to look into the possibilities of powered gliders. Lieutenant J.W. Dunne, who had been invalided out of the Army, was appointed designer of man-lifting kites at HM Balloon Factory, where he soon designed a tail-less glider, which was eventually powered by a pair of Buchet petrol motors. This proved capable of making short hops twelve months later.

But the advent of such devices did not mean that work on balloons had been abandoned. In 1903 and 1904 there were trials with a balloon flown from a destroyer taking place over Malta and Gibraltar. More reliable petrol motors were fitted to large balloons, creating a new form of transport – airships. Little more than an elongated, motorised balloon, *Nulli Secundus* – otherwise known as Army Airship no. 1 – was begun in 1904 by the Balloon Factory following Colonel Capper's visit to the pioneer aviator Santos Dumont two years earlier. It was launched in

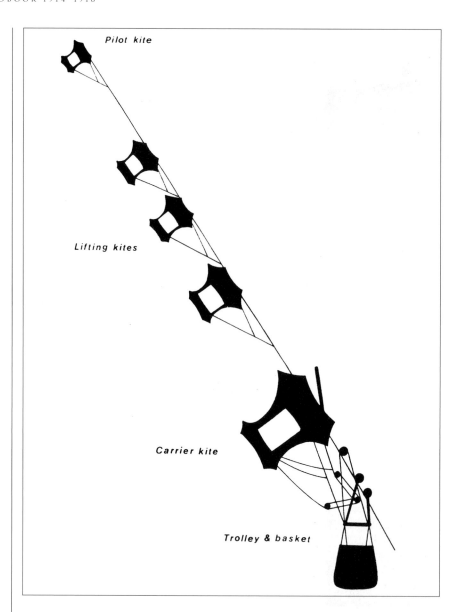

Pilot kite

Lifting kites

Carrier kite

Trolley & basket

*Cody man-lifting kite team.
(Author)*

September 1907 and in the following October it made its greatest – and last – flight. This was a 3½-hour trip, mostly at an altitude of 500ft to 600ft, from Farnborough to London via Frimley, Bagshot, Sunningdale and Brentford; crossing the Thames just north of Staines it passed over Kensington Palace, Hyde Park, Buckingham Palace and the War Office, from where it was watched by a number of people, including Sir William Nicholson. When it reached St Paul's Cathedral it circled the dome while Cody, taken along as he was the only man strong enough to restart the 50hp Antoinette motor which had a tendency to run hot, attempted to take close-up photographs of the cathedral. Unfortunately the pictures were spoilt because oil from the engine had coated the camera lens. Severe weather forced *Nulli Secundus* to land near Crystal Palace, and the balloon subsequently became too waterlogged ever to fly again. One eye-witness recalled: 'Sergeant Ramsay ripped open a sealing chamber,

With the aid of a woven wicker seat (a lighter alternative to the basket), an observer is lifted by a team of Cody man-lifting kites. (Author's collection [259/10])

remarking "And there goes £250 worth of hydrogen" as he did so.' In fact, it was later rebuilt as *Nulli Secundus II*, which first flew on 24 July 1908, perhaps to mark the renaming of 'His Majesty's Balloon Factory' (thus placing it on the same footing as the Royal Arsenal). In July 1908 the Admiralty made two important decisions: the first was the suggested appointment of a Naval Air Assistant to their Lordships; the second was proposing the construction of a large rigid airship, ordered from Vickers of Barrow-in-Furness. This was to be designated HMA [His Majesty's Airship] *No. 1*. Its fate may be read in Chapter Five. Meanwhile the Royal Navy was gathering a small band of qualified pilots, although Lieutenant G.C. Colmore RN had unknowingly achieved the distinction of being the very first on the 21st of the preceding month when he gained Aviator's Certificate no. 15 at his own expense.

The semi-rigid Army airship Nulli Secundus, *which made the epic journey of 5 October 1907 (the same year that it was launched). It was destroyed in a storm and was replaced by the slightly larger* Nulli Secundus II *in 1908. The special radiator for its 50hp Antoinette engine was designed by the youthful Geoffrey de Havilland. (Author's collection [178/13])*

With that sagacity associated with many naval decisions, the plan to create a nucleus of trained pilots was one that spoke well for the Admiralty's resolve to adopt a flexible approach to the likely new form of warfare. On 1 March 1911 four of its officers (selected from some two hundred applicants), Lieutenants R. Gregory, C.R. Samson, A.M. Longmore and E.L. Gerrard, the last being a member of the Royal Marine Light Infantry, were sent for training as aeroplane pilots. Their training was conducted at Eastchurch on the Isle of Sheppey, which F.K. (later Sir Francis) McClean of the Royal Aero Club had placed at the Admiralty's disposal, together with two of his Short aircraft, in the previous November. A further pair of aircraft were placed on loan by the RAeC later. Charles Samson gained RAeC certificate no. 71 on 25 April, Arthur Longmore no. 72 on the same day, Reginald Gregory no. 75 on 2 May and Eugene Gerrard no. 76 three days later. All had flown Short biplanes for their first solos.

On 30 April 1912 the proposed equipment of the RFC naval wing was set out as follows:

1 twin-engined Short biplane
1 new twin-engined Short biplane
1 70hp Gnome-engined Short biplane
1 Chenu-engined Breguet biplane
1 Nieuport two-seat 50hp monoplane
1 Short monoplane
1 Deperdussin two-seat 70hp monoplane
1 Etrich monoplane
6 set of Short floats for the above to convert them for hydro-aeroplane practice.

In their standard configuration all these were fitted with a normal (land) undercarriage, but the proposal also suggested a further fourteen machines described as 'hydro-aeroplanes' – seaplanes:

The car of the airship Lebaudy, *a vessel which had been purchased by the* Morning Post *newspaper in October 1910 and presented to the British government. It was subsequently based at Aldershot. (Author's collection [380])*

2 Short seaplanes with twin motors: one biplane, one monoplane
6 seaplanes (to be ordered from a British firm)
6 further seaplanes to be ordered from the firm supplying the most satisfactory design in the tender.

On 28 February 1912 the Royal Engineers were authorised to form an air battalion, with effect from 1 April. This had an eventual strength of 14 officers and 176 men under the command of Major Sir Alexander Bannerman, and consisted of two companies. No. 1 (Airships) was based at South Farnborough and equipped with *Beta*, *Gamma* and *Delta*. No. 2 (Aeroplanes) was based at Larkhill, its equipment consisting of a Wright biplane, a Bleriot Monoplane, a Paulhan, a de Havilland, a Henry Farman, a Howard Wright and four Bristols. At the same time plans were announced for a joint Army and Navy aviation school at Upavon on Salisbury Plain. This was staffed by 180 personnel including a commander and adjutant, 5 other officers, 63 NCOs and 2 Chief Instructors. A throughput of sixty-three pupils was envisaged. The school was officially opened on 12 June 1912, and consisted of fourteen sheds including hangars, workshops and accommodation. In the event, though, the school had been forestalled by the Royal Navy, whose Eastchurch training establishment became its official flying school in December 1911, the four aircraft now augmented by a further pair. The naval role in the event of war was officially defined as reconnaissance, shadowing submarines, identifying minefields and spotting for warships' guns after 'ascending from a floating base' – pointers to the practical application of flights such as the one that took place on 18 November 1911 when Commander Oliver Schwann made the first ascent from water in a British aircraft, flying an Avro biplane off Barrow-in-Furness.

The new year opened with a further achievement for the Navy's air pioneers on 1 January when Lieutenant Samson, one of the four pilots sent

The Admiralty took over the airship Gamma, *described with* Delta *and* Eta *as 'experimental', together with a Parseval and the civilian* Willows IV *before the outbreak of war in August 1914. (Author's collection [380/15])*

for training at Eastchurch, flying a Short S.38, 'T2', fitted with pontoons, took off from HMS *Africa*, anchored in Sheerness Harbour. HMS *Africa* was one of the King Edward Class warships, considered to be the finest pre-Dreadnoughts in the world. Completed in 1906, *Africa* was 425ft long, with a displacement of 16,350 tons, and had now been fitted with an experimental, wooden flying deck on the forecastle. Samson later repeated the experiment, flying a Short S.38 from the slightly longer deck of HMS *Hibernia*, a vessel of the same 'Wobbly Eight' Class, while it was steaming at 5 knots in Weymouth Bay during King George V's Review of the Fleet on 2 May. Although the aircraft carried air-bags so that it could land on the water, Samson elected to land ashore at Lodmoore. Later the flying platform was transferred to HMS *London*, one of the 15,000-ton Formidable Class ships completed during the first four years of the century, and another successful take-off was made on 4 July from this ship, steaming at 12 knots.

The year 1912 was turning out to be an eventful one for military aviation. The Committee of Imperial Defence appointed Brigadier-General D. Henderson, Captain F.M. Sykes and Major D.S. MacInnes to prepare plans for the formation of the Royal Flying Corps. Absorbing the Air Battalion of the Royal Engineers and the Naval Air Organisation, this was constituted by royal warrant on 13 April, the actual formation of the Corps also incorporating a Central Flying School ('to teach flyers to become soldiers rather than to train them to fly', said cynics) and the Royal (formerly Army) Aircraft Factory. The new Military Wing was to have a Headquarters, seven aeroplane squadrons, one airship/kite squadron and an Aircraft Park (termed a Flying Depot, Line of Communications).

The Military Wing was to be commanded by Captain (temporary Major) Frederick H. Sykes (1877–1954). Late of the 15th (The King's)

Hussars, with which he had seen service in India as part of British Intelligence during 1905–6, Sykes had gained Royal Aero Club Certificate no. 95 flying a Bristol Boxkite on 20 June 1911. He was just thirty-five years old and some people thought him too young to lead the Military Division of the Corps, but between 1915 and 1916 such doubts were forgotten under the pressures of war and he was to find himself in command of the RNAS in the Eastern Mediterranean. In 1918 he became Chief of Air Staff, and the first of his three books, *Aviation in Peace and War*

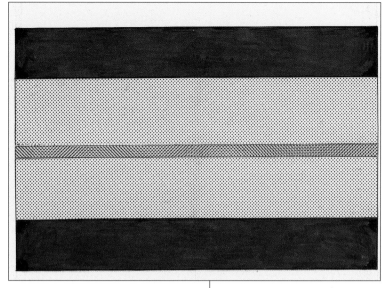

The Royal Flying Corps flag was light blue, with dark blue borders and a central red stripe. (Drawn from Army Form B2095 C. Author)

was published in 1922. As announced on 30 April 1912, the initial equipment of the Military Wing was proposed as:

    1 Nieuport three-seater 100hp monoplane
    1 Nieuport two-seater 70hp monoplane
    1 Deperdussin three-seater 100hp monoplane
    1 Deperdussin two-seater 70hp monoplane
    2 Flanders two-seaters
    2 Breguet three-seater 100hp biplanes
    2 Henry Farman three-seater 70hp biplanes
    1 Royal Aircraft Factory 'B'-type.
    3 Bristol-built Royal Aircraft Factory 'B'-types
    1 120hp Cody biplane
    1 Martin-Handasyde two-seater 60hp monoplane
    2 Bleriot single-seater 50hp monoplanes.

When war engulfed Europe in August 1914 Sir David Henderson (1862–1921) took command of the RFC in France, his appointment due partly to organisational qualities and partly to his work in 1911 as Director-General of Military Aeronautics. A patient dedicated Scot, described as determined but even-tempered, amiable and gentlemanly, he had earlier served in the Argyll and Sutherland Highlanders. At the age of forty-nine he joined the War Office and at about the same time he learned to fly at Brooklands, gaining his brevet on 17 August and Royal Aero Club Certificate no. 118 the next day, after a total of two hours instruction at Brooklands on a Bristol Boxkite. His instructor was C. Howard Pixton, who went on to win the Schneider Trophy for Great Britain in 1914, flying a Sopwith floatplane at Monaco.

No stranger to action, Henderson had joined the Army in 1883 and five years later was posted to the Sudan. He served in South Africa for two years until 1900; he was wounded, but twice mentioned in dispatches before returning home. He was awarded a DSO in 1902. Later his experiences in the field formed the basis of a book, *The Art of*

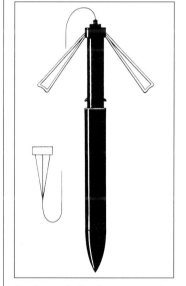

Ranken explosive darts measured some 5½in long and weighed 13 oz. Each dart had three sprung arms designed to catch in airship fabric once this had been pierced by the cast-iron nose. It was a non-explosive device, but its filling sent back a shower of sparks, fired by the jerk of their lodging in the fabric to ignite the volatile mixture of air and escaping hydrogen. They were carried in metal cases of fifty and dropped in groups of three from 60ft above the target. They were supported during their fall by a small rubber parachute. (Author)

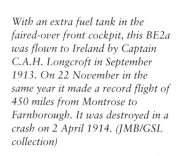

With an extra fuel tank in the faired-over front cockpit, this BE2a was flown to Ireland by Captain C.A.H. Longcroft in September 1913. On 22 November in the same year it made a record flight of 450 miles from Montrose to Farnborough. It was destroyed in a crash on 2 April 1914. (JMB/GSL collection)

Reconnaissance, which was published in 1907. He was again mentioned in a dispatch dated 8 October 1914, when Sir John French warmly commended his work in establishing the RFC in France. In August 1915 Sir David relinquished his command of the RFC in France to become its GOC.

Naturally the emergence of a new Army Corps took some time. Nos 1, 2 and 3 Squadrons were formed on 13 May 1912, and no. 4 in September. No. 5 Squadron was constituted in August 1913 (the year which saw the new Corps' first royal review), followed by no. 6 in January 1914 and nos 7 and 8 in May that year. No. 8 Squadron was formed out of the former no. 1 Airship and Kite Squadron. Meanwhile the redoubtable Samson was placed in charge of the Naval Wing's personnel, while its air bases came under the control of HMS *Vernon*, the torpedo school. On 25 November 1912 the Admiralty formed a new Air Department. Its director was Captain M.F. Sueter (later Rear Admiral Sir Murray) and although the new Wing was to fall into seeming decline over the next twenty-six months, his quiet organisational skills behind the scenes eventually earned him the nickname 'Father of the Fleet Air Arm'. Indeed in the year of his appointment to the new directorship, he had shown his grasp of the situation when he told a sub-committee of the Committee of Imperial Defence, 'war in the air, for the supremacy of the air, by armed aeroplanes against each other is likely. Thus flight . . . in future wars will be of the first and greatest importance.'

Meanwhile investigations into the practicalities of ship-launched aircraft had not been neglected, and the old cruiser *Hermes* had been fitted with a short wooden deck. During 1913 seaplanes (the term replaced 'hydro-aeroplanes' from 17 July) were experimentally launched with the aid of wheeled trolleys that fell into the sea and were lost at each take-off. But the aircraft were still equipped with floats or airbags and on their return were expected to touch down on the water alongside the vessel to be hoisted aboard. At the beginning of 1913 the total naval air strength was 5 monoplanes, 8 biplanes and 3 seaplanes, but by the summer the

At the military aeroplane trials in July 1912, this Maurice Farman S.7 is approaching after a 'good flight in a 30mph wind'. A later commentator described it as 'floating serenely, creating something of a sensation'. (Copyright Hampshire County Library)

position had materially improved, published figures listing the aircraft as 7 monoplanes; 14 biplanes and 10 seaplanes. They were made up as follows:

Monoplanes: 1 Bleriot, 2 Deperdussins, 1 Etrich, 1 Nieuport, 2 Shorts
Biplanes: 1 Avro, 2 Bristols, 1 Caudron, 2 Horace Farmans, 1 Maurice Farman, 5 Shorts, 2 Sopwiths
Sea and Floatplanes: 1 Astra, 1 Avro, 2 Borels, 1 Donnet-Leveque, 1 Henry Farman, 1 Maurice Farman, 3 Shorts.

There were bases at Calshot, the Isle of Grain, Harwich and Yarmouth.

The Army had been thinking along similar lines and in December 1911 announced that a Military Aeroplane Competition (better known as the Military Trials) was to take place at Larkhill on Salisbury Plain in August 1912. The specifications for the aircraft were based on the slight experience gained so far, although the requirements for military purposes were not fully understood at the time. The Navy was to take no part in the trials. There were thirty-two entrants, but some either failed to arrive or took little part in the competition. The unexpected winner was the Cody V biplane, a machine that was totally useless for military purposes. The winning machine was taken over by the new RFC's 4 Squadron as no. 301, but it was unfortunately destroyed in a fatal crash on 28 April 1913. The only other example, no. 304, was issued to the same squadron and allegedly also known as no. 2. This aircraft was eventually presented to the Science Museum, South Kensington, in November 1913 where it may still be seen.

But of greater import had been the creation in March 1913 of an Experimental Branch of the RFC's Military Wing. Commanded by Major H. Musgrave, its tasks were to look into the further development of balloons, man-lifting kites, aerial photography, bomb-dropping, meteorology, aerial gunnery, wireless and artillery observation. According to published sources the aeroplanes at Musgrave's disposal in mid-1913 were 22 monoplanes and 36 biplanes:

Cody military biplane no. 304, preserved in the South Kensington Science Museum. (Author [343/1])

BE2a no. 336, later to go to war with 4 Squadron, was equipped with wireless at the 'Concentration Camp'. (JMB/GSL collection)

Monoplanes: 2 Bleriots, 4 Bristols, 5 Deperdussins, 4 Howard Flanders, 1 Martinsyde, 6 Nieuports
Biplanes: 4 Avros, 22 BEs, 2 Breguets, 2 Caudrons, 6 Shorts.

The Experimental Branch had bases at Montrose (2 Squadron), Salisbury Plain (3 Squadron) and South Farnborough (Headquarters/4 Squadron). A footnote in one published source stated that the delivery of twenty aeroplanes of various types was 'awaited' and that of the sum total, fifty were 'effective for war'.

In the days when world events were rarely brought to the attention of the general public, the opening months of 1914 seemed to hold no portent of

The historic 'Concentration Camp' of 1914, where this photograph was taken, saw the appearance of BE2a no. 240, which had been allocated to the Military Wing of the RFC on 10 December 1913. It attracted much interest because it carried a Rouzet wireless, the aerial reel for which is visible under the front cockpit. The aircraft went to France on 13 August 1914 with 4 Squadron, but was struck off charge sixteen days later. (Flight International/Quadrant Picture Library [038])

the cataclysm that was to come, and life in general seemed to have set into a tranquil pattern of progress. Not so in the armed services, however. Throughout June a 'Concentration Camp' was held at Netheravon for the entire RFC, its purpose being to concentrate under canvas the total strength of the new Corps in order to test its mobilisation ability and efficiency by means of competitions, talks, conferences and demonstrations, the mornings being devoted to flying and the afternoons to lectures and discussions. This should have been a period of consolidation and progress for the RFC, with a budget of one million pounds called for in that year's Army Estimates, but there were damaging allegations that during the month of the 'Concentration Camp', serviceability and the condition of equipment made it impossible to put more than thirty machines into the air at any one time. In all, five squadrons were present at Netheravon – nos 2, 3, 4, 5 and 6 – although the latter was neither completely manned nor fully equipped. No. 1 Squadron was in the process of converting from airships to aeroplanes, while no. 7 was still being formed.

On 1 July came the announcement that future references to the RFC would indicate only the former Military Wing since the earlier structure had never been popular. The Naval Wing, which was henceforth to take responsibility for all airship operations, had from the beginning of the year claimed to have in excess of a hundred trained aeroplane pilots. From this time on it would follow an independent existence as the Royal Naval Air Service, a title that had already been in unofficial use for several months.

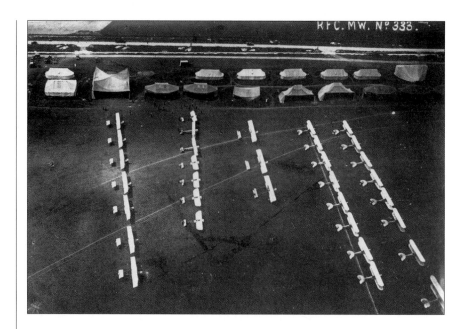

The 'Concentration Camp' from the air. The high-altitude RE5, bottom right, has extended wings. (Bruce Robertson collection)

Then, as if to endorse the new autonomy of naval flying, just twenty-seven days later, at RNAS Station Calshot, Squadron Commander Arthur Longmore dropped a 14in 810lb torpedo from a seaplane for the first time. The Short Folder Seaplane, no. 119, was specially modified for the task, with a quick-release gear designed by Flight Lieutenant D.H. Hyde-Thompson. The experimental drop was the result of a request from the First Lord of the Admiralty, Winston Churchill, encouraged by the enthusiasm of Commodore Murray F. Sueter, Director of Air Operations, for the development of this weapon.

Seven days later hostilities opened between Great Britain and Germany – the First World War had begun. This cataclysmic event not only demanded the best efforts of the men and machines in the front line, but also the vast support system required to keep them flying. This included the RFC's now largely forgotten Chinese Labour Corps: civilian 'pick and shovel men' who prepared aerodromes in France as well as laying roads. This was hard physical work and one RFC veteran remembered that 'these lads did a fine job, many of them only to die far from home in a foreign country'. Sometimes referred to as 'Annamite Coolies', they were recruited from an area on the east coast of French Indo-China; there were some 250,00 of them in France, organised into companies and regiments along military lines. The uniformed RNAS Air Construction Corps did much the same tasks.

In 1915 the RFC founded the Air Accidents Investigation Branch (which continues today under the aegis of the Department of Trade and Industry), ensuring safety in air operations and travel.

From mid-1916 the little-remembered Intelligence Division of the Admiralty pioneered the production of numbered Air Packets containing specially prepared air maps to obviate the need for naval pilots to use their old school atlases and road maps for navigation, as they had done in the earliest days.

Cast bronzed RFC cap badge and 'collar dog' (left). (Author [700/0])

One of the RFC's most bizarre duties was dropping copies of genuine letters and postcards written by German POWs over the front line trenches in France as part of the silent propaganda struggle.

The first pilots quickly had to become familiar with the phonetic alphabet for safer communications. In 1917 J.M. Grider, an American who served in France with 85 Squadron, listed the small number in use as: Ak, Beer, Cee, Don, E, F, G, Haiches, I, J, K, Ella, Emma, N, O, Pip, Q, R, Esses, Toc, U, Vic, W, X, Y, Zed. Grider was killed in action in late 1918.

THE CRUCIBLE
OF WAR

The RFC was officially recognised as a Corps of the Army with effect from 13 May 1912. The precedent of Army organisation had already been set by the RFC's predecessor as an Air Battalion of the Royal Engineers from 1 April 1911 (following the issue of an Army Order dated 28 February 1911), so it naturally followed that the new Corps would be organised along similar lines, with the basic units being the squadrons, which were then subdivided into flights.

The first member of the new RFC had been Private H. Edwards who was identified by the historic service number '1'. He had joined the Army in 1895 but had left to join the RFC on 16 October 1913, so that although his identity was preserved as the nominal first member of the RAF in 1918 (RFC numbers were adopted without change) the first serving member of the RFC was by that time no. 5, Warrant Officer E. Moore who had enlisted in the Army on 9 December 1889. Neither of these men would have seen anything strange in the adoption of the term 'squadron' for the basic unit. Whereas the Army favoured larger units such as the battalion, brigade or regiment, the RFC's unit was much smaller, rather akin to the cavalry's small force of some 120–200 men. One also suspects a certain maritime influence, since a naval 'squadron' had denoted a detachment of vessels for special service since the seventeenth century.

At the outbreak of war on 4 August 1914, the strength of the Military Wing of the RFC was quoted as 147 officers and 1,097 men with 179 aeroplanes, all those in France being commanded by Brigadier-General Sir David Henderson. However, despite Henderson's able leadership, as early as mid-November it was realised that a more flexible command structure would need to be introduced to enable the RFC to cope with the tremendous demands being made on it. The Wing system was introduced on 29 November, with GHQ at St Omer keeping control of 4 Squadron, the wireless unit and the Aircraft Park. The field base was commanded by Major A.D. Carden, with 9 BE2s, 1 BE2c, 3 BE8s and 4 crated Sopwith Tabloids. It was staffed by a dozen officers and 162 other personnel. Nos 2 and 3 Squadrons made up No. 1 Wing RFC at Merville, serving the IVth and Indian Army Corps. No. 2 Wing, the second of the new Wings, was administered from St Omer and comprised 5 Squadron serving III Corps and 6 Squadron serving II Corps, both Army units having their own RFC wireless section detached from the parent unit at St Omer. On 25 December a further change took place when the British Expeditionary Force in France was divided into the First Army, comprising I, IV and Indian Army Corps served by No. 1 Wing, and the Second Army made up of II and III Corps with the 2nd Wing.

This system proved convenient for the next two years. During this time the demands made on the Royal Flying Corps' Military Wing had resulted in greater specialisation and a consequent move away from the early idea that every squadron was expected to perform multitudinous functions: bombing, fighting, reconnaissance, artillery observation, photography and contact patrols. With effect from 30 January 1916, it was decided that each Army would have two Wings, a 'Corps Wing' made up of squadrons directly committed to assistance of ground forces, and an 'Army Wing' to carry out those operations called for by the Army commander, such as air fighting, long-range reconnaissance and strategic bombing. The Corps and Army Wings were now termed an RFC Brigade, each of which had also its own kite balloon section and Aircraft Park.

Not all aircraft flew to France: some were sent by sea, including this RE5, no. 651, which went to 2 Squadron on 27 September 1914 and to 16 Squadron on 10 February 1915, only to be SOC four days later. Also sent to France by sea was an Aircraft Park, which perplexed the Landing Officer at Boulogne who described it as 'An unnumbered unit without aeroplanes', adding 'What are we to do with it?' (Author's collection [700])

March 1916 saw the creation of a further Wing, brought about by the formation of the new Fourth Army, its Wing being formed on 6 May. Eight days later those RFC units retained at the Corps Headquarters for air operations required by the Commander-in-Chief of the BEF, Douglas Haig (who had succeeded John French in December 1915) were renamed the 9th (GHQ) Wing. Throughout the war the composition of Squadrons, Wings and Brigades was never fixed, instead varying according to the situation and requirements of Corps and Armies in the field.

Meanwhile a comparatively unknown name was becoming associated with the Corps. On 7 August 1914 Temporary Lieutenant-Colonel Hugh M. Trenchard (1873–1956) had been appointed officer commanding the RFC at Farnborough and thus was in charge of all home activity. An ardent admirer of Henderson, Trenchard had seen service abroad, where he was wounded in South Africa. Taking the advice of a friend, he learned

Described today as Farnborough's 'Building G5' (or unofficially as 'Trenchard's Building'), this is the original Royal Flying Corps Headquarters. (Falcon Aviation)

to fly; after instruction by none other than T.O.M. Sopwith, he took ticket no. 270 on 13 August 1912 at the controls of a Farman biplane over Brooklands. He later succeeded Henderson in command of the RFC units in France, although he was widely regarded as a less-than-skilled pilot.

Towards the end of the official existence of the RFC, on a bitter February morning in 1918, a strange Avro came in to land at 40 (Training) Squadron. Captain Taylor, a superb pilot and fanatical perfectionist, was so absorbed in drilling his pupils that he failed to notice the aircraft. The first attempt at landing was much too high so the pilot had to go round again and finally made a less-than-perfect landing. As the machine taxied up to a hangar and the pilot alighted, Captain Taylor sauntered over and sneered 'Where did you learn to fly like that? Fancy coming to a place where I'm trying to teach. What sort of example do you think you are?' During this tirade the Avro pilot loosened his flying jacket, revealing the red tabs of a Staff officer and a general's insignia on the tunic underneath! A moment later he removed his goggles and wool hat, revealing himself to the astonished Taylor as none other than Trenchard himself, commander of the entire Flying Corps! For once Taylor was lost for words and merely gaped as Trenchard answered. 'Well Captain, I'm sorry I put up such a bad show. I'm rather a poor pilot, I'm afraid, as I'm at a desk most of the time and very seldom get a chance to fly. This is the first time I've had an Avro up but I won't come back and give another poor exhibition after this! I've heard all about you and that you're a good instructor and how

A pristine Avro 504K. (Author's collection)

The RNAS Eastchurch Squadron at Dunkirk, probably in late August 1914. Below the Astra Torres (Naval Airship no. 3), which flies a White Ensign, are Commander Samson's BE2a no. 50 and a Short biplane no. 42, while a Sopwith Tractor biplane stands in the distance. (Author's collection)

you tick people off if they don't show up properly.' The slightest wink seemed to be directed at the grinning pupils (or did the general's eye simply water in the cold wind?), as he patted the instructor on the shoulder, adding 'Come on Captain, don't be ashamed of having done a good job.'

Trenchard took with him to France as his ADC Maurice Baring, the fifth son of Baron Revelstroke, who had been educated at Eton and Trinity

College, Cambridge. He had already won a reputation as a wit, and as a man of letters; he wrote poems, books, plays and essays, and was fluent in seven languages. He had earlier excelled in the diplomatic services and was to write the lengthy work *Per Ardua*, and the poem 'In Memoriam' after the death of Captain Lord Lucas RFC on 3 November 1916. Trenchard wrote of Baring: 'There never was a staff officer in any country, in any nation, in any century, like Major Maurice Baring. He was the most unselfish man I have ever met or am likely to meet . . . words fail me in describing this man.'

The RFC and its pilots had to learn the rules of war as they went along, and constantly had to adapt to meet the changing pattern of requirements. Combat experience proved a source of serious study as the conflict progressed and the degree to which this information was acted upon is shown by the figures given below.

29 September 1916:
Aircraft abroad: 1,035
Aircraft at home: 1,677
Aircraft SOC since 12 June 1916: 1,195
Aircraft added since 12 June 1916: 1,725
Operational squadrons: 64
Reserve squadrons: 33
Operational stations: 28
Training stations: 22 plus 12 buildings
Personnel: 46,257
Personnel under training: 1,392
New pilots since 18 June 1916: 952

The figures from 1917 illustrate not only the scale of the RFC's expansion but also the new directions the Corps was taking:

Operational squadrons: 115
Training squadrons: 109
Aircraft (France): 4,227
Aircraft (Middle East): 941
Aircraft (Home): 5,770
Qualified pilots: 1,679
Kite balloons: 89
Cadets under training: 14,097
Personnel (total): 114,260
Personnel overseas: 24,895
Air photos taken: 127,000
Prints developed: 3.9 million
Juveniles for labour: 9,601

By 1917 the RFC was vastly different from the force that had gone to France in 1914, but it still remained almost entirely a biplane force. This was largely due to a ban on monoplanes after a series of accidents in 1912 (although on Sunday 17 September 1911 Lieutenant R.A. Cammell of the Air Battalion had died when his Valkyrie biplane side-slipped into the ground at Hendon). Official opinion hardened against monoplanes following an accident on Sunday 5 July 1912 near Stonehenge, when Captain E.B. Lorraine and Staff Sergeant H.V. Wilson of 3 Squadron died in a Nieuport monoplane from the Central Flying School. Two more

The RFC had two hospitals in London. This is the one in Eaton Square. (Author's collection [701/14])

monoplanes were lost in the following September, the first on Friday the 6th when Deperdussin no. 258 broke up over Graveley, near Welwyn, resulting in the deaths of the pilot, Captain Patrick Hamilton, and his observer, Lieutenant Athole Wyness-Stuart. On the 10th Bristol-Coanda no. 263 came down at 8.15a.m., crashing at Lower Wolvercote, Oxfordshire, killing the pilot, Second Lieutenant Edward Hotchkiss, and the observer, Lieutenant Claude Albemarle Bettington. (This machine had been fitted with quick-release flying wires when it was entered in the Military Trials of the previous month, and the crash was undoubtedly brought about by the accidental operation of this device.) Four days later the monoplane ban was imposed but applied only to the Military Wing.

These were peace-time operations conducted by single aircraft, and contrast with the large number of machines accepted as the norm six years later. By this time an operational pattern had evolved, shaped by the needs of operational flying, and the accepted composition of a Royal Flying Corps Brigade was as follows: a Corps Wing, made up of an Army

During the war years the Crossley tender was to become the best remembered of the RFC's motorised transport. Here 20911 1/AM Bassett sits at the wheel of one at Hounslow Heath. (Author's collection)

Co-operation Squadron for each Corps in the Army on the ground; an Army Wing consisting of Scout (Fighter) Squadrons, for day and night bombing; a Kite Balloon Wing; and, as a supply source of aircraft, parts and equipment to squadrons, an Aircraft Park. By December 1915 the original allocation of motor vehicles per squadron had proved inadequate and the numbers were increased at this time, bringing the total to over thirty vehicles as follows:

6 Crossley light tenders
6 Crossley heavy tenders
3 lorries for reserve equipment
3 lorries for the transport of sheds
3 lorries carrying power tools, etc., for repairs
1 lorry (heavy) with machine tools
1 lorry with parts and materials for motor transport
(All the above lorries were generally Leylands.)
2 other lorries (one for baggage)
8 (formerly 6) aircraft trailers
8 (formerly 6) motor-cycles/motor-cycle combinations.

In addition to this, Squadron Commanders above the rank of Lieutenant-Colonel had a Crossley touring car placed a their disposal.

Training was carried out at a wide variety of instructional establishments, some of them already regarded as 'old', one such being the 600-acre site set up in November 1910 at Eastchurch in Kent for the flying training of Royal Navy officers. Officially titled the Naval Flying School, this was also known in maritime circles as HMS *Pembroke II*. The first designated Commandant of this school was Captain Paine RN, but when he took command of the Central Flying School at Upavon his place at Eastchurch was taken by 28-year-old Commander Charles Rumney

Samson (1883–1931). There are countless legends concerning this resourceful, bearded, Lancashire-born officer. He joined the Royal Navy at the age of fifteen and proved to have a natural ability as a pilot; on the outbreak of war in 1914 he took the first Royal Naval air unit to Europe and operated it with distinction against the enemy in the manner of a private air force, despite orders to the contrary. In 1915 he went to Gallipoli and later commanded the first carrier task force in history, only to become a colonel in the new RAF in 1918. He eventually died of cardiac problems, largely the result of his immensely demanding (and largely self-inflicted) workload.

The RNAS had numerous training establishments, set up by the Admiralty in 1915 and 1916, where Navy pilots learned the art of flying. There were also specialist establishments, such as Stonehenge Aerodrome (now straddled by the A303), which was the home of the RFC's School of Navigation and Bomb Dropping, the buildings of which were not to vanish until 1927. Other specialised stations included Orfordness, the Armament Experimental Station; Martlesham Heath, an Experimental Establish-ment; and Marske, the School of Aerial Fighting. Many other schools, such as those above West Marina Gardens, St Leonards-on-Sea, East Sussex, and in nearby Cornwallis Terrace, Hastings, existed to teach men to be officers, or perhaps just service personnel.

The RFC Club, Bruton Street, London. This was set up by former president of the Air Board (later Air Ministry) Lord Cowdray with a gift of £350,000, and was in the nature of a memorial to his son, killed in France, but simultaneously paying tribute to 'the brilliant, heroic work of the RFC'. (Author [492])

The subject of pilot instruction had for many of the war years been approached in a haphazard manner, instructors often being seconded to the work during periods of recuperation and rest from first-line duties. Although the Central Flying School had been established at the same time as the RFC, in practice standards of instruction varied, with poor teachers producing second-rate pupils. In addition there persisted the system of rewarding men accepted as pilots with £75 in payment for their course of civilian instruction, a legacy of the very earliest days of the Corps. This meant no control could be exerted over the standards achieved by civilian training schools.

The Central Flying School's first tentative steps towards perfection were

The first officers' course at the Central Flying School in 1912. In the centre is Captain Godfrey Paine RN, while Lieutenant Quartermaster F. Kirby VC is in the front row, extreme right. Behind him stands Major H.M. Trenchard DSO. (Author's collection [700])

somewhat shaky. Major Trenchard himself was a pupil there, when he was also acting as the Senior Staff Officer. His Staff duties included invigilating and marking the papers of the final written examination before the award of pilots' brevets and rumour has it that he set himself a special examination, marked it and then awarded himself his 'wings!' – although he never completed a flying course at the school. Sadly, the tale is almost certainly apocryphal!

The original staff at the CFS were under the command of Captain Godfrey M. Paine MVO, RN. They were:

2/Lt R. Abbercromby	Asst Pmr J.H. Lidderdale RN
Lt A. Allen	Lt-Cdr A.M. Longmore
Lt E.V. Anderson	Lt R.B. Martyn
Lt P. Atkinson	Lt J.W. Pepper
Capt. J.H. Beke	Eng. Lt C.J. Randall RN
Lt R. Cholmondeley	Capt. C.E. Risk
Lt-Col. H.R. Cook	Lt D. Shephard RN
Capt. R.H. Cordner	2/Lt R.R. Smith-Barry
Lt I.T. Courtney	Lt G.B. Stopford
Capt. J.D.B. Fulton	Maj. H.M. Trenchard DSO
Maj. E.L. Gerrard	Lt F.F. Waldron
Maj. J.F.A. Higgins DSO	Lt G. Wilman-Lushington
2/Lt T.O.B. Hubbard	Lt S. Winfield-Smith
Lt Qmr F. Kirby VC*	2/Lt D. Young

*Frank Howard Kirby VC was born at Thame, Oxfordshire, on 18 December 1871 and as a 28-year-old corporal in the Royal Engineers was serving in South Africa. On 2 June 1900 he was part of a small detachment pinned down by heavy enemy fire while attempting to retire from the vicinity of the Delagoa Bay railway line. During the retreat, one man's horse was killed under him and Kirby immediately galloped to his rescue. Despite the heavy Boer fire, he managed to get the man up behind his saddle and his horse carried them out of range. This was the third occasion on which Kirby had displayed gallantry in the face of the enemy and he was gazetted with the Victoria Cross on 5 October of the same year. He served with the RFC throughout the First World War, rising to the rank of lieutenant-colonel. He stayed in the RAF after the war until 1926, attaining the rank of group captain, and died at Sidcup, Kent, on 8 July 1956.

Despite their reputation for instability, Valkyrie monoplanes were used as instructional aircraft. (Author's collection [L16])

The staff at the CFS were soon joined by the renowned Robert Raymond Smith-Barry (1886–1969). Of Irish aristocratic descent, he was the son of a Grenadier Guards officer. After leaving Eton he joined the Consular Service and was posted to Constantinople in 1909. Two years later he was back in England, learning to fly at the Bristol School, Larkhill, Salisbury Plain. The following year he was himself an instructor there. On 10 August 1912 he joined the Royal Flying Corps and became a member of Course no. 1 at the CFS where the top five pupils were automatically delegated to teaching. At Upavon Smith-Barry established a new altitude record for the School when, on 28 November, he took Short Tractor Biplane no. 413 to a height of 7,000ft. Already with a commission, he later joined 5 Squadron at Fort Grange Aerodrome, Gosport.

On 14 August 1914 Smith-Barry was sent with his squadron to France, where he was severely injured four days later. He was flying BE8 no. 391 when it developed a control fault, and crashed into the ground near Peronne from a height of just 60ft. His observer/mechanic, Corporal F.J.P. Geard was killed in the crash. Smith-Barry was taken to the local hospital, where doctors tended his injuries: two broken legs and a smashed knee-cap. Only a few days after he had been admitted it became clear that enemy forces were already entering the outskirts of the town, so he persuaded the nurses to transfer him on to a stretcher. This was then placed in an old horse-drawn cab which took him to St Quinten, whence he escaped to Rouen in the guard's van of a train, before arriving in

Flying training schools, in common with all RFC stations, had their crop of crashes. This one took place later in the war at No. 2 Fighting School, Marske-by-the Sea, Yorkshire, when Martynside G.100 Elephant no. A1592 landed on a roof. (Author's collection [91])

England for further medical treatment and convalescence. He recovered well from his injuries, though he always walked with a limp, sometimes needing a stick to help him get about.

Promoted to the rank of Captain, Smith-Barry was posted to 60 Squadron where he became a flight commander alongside Lieutenant H.H. Balfour (later Lord Balfour of Inchrye) and Lieutenant C. Portal (another CFS graduate and later Sir Charles Portal, Chief of Air Staff in 1940). Between July and 24 December 1916 Major Smith-Barry became the squadron's commanding officer. He was appalled when he realised how poorly trained most of the new pilots were, some of them having received only three hours tuition. His concern came to a head when a visiting Australian pilot, Balcon Browne, gave a demonstration of how to initiate and then recover from a spin (a manoeuvre regarded as highly dangerous and not to be attempted). Smith-Barry approached Trenchard on the question of flying instruction, supporting this with a paper advocating the adoption of Avro 504 dual-control trainers, with the pupil seated in front, the two occupants being able to communicate with the aid of a 'telephone' – later widely known as a 'Gosport tube'. This consisted of twin 18in lengths of tube with acoustic caps and a 'Y' union for the pair at the other end. This replaced the confusing system of flags formerly used to give directions to a pupil, and the new method was a significant advance. Funnel attachments were introduced shortly after. Further, it was recommended that the status of instructors be improved by training at a special school, their number being selected from good scout pilots who displayed dash and confidence, with pupils staying with a particular instructor throughout the course.

Smith-Barry's timing was perfect, since RFC casualties at the front were mounting dramatically. Trenchard ordered him to 'Go to England and try out your ideas – and don't let me or yourself down!' As a result the School of Special Flying was established at Gosport. Its instructional policy was

Less well-known than the Avro 504K was the 504J. This example of the latter, D5509, was of late assembly in Egypt and was still in service in 1919. (via Mrs I.W. Austin)

summed up by its architect with the words: 'The object of training is not to prevent flyers from getting into difficulties, but to show them how to get out of them satisfactorily, and having done so, to make them go and repeat the process alone.' With (Temporary) Lieutenant-Colonel Smith-Barry in command from 23 August 1917, the No. 1 Training Squadron, designated No. 1 School of Special Flying in May 1918, was later joined by No. 2 at Redcar (renamed the South-West Area Instructors' School in July 1918), and others at Ayr, Lilbourne, and on the Curragh in Ireland as well as in Canada. At Gosport Smith-Barry had a well-appointed office, with a genuine Persian rug on the floor, and he relaxed in the Mess by playing Chopin waltzes on the piano. He retired from the RAF in 1921 but rejoined the Service in 1940. A former instructor summed up the value of his work: 'By shedding a flood of light on the mysteries of aircraft control, he drove away fear – which was really the greatest danger which existed for a pupil.' Smith-Barry died on 23 May 1949, following an operation intended to relieve the pain he still felt from the crash so long before.

The officers under Smith-Barry's command at Gosport included the following. (The list of instructors is not exhaustive.)

Adjutant Capt. George Phillipi
Eng. Off. Capt. J.N. Dundas Heenan
Flying Staff Capt. H.H. Balfour (later Lord Balfour PC, MP)
Capt. Norman Brearley (later Group Captain)
Capt. Duncan Davis (later of Brooklands Aviation Ltd)
Capt. E. Leslie Foot (later aerobatic expert)
Lt W.L.S. Keith Jopp (later of the ATA)
Capt. J. Noakes (later Group Captain and 'crazy flyer')
Capt. J.M. Robb (later Air Chief Marshal Sir James)
Lt R.H. Stocken (later light aircraft expert)
Capt. S.F. Vincent (later Air Vice-Marshal)

It soon became clear that national markings were necessary for RFC aircraft, and the Union Flag was the first identification mark to be adopted. This BE2c was still in service a year after war had been declared. (JMB/GSL collection)

The aircraft used were Avro 504J and K types, with at least one Sopwith 1½ Strutter and a pair of Sopwith F1 Camels. The School was organised into six flights. A Flight aircraft were identified by white wheels and a black or white triangle (according to the main dope finish) on the fuselage aft of the roundel; B Flight had equally divided blue and white wheel discs; C Flight had dark blue wheel discs; D Flight had red wheel discs, some with red tips to the propellers; E Flight had white wheel discs with a red centre; and F Flight had black wheel discs with a white centre and a small red disc aft of the fuselage roundel. The Special Instructors Flight of the South Eastern Area School at Manston (derived from the Gosport School in 1918) distinguished its Avro 504Js by means of narrow vertical bands on the nose and cowling – usually five silver and four black, although the number varied.

When an artillery observation pilot was asked how long it took to learn to fly, his answer was 'Four hours and forty minutes', this being the dual instruction time with his instructor (who had laid particular emphasis on 'split-arse turns') in a de Havilland DH6, the type also used for his first solo. The successful outcome of this, he was anxious to make clear, was not in itself sufficient, for ten examinations had first to be taken, five preliminaries and five finals, and it is an interesting point that he preferred the operational BE2es and later the RE8s to the 'heavy types such as Bristol F2Bs'. He also recalled that 'turns on all these were always made anti-clockwise', with 'particular attention on the REs to keeping the nose up'. This man had learned to fly at RFC Station Yatesbury in Wiltshire, where the commanding officer was Major Whitlock. The latter flew an SE5a as his personal aircraft although he later displayed a preference for the Sopwith Triplane.

Among the staff at this time were Captains George, Webb and Kelly, the latter earning transient fame for flying a Bristol Fighter through an open hangar, while 'Reckless Reggie', 6ft 2in tall and a former Grenadier

Guardsman, took pleasure in flying through Clifton Suspension Bridge over the River Avon as a relief from hedge-hopping at near zero altitude! The same informant also remembered that as the official existence of the RFC drew to its close only 40 per cent of the volunteers then coming forward were regarded as sufficiently fit for the job: a grim reflection of how the war was decimating the health of the nation's available manhood.

In addition to the instruction of pilots, a vast part of the RFC organisation was devoted to the many other trades and responsibilities allied to flying. The following list indicates their great variety:

RFC Machine Gun School	Dover
RFC Machine Gun School	Hythe
RFC Observer School	Hythe
RFC Observer School	Oxford
RFC Observer School	Reading
RFC Officers Training School	Reading
RFC School of Aerial Gunnery	Hythe
RFC School of Aerial Gunnery	Loch Doon
RFC School of Instruction	Reading
RFC Wireless School	Brooklands
RNAS Central Depot	White City
RNAS Central Training Establishment	Cranwell
RNAS Gunnery School	Eastchurch
RNAS Observer School	Clement Talbot Works
RNAS Observer School	Eastchurch

For all grades, serving at home and abroad, the pay structure for the rank and file of the RFC was as follows:

Rank	Duty	Pay Per Day
3/AM	Clerk	1s 8d
	Storeman/Other	1s
2/AM	All	2s
1/AM	Clerk/Storeman	3s
	Other	5s
	Clerk	4s
Corporal	Storeman	4s 9d
	Other	5s
Sergeant	Clerk/Storeman	4s 9d
	Other	6s
Flight Sergeant	Clerk/Storeman	5s
	Other	7s
W/O	Clerk/Storeman	6s 9d
	Technical/Disciplinary	9s
Quartermaster Sergeant	Technical	8s
	Non-technical	4s 6d

UNIFORMS, FLYING CLOTHES AND BADGES

The addition of a new corps to Britain's services with effect from April 1912 meant that fresh insignia and badges were required, as well as new uniforms in the Army. Resolution of the first was a simple matter for the Military Wing, only three being necessary, and since the new service had sprung from the Air Battalion of the Royal Engineers, it was logical that the RFC's badge should be based on this but with the royal cipher and motto deleted to make room for the initials of the Corps. There existed a number of forms of this, the most common having the initials voided (fretted-out). Least common were those badges moulded from brass so that the unvoided letters were merely in relief against a filled, slightly convex background which was usually plain, but very rarely had a hammered finish. For wear, these were usually mounted on lugs through which a split pin passed, but a few could be found with either vertical sliders or horizontal tags. Finish was either dull, giving an oxidised appearance, or brass, while those for wear on full-dress uniforms were gilded.

Although the Royal Flying Corps was created in May 1912, it was not until the following year that the pilot's insignia was introduced, this being formally announced by Army Order 40 published in February of the following year after being approved by King George V. Consisting of a pair of swift's wings stitched in white silk, it bore the monogram of the RFC encircled by a brown laurel wreath, all surmounted by a crown and on a backing of black cloth. It measured 4in across and in this form was worn centrally above the left breast pocket and medals on Service dress, or in the form of a gilt metal brooch, having a larger 'span' than that of the woven version, with full dress. It had been jointly designed by Brigadier-General Sir David Henderson, the RFC's first commanding officer, and his deputy in charge of the Military Wing, 36-year old Major (later General Sir Frederick) Sykes.

Only one other flying badge was introduced for the RFC, but not until after the outbreak of the war. The observer's stitched half-wing protruding to the wearer's left of a letter 'O' was announced in Army Order 327 of

A brass RFC badge compared with a 'collar dog' of the Royal Engineers (full dress). That the former was based on the latter is clearly shown. The RFC badge is unfretted. There were also a few unfretted badges with a 'hammered' backing, but these are rare. (Author's collection [701])

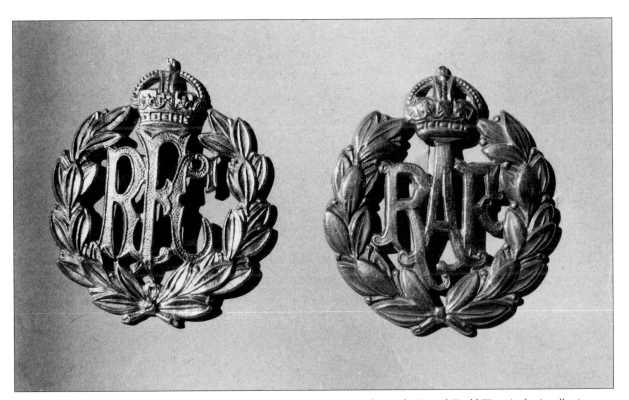

A gilt, full dress RFC badge compared with a much-polished RAF badge worn during the Second World War. (Author's collection [701])

RFC pilot's wings. These could have either black (as here) or khaki cloth backing (though this did not indicate the colour of the uniform on which they were worn). This pair belonged to Captain Frank Barnard. When RAF wings first appeared they were less arched and had thicker roots. (Author's collection [206])

September 1915 which restricted its wear to officers only. Not until November 1915 was its use extended by AMO 404 to 'Warrant Officers, Non-commissioned officers and men'. It was worn by observers of both powered aircraft and observation balloons.

The Naval Wing of the Royal Flying Corps went its own way almost from its inception, with the result that its pilot's brevet, introduced in December 1913, consisted of a gilt brooch in the form of an eagle with its wings outspread, and measuring 2in across. The design had its origins in a brooch purchased in Paris by Captain Murray Sueter's wife, who liked its French Imperial design. Murray Sueter borrowed the brooch, and showed it to the Admiralty Air Department with the suggestion that it be adopted as a flying badge, an idea that was accepted by the Lords Commissioners. Indeed, it was used again, for a small copy in gilt finish replaced the anchor on an officer's cap badge and a larger copy was worn by pilots above the RNAS officer's gold rings on the tunic cuff, at first only on the left cuff and shoulder, until 8 June 1917 when its use was extended to both right and left sides. It is interesting to note, however, that on caps the head of the bird was inclined to the wearer's right until about 1915, when the reverse was adopted and it is probably due to the association of this badge with the Navy that it has on occasion been erroneously described as representing an albatross. Otherwise non-pilot officers wore a winged 'A' on the cuffs.

However, the change-over from anchor to eagle in the centre of an officer's cap badge was not universal, and many of the former type were retained with flying insignia, while other photographs show that a few RNAS pilots followed the Army custom when wearing khaki, pinning the eagle brooch on the left breast of the tunic, over pocket and medal ribbons, often combining this with the cap badge already described, on an otherwise army-style khaki cap!

The tunic designed for the Military Wing of the RFC was humorously referred to as the 'maternity jacket'. It consisted of a high-collared khaki jacket without external buttons (which might catch in the wires or

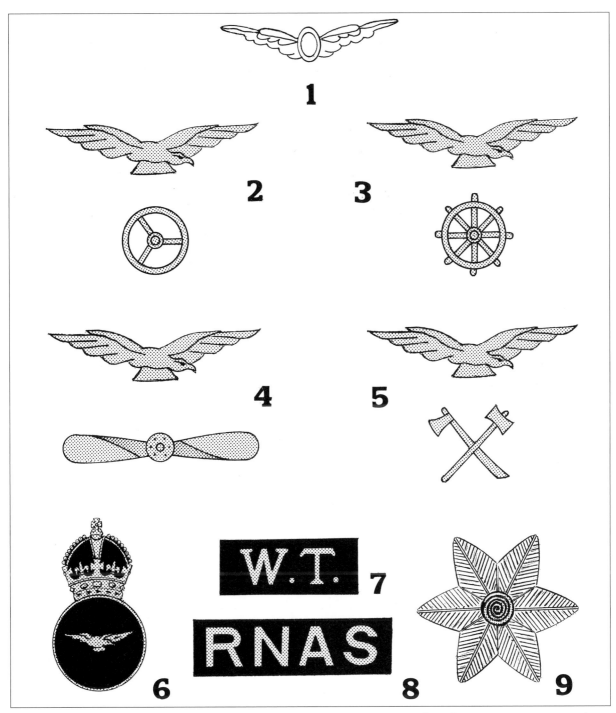

RNAS rank insignia. Unless otherwise stated, all were woven in red thread. (1) Gilt metal officer observer's insignia; (2) NCO pilot; (3) Airship coxswain (worn on the collar by CPOs and in gilt thread by ratings); (4) 1st Class Air Mechanic, authorised in October 1916; (5) Artisan (i.e. Rigger/Fitter); (6) CPO's cap badge; (7) Wireless Telegraphy operator; (8) RNAS shoulder title; (9) Gold thread officer's sleeve/shoulder strap star as laid down in AMO 2590 of 13 July 1917. Other red thread insignia (not illustrated) included that worn by Dispatch Riders (a winged wheel over the letters RNAS) and the Anti-Aircraft Corps (RNAS over AAC). (Author)

'Darkie' Romford of 3 Squadron sports an RFC 'maternity jacket' early in 1914. (Author's collection)

Royal Flying Corps shoulder flash, in white on black. (Author)

structure of an aircraft), and one contemporary writer describes it as giving 'as it were, a breastplate of cloth across their chest', adding that it was worn with 'a forage cap, which can occasionally be pulled down to tie under the chin'. In fact there was nothing unusual in the RFC having an adaptable cap – this is true of all caps of this type – but they differed from later practice in having the badge already described rather further back than was the later custom. When the Corps was first formed, peaked caps had been worn by the Military Wing.

All ranks wore clothing similar to this, with Bedford cord breeches and puttees; although khaki or fawn was acceptable with the breeches, officers could alternatively wear riding boots or long socks, and they were further distinguished by epaulets with 'pips', either metal or woven, denoting rank. Overseas officers had their country of origin stitched in lettering below the pips. Most collars carried a smaller copy of the cap badge on each side of the fastening. Also worn was the 'Sam Browne' – an item that one contemporary drawing, still frequently reproduced, shows being worn over the wrong shoulder! Buttons carried a king's crown above the letters 'R.F.C' (sic), in an arc parallel to the lower edge. Retention of pantaloons by the RAF into the 1920s meant that since the issue pattern tended to droop, they were often 'doctored' – and these must therefore have been among the first 'private amendments' to a standard uniform. Puttees were retained by the new service, but these were widely replaced by privately purchased ones, those issued being described as 'real horse bandages'.

On the upper part of the sleeves of the uniforms of both NCOs and other ranks was a crescent of black cloth bearing in white stitching the words 'ROYAL FLYING CORPS', the word CORPS appearing below the others on an integral rectangle below the arc. This was carried on 'maternity jackets' and greatcoats, garments which were shorter than usual for the period, having an almost modern appearance. There also existed a very rare shoulder flash worn on the tunics of those serving in the Middle East. This consisted only of a small rectangle of black cloth with the white letters 'R.F.C'. Hats worn in this theatre and described as 'Middle East Type Side Caps' were made from a khaki-coloured, hard-wearing cotton, similar to corduroy.

The traditional sergeant's and corporal's stripes were adhered to, as were the four inverted chevrons of a Quartermaster-Sergeant, the stripes being alternatively either conventional stitching or a discernibly looser weave and it is interesting to note from photographs that the very earliest examples (and a few from considerably later) lacked the four-bladed propeller above the sergeant's stripes that distinguished an NCO of the Army's Flying Corps.

The solution to this mystery may be found in a publication of November 1914 which refers to an NCO wearing the 'new badge' of a propeller on his arm. Above this and the chevrons of rank, a flight sergeant wore a crown insignia, his

An RFC sergeant wearing overseas uniform with shorts and pith helmet has his pack adjusted. (Author's collection)

woven propeller like that on the sleeve of a quartermaster sergeant having a small, four-pointed star on its boss. No such emblem was carried above a corporal's stripes, while an air mechanic first class was distinguished by the insignia of a small two-bladed propeller on his sleeve. At work, fitters and riggers wore one-piece dark blue overalls.

Officers' alternative uniforms were no different from those worn by the rest of the Army, the only distinguishing features being the buttons and the RFC badge at each side of the collar above the lapel. This was also worn as a badge on the peaked cap which was generally more popular than the 'fore and aft' cap (also known as 'the Austrian type').

Rank insignia was by means of lace and pip combinations on the jacket cuffs, later gradually replaced by pips only on the epaulets. As before, breeches tended to be worn with puttees or riding boots, or alternatively slacks with turn-ups and ankle boots. Nevertheless many officers, after transferring from their regiment to the Flying Corps, continued to wear their former uniform without change apart from the addition of pilot's or observer's brevets if they were flyers, and often a change of cap badge.

As with the Army, the Navy saw no reason for an alternative uniform for the RNAS, even the prevailing fashion for white cap-tops being adopted from May to October, with the result that apart from a pilot's

Working dress for RNAS mechanics. (Author via Chaz Bowyer)

eagle brooch, the only additions for officers was a smaller reproduction of this worn on each sleeve above the cuff rings and those on the epaulets, to denote that the wearer served with the service's aerial arm. Thus it was that not until the issue of Admiralty Fleet Order on 22 June 1917 that a gilt observer's badge was introduced, consisting of a letter 'O' supported by a pair of birds' wings. At first this was confined to officers who wore it on each sleeve above the gold lace and on each epaulet; in December 1917 the design was extended to sword belt and buttons which in general carried the eagle once more, instead of the traditional anchor and a rope design round the edge.

NCO pilots in the Royal Navy were identified by the familiar eagle, worked in red above a three-spoked wheel, carried on the right arm. Chief Petty Officers wore this badge on their collars while CPO coxswains of airships had a similar insignia but incorporating an eight-spoked ship's wheel in red on their collars. These badges for ratings were worked in gilt, with two similar sleeve badges, but worked in red for engineers, where the wheel was replaced by a horizontal two-bladed propeller, while the version for 'artisans' had a crossed axe and mallet below the eagle. A slightly smaller version of this, executed in gilt wire, was worn with full dress.

By June 1917 it became necessary to formalise the designations of ranks and duties in the RNAS, and the original orders were supplemented to cover the observers' ranks thus:

Description of Responsibilities	Equivalent Rank	Insignia
Wing Captain, with the rank of Captain RN	Captain RN	
Wing Captains holding other rank	Commander RN	
Wing Commander	Commander RN	
Squadron Commander (with 8 years seniority) as Flight Lieutenant, Flight Commander or Squadron Commander)	Lieutenant-Commander RN	
Squadron Commander (with less than 8 years seniority as specified above)	As Lieutenant RN	Two stars over sleeve eagle
Flight Commander	Lieutenant RN,	Star above eagle
Flight Lieutenant	Lieutenant RN	
Flight Sub-Lieutenant	Sub-Lieutenant RN	
Observer Captain with rank of Captain RN	Captain RN	
Other Observer Captains	Commander RN,	star above winged 'O'
Wing Observer	Commander RN	
Squadron Observer (with 8 years seniority as Observer Lieutenant, Flight Observer or Squadron Observer)	Lieutenant-Commander RN	
Squadron Observers (with less than 8 years seniority as specified above)	Lieutenant RN	Two stars above winged 'O'
Flight Observer	Lieutenant RN	One star above winged 'O'
Observer Lieutenant	Lieutenant RN	
Observer Sub-Lieutenant	Sub-Lieutenant RN	

(Top) RNAS officer-pilots wore a small gilt eagle badge above the rank lace on both cuffs and shoulder straps. (Below) Photographs prove that the eagle centre of officers' cap badges could be either 1¼ or 2⅛in wide, both being 'handed' and either gilt or bronze, the latter probably for wear with khaki. (Author)

These woven sleeve stars were defined on 13 July 1917 in AMO 2590 as being the same as those worn in gold on the epaulettes of officers below the rank of rear-admiral but in silver, and when worn above the rank lace on epaulettes they were to be half the diameter. When two such stars were worn they appeared in a horizontal line on the shoulder and as a vertical line on the cuff.

The every-day attire for naval airmen, aircraftmen, mechanics, leading mechanics and so on consisted of the traditional 'monkey jacket' with dark blue breeches and either field boots or black ankle boots, with dark blue puttees and a white flannel shirt with a soft white collar and black

Sergeant Carter (left), 1175 AM2 Percy E. Butcher of 2 Squadron (centre), both in working dress, and Provost Sergeant Urquart in front of an Avro 5O4K. (P.E. Butcher)

tie. Cadets at Cranwell, then known as HMS *Daedalus* wore 'square rig' jackets with patch pockets, open neck grey flannel shirts and a cap with a glossy peak and a woven RNAS badge at the front. This consisted of a vertical black oval with a narrow red inset edge, bearing in its centre a red eagle device, the whole surmounted by a red crown. This badge was worn by Petty Officers but with the red areas replaced with 'gold', thus allowing the areas below the arches of the crown to be red instead of black. A similar cap was combined with a khaki light-weight tunic fastened with four buttons and with buttoned lower patch pockets for wear on postings to hot climates, the sleeves having a red RNAS eagle on a khaki rectangle worn at the mid-point of the upper arm. Khaki shirts were worn with a tie of the same colour as appropriate.

As in the RNAS, the Military Wing of the RFC issued lighter clothing for men posted to warmer climes. This consisted of a long khaki tunic, with five brass buttons fastening to the neck and usually buttoned breast pockets only. It had epaulets and a hacking back and was worn with knee-length shorts, ankle boots, puttees and forage cap or frequently a sola topi. Belts, equipment, rank insignia and shoulder titles were similar to those worn at home.

Since the RFC enjoyed only twenty-six months of peacetime existence and the regulations for such a uniform were not promulgated until an Army Order of November 1913, only a relatively small number of full dress uniforms ever existed. However, for both officers and men these were dark blue, having high 'mandarin' collars. For the men these were scarlet with a wide blue border and an RFC gilt badge set some way back from the fastening; the epaulets bore the letters of the service as a shoulder title, with a button, similar to that of service dress at the opposite end. Cuffs were deep and of scarlet cloth, ending in an inverted chevron of Petersham, half an inch wide, while the tunic was secured down the front with seven buttons.

Officers' full dress uniforms were basically very similar to those already described, being dark blue in colour with a red stripe, two inches wide, running down the outer seam of the overalls, while the tunic was fastened with eight buttons down to the sash which did duty as a belt. This was made of Petersham, 3 in wide, and fastened by three gilded wire toggles, and of a darker blue than the main garment. Scarlet piping edged the front fastening and the collar which was otherwise similar to that already described except that the blue edging was narrower, thus allowing a wider red area. Gilt metal badges were worn as before, but nearer the fastening. Also similar were the cuffs, except that those of officers had the upper edge of the narrow blue Petersham piped in red. Epaulets were entirely different, consisting of three loops of gold cord, while the back had an RFC button immediately below the sash at each side of the centre-line; at each side of the single vent, occupying the space between waist and hem, were three broad bands of blue cord decoration.

With a gilt badge in its centre, headwear consisted of a dark blue cap with a black, patent leather peak and a scarlet headband.

Mess dress consisted of a dark blue jacket, a little more than waist length, with scarlet lapels and pointed cuffs of the same, while rank badges were worn on blue cloth shoulder straps and gilt collar badges. The vest or waistcoat was also of blue cloth while the overalls were as for full dress. The resemblance of all these patterns to the patterns for full and mess dress of the Royal Engineers is obvious.

The main flying garment for the RFC was a knee-length, double-breasted chrome-leather coat with three pockets, brown for the Military Wing and black for the RNAS. Near identical copies of these were available for private purchase, the 'Burfron' being advertised as being so shaped as to 'shoot wet clear of the legs when seated'. Alternatively a short version existed which was often worn over an Army greatcoat or with a short fur jacket to combat the winter cold at altitude when, as one aviator recalled, the protection 'was never enough' and experienced flyers would only don thick clothing immediately before taking off since perspiration would freeze, as could urine if one had drunk more than a single cup of tea so that there was a risk of frostbite. One pilot recalled that the cold caused his penis to 'shrink to the size of a periwinkle'. Similar restrictions applied to preparations for the dawn patrol when the pilots and observers gathered in the mess 'for cocoa and biscuits, everyone silent and miserable as sin', while outside 'the mechanics were frantically pouring hot water into radiators in order to raise engine temperature'.

The Mk I version of the famous Sidcot suit, a greatly prized garment, became generally available in March 1918. In effect airtight overalls, they were said to have been inspired by the protection given by an oil-soaked,

Lieutenant Frank Marlowe RNAS, ready to go on patrol in a Short Type 827 floatplane from Yarmouth in 1916. (Author's collection)

An amusingly theatrical farewell! The men still wear their RFC tropical uniform, with standard high-collar jackets instead of the 'maternity' tunic, despite the sign on the wall headed Royal Air Force. (Author's collection)

An aircraftman wearing overseas khaki dress, possibly in Palestine. His tunic carries the letters RFC on a shoulder patch. The original photograph is dated 6 November 1917. (Author's collection)

cotton flying suit, trials of which were held and a report published in the previous September. The Sidcot suit was made from light Burberry material thinly lined with fur and silk with additional fur at the neck and cuffs. It was worn with the Mk I helmet which was fur-lined and retained the cylindrical leather pads in front of the ears (intended to reduce wind noise) which had been a feature of its several forerunners. The helmet was lined with fleece or gabardine, or worn with a wool under-cap if unlined. Pilots also wore long undercoats with sleeves lined with camel fur and

Outdoor sick parade, possibly in Palestine. The corporal wears a black patch on his upper sleeve with the letters RFC instead of the full title as worn by the sergeant. Quarterly reminders were read at parades warning of the severe penalties resulting from the failure to report cases of VD. (Author's collection)

Lieutenant Donald C. Austin (centre), with colleagues. They are wearing flying overalls of late 1918 design. The DH9A behind is likely to belong to 47 Squadron. (via Mrs I.W. Austin)

A 7 Squadron observer about to go on patrol. (Dr A.G. Wilson MC)

thigh-length leather 'fug-boots'; these fleece-lined boots were said to have been introduced by Lanoe Hawker, later to be awarded the Victoria Cross. Some members of the RNAS favoured the hard Warren helmet. This was distinguished by a domed crown and close-fitting fastenings round the face. Meanwhile long coats began to be adopted as the range of aircraft increased and sorties of greater duration became possible.

A 1918 advertisement for Messrs Gieves of Old Bond Street. (Author's collection)

Developed primarily for the RNAS for carrying out long patrols and for bomber crews towards the end of 1917, electrically heated suits consisted of a heated wash-leather waistcoat, again of Burberry material, under-gloves of horse skin (dogged by problems caused by wires broken by flexing of the fingers) and heated boot soles (equally unreliable since the mica tended to crack). A persistent and unresolved problem was that of over-heating, which could cause burns to the fingers if the wind-driven generator increased the electrical charge when the aircraft dived steeply.

The long patrols undertaken by RNAS airship crews posed special problems which were largely solved by the adoption of the loose, hand-knitted sweater commonly known as a 'submarine frock'. Those in static duties in exposed positions covered this with a 'Lammy coat', which had a hood with a cord around the front to draw it close to the face, and toggles and loops to fasten the front; these coats were proof against almost anything the elements could throw at them.

Goggles were available in many forms, with various brands being described as non-flammable and shatter-proof. Indeed, so important were such items that pilots were warned never to fly without them and some even took the precaution of carrying a spare pair in case of emergency. Triplex marketed two types, clearly based in the firm's experience in producing motoring goggles, with a choice of tinted or non-tinted lenses. These might be worn with one of several types of face protector. All were made of cloth or thin leather, which covered the face (or even the whole of the front of the head) with a small breathing hole and aperture for speech and large cut-outs for the eyes. Again intended to combat the extreme cold pilots might encounter and ensure protection against frostbite, there were several types. One type was made from skin with the outer surface covered in fur. As a precaution against drowning, should a crew have to crash land in the sea, it was possible to purchase privately (along with practically everything else listed as 'extras' such as fur collars) either a black, chrome-dressed leather jacket with kapok lining to ensure buoyancy or a flotation waistcoat which was worn over all.

Captain Jack Lawson, commander of A Flight at No. 46 Training School at East Retford's Ranby aerodrome in early 1918. He appears to be wearing braces in RFC colours. (Author's collection)

The RFC foresaw the provision of oxygen for its air crews, some forty pieces of breathing gear being available as early as the end of 1917. This equipment was produced by the Sieb-Gorman organisation and was based on their experience of a wide range of oxygen apparatus design. It was fitted with a delivery valve capable of three settings, for altitudes up to 29,750ft, the oxygen being supplied from a pair of 500-litre bottles, but this was superseded by a regulator controlled by an aneroid barometer designed by Major Dreyer of the Royal Army Medical Corps, manufacture beginning in April 1917. The rubber mask accompanying this design is recorded as being comfortable to wear and light.

The only means of escape from an aircraft in difficulty was by means of a parachute. These were not issued to RFC pilots, and a legend has grown up that their use was discouraged by General Trenchard. Yet there is nothing to indicate this in any records, official or unofficial; moreover at the time in question he was not the dominant figure he was later to become. At the outbreak of war, observation balloon observers were issued with Spencer-type free-fall parachutes (i.e. ripcord-operated), but these were little better than those used by showmen, although retired engineer E.R. Calthrop was experimenting with a non-free-fall parachute in 1914 which relied on the action of the wind to pull the canopy open. Other than those issued to balloon observers, and a few ordered with black canopies for spy-dropping, no wider issue was made – due not to an individual's opinion but rather to technical ignorance at War Office level.

Under everything members of the new flying service, being until April 1918 either soldiers or airmen, would wear their fibre identity tags on a

While the RFC's Naval Wing officially existed, ratings wore caps such as this. (Courtesy Peter F.G. Wright)

'Peter' Wilson of 7 Squadron still wears his regimental uniform but with his Observer's wing in 1918. (Dr A.G. Wilson MC)

length of string around the neck. The information these bore was of the simplest, giving name, initial, religion and number, these details being stamped on both the red fibre disc, which was 1⅜in in diameter and pierced by a single hole to one side, and its octagonal green-grey fellow, measuring about 1½in wide by 1¼in, and with two holes opposite each other to each side. Typical were Major Edward Mannock tags on which the legend MANNOCK ran parallel to the upper rim, while adjacent to the lower edge appeared the number 'I 1748297', the middle being occupied by the initial 'E' with below it the letters of his faith, 'CE'.

The earliest uniforms of the short-lived Naval Wing of the RFC featured identification carried by attached naval ratings between 1912 and the official emergence of the RNAS in 1914. These were issued with tallys (cap-bands) carrying the words 'ROYAL FLYING CORPS' in place of the name of a ship, worked in gold serif lettering. These caps also boasted the substantial regulation chin-strap for working on exposed stations; they were dark blue and soft-topped and were worn with normal ratings uniform by those under training.

Uniforms for the new service, the Royal Air Force, did not appear immediately although 'sealed patterns' were drawn up. The colour remained khaki. The tunic for NCOs and men was no longer the 'maternity jacket' but one similar to that issued to the Army, with a high collar and four brass buttons. This was worn with a standard wide canvas belt and a cap with a soft peak and a brass badge clearly based on that of the RFC. Buttons throughout were similar to those of the present day, but had in addition, a 'rope pattern' rim.

On the sleeves were worn the usual Army rank badges for NCOs, with at the top the later familiar cloth eagle insignia in red and immediately below, also in red, the well-known 'fist with lightning flashes' indicating a wireless mechanic or the two-bladed propeller of an air mechanic first class. This was worn immediately below the eagle at the top of the sleeve. However, before the eagle arrived at shoulder level there was a brief period when it was worn perhaps 9in lower down, the extreme top of the sleeve having a black crescent exactly the same as that of the RFC but now bearing the words ROYAL AIR FORCE, again stitched in white but in slightly larger lettering than hitherto. As before, the final word appeared below the others.

The uniforms of commissioned officers differed little from those of the Army, except for the cap badge, identical to that of the present day, which was worn on the black headband of a cap with a shiny peak. Rank insignia consisted of bands of fawn lace with a thin, sky blue centre on the cuffs, surmounted with a gilt eagle and crown (clearly borrowed from the

Sergeant Reynolds William Smale (above), having been issued with his new khaki RAF uniform on 10 December 1918, poses with a friend on becoming 'Attached, RN', his number 207158 having become F7158. Note how the former RFC sleeve insignia is retained, although the petty officer's cap badge with an eagle has reverted to the earlier RN pattern with an anchor. (T. Smale collection via Author [702/L])

A brass cap badge sometimes seen with RFC wings on the wearer's tunic indicated a member of the Australian Commonwealth Military Forces. (Author [701/23])

Early RAF greatcoats. While the one on the left has no shoulder badge, that of Sergeant Smale appears to have the eagle on a lighter patch. The form of the first seems similar to that shown on the opposite page, with a straight line to the top of the wings. (T. Smale collection via Author [702/L])

Navy). This was worn without a rank ring by second lieutenants and 9in below the top of the sleeve by warrant officers first class.

Rank insignia, based on that of the Royal Navy, was laid down for senior officers above the rank of full colonel, though it was worn by only a small minority. This was doubtless because of the brief period during which these early uniforms were current. They were replaced by 'sky blue' dress with effect from 1 October 1919. Nevertheless at least one photograph exists, dated 6 August 1918, showing King George V with a brigadier-colonel wearing a tunic with RAF rank insignia. All officers wore khaki shirts with black ties during the period of khaki dress.

Perhaps the most unusual uniform was that worn by RNAS personnel in the fortified Indian town of Aden. This khaki uniform consisted of a light drill single-breasted jacket and trousers, the former for ratings being unique in that it was worn with a collar and tie. The black composition buttons bore the usual RN insignia while on the sleeves was a patch marked with a red, printed eagle design which was slightly larger than some of its contemporaries. All ranks wore a standard navy blue peaked cap, on the front of which the cloth badge retained the usual standard eagle in the centre (instead of the stitched red eagle).

The greatest change took place with the official adoption from 1 October 1919 of a replacement for the RAF's khaki uniform. The new clothing was announced by Air Ministry Order 1049/19 of 15 September 1919 and approved for wear from 1 October 1920; it was not today's blue-grey shade, but a lighter colour which gave it a distinctly 'Ruritanian' appearance, added to by rank insignia in gold lace. Small wonder that the service quickly became known as 'Gertie Millar's Own'.* The shade of the

---

*Gertie Millar (1879–1952), a beautiful and much-loved actress of the day associated with the Gaiety Theatre in the Strand, where she is best remembered for her lead in *The Quaker Girl*. Later the Countess of Dudley, her grey-cloaked ghost is said still to haunt the fifth floor of the old theatre building.

Showing the uniform transition that took place after the war, the officers pictured here in front of an RE8 are mostly wearing RFC and RAF khaki dress with patent leather peaks to the caps. Exceptions are the squadron leader in the middle who wears one of the new 'sky blue' uniforms with gold cuff rings, and the RNAS officer behind him who wears a cap with a large eagle in the badge facing towards the wearer's right. On the left of the front row is Lieutenant G.P. Olley (who went on to form Olley Airways), and at the back on the right is Olley's friend Peter Wilson. (via Dr J. Cunbrae-Stuart)

new cloth was said to reflect this lady's eyes. The change was slow, one veteran summing up the uniform position of the earliest post-war years of the RAF in the words, 'We never wore the blue, it was the khaki we'd always had'.

The steel helmets (officially termed 'shrapnel-proof helmet') designed by John Brodie and issued to British troops from late 1915 (and fondly referred to by them as 'tin hats') were never issued to Royal Flying Corps personnel, but any examples which did come their way might be strapped to the underside of a flyer's seat (likely to

An early version of the RAF eagle as worn at the top of the sleeve by non-commissioned ranks. By 1920 some of these had had the bottom line of the patch cut into a shallow 'V' shape. (Author [700])

The two figures on the left wear new blue-grey uniforms with white shirts, but non-standard light breeches. On the right, an army-type khaki RFC uniform and cap are retained. The aircraft is believed to be F4440, a Bristol F2b of 18 Squadron. It is marked 'Presented by the MAHARAJA OF BAHADUR. Sir Rameswar Singh of Darbhanga no. 1 'The Lord Hardinge', and it replaced B1331 which had been struck off charge. (Dr A.G. Wilson MC)

be made of wicker, woven like a basket) as a crude form of armour against ground fire. These helmets weighed 2lb and had a wider brim than the Mark IIs produced from 1938, which also had an improved lining and sprung chin-strap. Mk I was the correct designation for a version made from manganese steel and manufactured from early 1916.

CHAPTER FOUR

LIGHTER THAN AIR

At the beginning of the twentieth century the Balloon Section of the Royal Engineers was small but efficient, with a staff of 150 officers and men, 36 horses and 20 carts. On 13 April 1912 all these were absorbed into the new Royal Flying Corps, the former Balloon Section ceasing to exist. However, when the First World War broke out in August two years later, the Army found itself in a difficult position following the decision that, with effect from 1 July, the Naval Branch of the RFC, henceforth to be known as the RNAS, would be responsible for all lighter-than-air craft. The result was that although the Military Section had gained valuable experience with balloons, it was now left at a disadvantage, since by the end of the year Germany had begun using kite balloons for artillery observation on the Western Front. Clearly there was considerable potential in the idea and plans were formulated to fly tethered balloons between 2 and 5 miles inside friendly territory at about 5,000ft for similar work.

Quick to seek a remedy for the problem, the commander of the British Expeditionary Force, Sir John French, appealed for assistance from the Royal Navy, a request that finally filtered through to the tiny department staffed only by a major and a corporal of the Royal Marines, accommodated in Room 1005 over the chilly, three-year-old Admiralty Arch. In the meantime spherical balloons were pressed into service, although totally unsuitable for the job, and plans were started to produce a British copy of the German Drachen (Dragon) type balloon. The envelope of these balloons measured 64ft in length with a diameter of 27ft, the British Spencer-Drachens being slightly larger with a length of 81ft. These were known as Type 'H' and made their appearance in September 1915, the date on which the Royal Flying Corps took the first steps to increase the existing four balloon units to twenty. During December the Air Board, in an attempt to meet manning problems, announced that 'men over 33 years old and [in] B1 and B2 medical categories, even though unskilled, can be accepted for balloon parties of the RFC'. These were the men who knew their kite balloons as 'Ruperts' – probably a derogatory reference to Crown Prince Rupprecht of Bavaria who commanded the Kaiser's 6th Army.

The first winches for military balloons were manual and consequently slow, taking some 45 minutes to haul in the 1,500ft (later 6,000ft) of cable

Spherical Army balloons photographed at Aldershot in about 1913. One begins to climb while another is inflated behind the trees to the right. (Copyright Hampshire County Library)

suspended from a balloon. In the field these remained mounted on horse-drawn wagons as they had been from 1889; in fact these were favoured by some as being more mobile than motor vehicles in the tenacious mud of the Somme. Aveling & Porter tractors were also tried, towing Sykes steam-winches with vertical boilers; these were soon adopted, a few remaining in service until 1918, although by then they were mounted on a motor chassis.

By 1915 the Army, which had lent men to the RNAS balloon units that had provided the first lighter-than-air presence over the Western Front, had taken over the kite balloons, although the Navy's No. 4 Kite Balloon Section was still in France where it would remain until well into the following year (uniquely using railway transport). At much the same time, early in 1916, Scammell & Nephew had been commissioned to produce a winch capable of giving a 500ft/min. rate of haul-down; later Lancaster, Panhard and Aster winches were substituted. Once mounted on a 3-ton Leyland chassis, these turned out to be a heavy combination which was liable to get bogged down on any but a proper road. Many people claimed it was insufficiently powerful to handle the Caquot balloon, pointing out that the ideal was a haul-down rate of 800ft/min. in a 30mph wind; the best then available was the Scammell with a haul-down rate of 800ft/min. in a light wind, although 600ft/min. in a 25mph wind was the designated rate not to be exceeded and the routine speed was just 450ft/min. Later a winch with a 900ft/min. haul-down rate was introduced which could be mounted on either an American 4-ton four-wheel-drive vehicle or a 35hp Lancia Z Type.

The usefulness of observation balloons was indicated both by their heavy defences and by the enemy pilots anxiety to attack them. Another method of dealing with balloons spotting for the artillery was by making their winches targets for the guns. Second Lieutenant A.C.D. Gavin, who had joined the RFC from the Royal Highland Regiment, had been ordered to keep watch in an artillery spotting balloon, despite the high wind that sent

A British Drachen balloon of No. 2 Kite Balloon Section at Locre, Belgium, in March 1916. (IWM Q449 via Bruce Robertson)

the 'Rupert' bucking, twisting and straining at its cable even as it was paid out by the winch to an altitude of 4,000ft. After a successful bombardment of the trenches, throwing up great fountains of earth, chalk and stones, the enemy turned his guns on to the area from which the balloon was being flown. Lieutenant Gavin in the meantime was kept busy distinguishing between genuine explosions of shells from the guns he was directing and decoy explosions from the German lines. Suddenly, he became sharply conscious of the fact that his own winch lorry was now a target for the enemy gunners: a thunderous explosion from below indicated that they had found the range. A well-aimed shell wiped out the winch and its attendant crew, at the same time releasing the balloon which bounded higher and began to drift towards the enemy lines.

Gavin ordered his companion to take to his parachute, and such was the height at which the balloon was

Six Leyland three-tonners that had seen service in the Middle East were the first mechanised transport purchased by J. Sainsbury and Chivers & Sons Ltd. Robust, cheap, with hard tyres and oil lamps (replaced by their civilian users), they are remembered as being like 'driving a pneumatic drill'. (via Mrs I.W. Austin)

A balloon observer heavily clad for a high ascent in winter. (P. Lamb collection via Author [374/6])

now riding, that his canopy was still visible below when the officer also plunged out of the basket. But valuable time had been wasted and only the front British trenches lay below; in a few minutes the balloon would be over no-man's-land. If the balloon crew landed beyond the enemy lines they would spend the rest of the war as prisoners. More by luck than judgement, Gavin landed among friendly forward trenches, and in the hail of machine-gun fire crawled into the shelter of the nearest dugout.

Although the RFC had taken over all kite balloons in France the RNAS continued to provide both the balloons and their support equipment until July 1916 when the War Office began to place contracts on behalf of the Corps. In the same year steps were taken to re-equip with a new type of balloon, although free sphericals continued to be used for training at home, operating from two new schools. One of these was established by the RFC with an attendant Balloon Centre at Roehampton Park, and the London public saw one of the new spherical balloons for the first time in the summer of 1917 when one made a forced landing in High Holborn, outside Chancery Lane underground station, causing considerable disruption to the traffic!

The new kite balloons were of the French Caquot design, named after their designer, Capitaine Albert Caquot. Whereas the Spencer-Drachens had a single, ventral, air-filled fin, the new kite balloons had three stabilisers, set at 120° to each other, which allowed them to be used in winds of up to 62mph. The barrage balloons of the Second World War were very similar in design except that the early balloons were more elongated fore and aft.

The first two Caquots were either of the rare Type L or of Type P, the latter having a 26,486cu.ft gas capacity (the Type P.2 was bigger, with a capacity of 28,958cu.ft). Both types were capable of taking two observers to 1,640ft. The Type M (32,843cu.ft), the most common type, was capable of attaining an altitude of 13,124ft. There also existed the Type R of 35,315cu.ft capacity, which could lift three men to the same altitude as the Type P. Caquots were introduced fairly rapidly into service with the RFC, at first being used

An observation balloon of No. 2 Balloon Section, No. 2 Wing, in France, 1917. (P. Lamb collection via Author [374/5])

alongside Drachens, although by the end of 1916 a Swiss source stated that only twenty-seven examples of the earlier design remained.

The handling ropes on all these, formerly made of hemp, were replaced by thicker cotton ones which gave a better grip when the guys became coated with mud and slush. This then ran down the inside of the men's sleeves, although some ropes were fitted with a series of toggles to make them easier to grip. The envelopes themselves were made of a fabric described as 'doped, waterproof cotton'. This substance seemed to have a peculiar attraction for the many rats on the Western Front, which tended to cause leaks by gnawing the envelopes.

From 20 November 1916 the Army established five Balloon Wing HQs on the Western Front, one for each of the British armies. Each Wing was attached to an RFC brigade which controlled the balloon companies. These companies were further divided into two sections. In July the same year the RFC had established the Roehampton Balloon Depot, plus two Training Schools; by 1917 there was another in Richmond Park where there was also a Free Balloon Section. No. 1 Balloon School was at Rollestone Camp (HQ) and Larkhill, with No. 2 at Lydd in Kent. The following year saw the creation of No. 1 Training Wing HQ and also depots at Roehampton, and No. 1 Training Base at Sheerness. No. 2 Training Wing had an HQ at Upper Richmond with its training depot in the nearby park.

Each Caquot balloon required eight men to handle the picketing ropes, with a further twenty-three looking after the ground rigging, fifteen on the bow guys, four at the mid-point and three on the stern guys. In addition there were men in charge of gas pressure, valves, fin sleeves, car suspenders, ballast, shock absorbers, winch and parachutes, all under the charge of a flight sergeant. The parachutes were usually of the Spencer static-line pattern and were stored in conical canvas bags known as 'acorns' suspended outside the rim of the basket.

An RFC Drachen balloon shows its distinctive lines, with the massive ventral lobe. (Bruce Robertson collection)

Introduction of the new kite balloons was not without its problems, however. On the Spencer-Drachen balloon the telephone line ran down the main cable in the manner of a core, but on the new aerostat this could prove dangerous for an observer having to bale out. After some experiments, the cable was led up over the trapeze. The very earliest use of kite balloons by the RFC posed problems when handling orders were being given, largely because in open country where they were usually deployed it was difficult to hear. This was quickly resolved by the introduction of a simple code of whistles. Thus the operational signal (or Balloon Alarm) was indicated by a single long blast followed by one short, 'Let Up' by one short one, and 'Stop' by a long blast on the NCO's whistle.

Except in overseas theatres (observation kite balloons being used by the RFC in Egypt, Salonica, Mesopotamia and Palestine), observers usually wore similar clothing to other flying crews. They went aloft in a basket with a floor area of just 20sq.ft, lined with canvas. Their comprehensive equipment included:

Stratoscope to determine true altitude
Hand anemometer to determine wind velocity
Thermometer
Map board (seen protruding over the basket edge in photographs)

The basket of a Caquot balloon. Note the parachute container hanging over the side. One officer is holding a pair of binoculars and the other wears a telephone headset. On the right is a map-board. (Bruce Robertson collection)

Telephone, plus batteries

Parachutes for the crew

1/20,000 map on rollers

1/10,000 map on rollers showing position of ground troops

Photo-reduction to 1/50,000, showing main sector and the two adjacent

Card-mounted sections of a 1/5,000 map

Cloth-mounted 1/50,000 map showing roads, railways, camps, etc.

Map of gun batteries showing their fire zones

Three pairs of binoculars of varying powers, one marked with an artillery scale, plus cleaning chamois

Scale-rule for use on maps

Hard pencils, note pads, India rubbers, map scales
In addition, they also carried for emergency use:
Spare telephone capsules
1,500ft telephone wire
Signals table (for use in event of telephone failure)
Weighted message bags with streamers to drop messages
1/200,000 map for navigation if the balloon broke away.

All crewmen at some time or another were rendered temporarily deaf on landing as a result of forgetting to keep their mouths open during the descent. But deafness was not the only problem encountered by kite balloon observers. One officer surprised himself with a flow of obscene language that he freely used for some five minutes after landing, this being accompanied by a pronounced stammer. He was not alone in this and it was soon realised that this was one of the effects of a swift descent from high altitude. Different wings developed their own individual techniques to cope with the problems. For example, No. 2 Wing's procedure called for a pause at about 14,000ft, even if the balloon was under attack. (This was especially alarming for new or inexperienced basket crews.)

The basic operational unit was the balloon section, two of these making up a company. One company was originally allocated to each Army Corps. However, after the reorganisation of 1916 these companies became components of a brigade balloon wing; thus, for example, No. 2 Balloon Wing served the Second Army. Six qualified observers were allocated to each balloon, generally working in pairs. Each section was manned in the following manner for a Caquot balloon, making a total of ninety-six personnel:

1 flight sergeant
2 sergeants
45-man balloon handling party
3 corporals attached to the above
2 balloon riggers with a corporal
1 clerk
2 cooks
14 motor drivers
3 motor-cyclists
6 telephonists with a corporal
2 storemen with a wireless operator
4 winchmen
4 batmen
5 officers
(From 1918 an NCO Observer was added.)

The average strength of a balloon wing on the Western Front was fourteen or fifteen sections. At its peak the balloon service employed around 9,000 men operationally, not including those serving at Headquarters and with the supply units. There were forty-four balloon sections committed to operations, with a further thirty-nine in reserve, each section consisting of around one hundred men. The most common operational altitude was

An RFC balloon observer steps from the basket of a Caquot. His lack of heavy clothing suggests a posed picture. (IWM via Bruce Robertson)

1,000ft, but this could vary according to the weather and activity. Extremes of temperature and stress could affect the observers' efficiency so the time aloft was usually restricted to three hours, with a maximum of five. The observers controlled artillery shoots, monitored enemy activity and took photographs using cameras fitted with lenses of enormous length. These pictures were used to compile mosaic maps and were particularly valued as they did not suffer from the effects of vibration associated with those taken from powered aircraft. Once the balloon had landed, any information gathered by the balloon crew was immediately taken by motor-cycle dispatch riders to various headquarters, while film would be delivered by the same means to a mobile darkroom to be developed. These were housed in modified Leyland lorries, which resembled a horse-box.

The motor-cycles used from the end of 1916 onwards were 3½hp (489cc) Phelan & Moores, a type on which the RFC was beginning to standardise, replacing the earlier Douglas and Triumph machines which were also favoured by the RNAS. Two of the four Phelan & Moore machines were fitted with side-cars for the transport of inspecting officers. Six (later eight) motor-cycle/motor-cycle combinations were allocated to each balloon unit but it was not until 1917 that re-equipment with 550cc Triumphs began, but 3,380 Phelan & Moores were still in use in November 1918.

The early motor tenders operated alongside these early motor-cycles were of Mercedes and Daimler manufacture, but these were later superseded by the ubiquitous standard Crossleys for the RFC and 15cwt Clement Talbots for the RNAS. Other vehicles included a telephone cable trolley, mobile chart room, Leyland three-tonners and (usually) a pair of anti-aircraft machine-guns mounted on chassis, and the cylinder wagons to supply the necessary hydrogen. Filling a Caquot balloon with gas was a lengthy process which could take up to half a day for a new balloon and exhausting the contents of 180 cylinders in the process

The box-like mobile telephone exchange trailers enabled the telephonists seated inside to connect the observers in the balloon to any branch of the service telephone system. This offered immediate two-way conversation and was much more efficient than either a motor-cycle dispatch rider or the one-way Morse communication possible from an aeroplane.

The line of observation kite balloons was soon extended to run practically the whole length of the Western Front. This resulted in a huge demand for trained observers so at home a series of balloon depots and schools were rapidly set up in addition to the established artillery schools. One was even founded on Kennington Oval

This Crossley tender, marked M.55257 on the bonnet and pictured in Egypt, carries on the side the bell insignia of 80 Squadron. (via Mrs I.W. Austin)

An observation balloon of No. 2 Kite Balloon Section at 'Suicide Corner', Kemmell, Belgium, in November 1917. Minutes after this photograph was taken the crew lost control of the balloon which blew away. A Delahaye motor winch with an extra drum, possibly for a telephone cable, stands on the left. (Captain G.D. Machin DFC, via Cross & Cockade, Hastings.

cricket ground, although this was short-lived, closing in May 1918. Instruction at these schools taught such unexpected techniques as keeping the binoculars trained on a target irrespective of the behaviour of his basket, for balloons were not a static platform but could roll, leap, jerk, sink or soar according to the prevailing conditions.

Many of the balloons used at home were for the instruction of RNAS cadets or Probationary Flying Officers. Their introduction to flight began in a captive balloon sent aloft to about 500ft to 'listen for Zeppelins'; they took some comfort in being equipped with a grappling hook for use if their balloon broke away. Later, in company with some twelve of fifteen others, they were obliged to make six cross-country flights in the 8ft basket of a spherical balloon filled with coal-gas. One such balloon landed at Norfolk House, near Norbury, south of London, and the passengers began to disembark. To compensate for their weight in the balloon, a tarpaulin was filled with earth by the estate gardeners, but before this had been completed the balloon suddenly rose again, taking the only occupant, Cadet Woodman, with it. His last impression was of his red-faced instructor on the ground bawling instructions not to panic! Woodman was still hanging on to the valve, without losing much gas, when he reached an altitude of 15,000ft over Croydon – where he occupied himself in trying to identify a road where an uncle lived! Shivering with cold despite his British warm and kid gloves, Woodman tied himself to the valve rope so that if he fainted, gas would continue to be evacuated. Just as he did so a hailstorm reduced the temperature further. He then became aware that the balloon was losing height at an alarming rate, so he began dumping the sand ballast, not in the prescribed small quantities, but by the bag full. His descent was still so fast that when he finally touched down on a railway line near Chislehurst the balloon bounced back into the air. Woodman's brave attempt to use the grappling hook to foul a May tree only uprooted it and towed it below! Then, at an altitude of about 25ft, Woodman pulled the rip panel. The balloon hit the earth at some 30mph, and the basket

A naval Caquot observation kite balloon being flown from a winch-equipped trawler. (Bruce Robertson collection)

rolled over and trapped him inside. He was finally released by a group of men, the first potential rescuer being informed by a disembodied voice from inside the basket that the car was too heavy for one person to lift.

Considerably less well-remembered are the operational balloons flown by the Royal Navy. For the most part these were of the Caquot Type M, and they differed little from those of the RFC except in the rigging of the envelope. A total of eleven balloon stations came under Admiralty command between 1914 and 1920:

Caldale in the Orkneys
Immingham, Lincolnshire
Lowestoft, Suffolk
Merryfield, Somerset
Milford Haven, Pembrokeshire
North Queensferry, Fife
Rathmullan, Donegal
Richmond Park, Surrey
Sheerness, Kent
Shotley, Suffolk
Tipnor, Hampshire
The Navy shared with the Army the centre for certification flights at Hurlingham.

The role of the RNAS balloons included convoy protection and U-boat spotting; for these roles they were flown from monitors. A total of twenty vessels were equipped with balloon winches. They included the light cruiser HMS *Birmingham*, a 5,440-ton vessel completed in 1914 and capable of 25½ knots, with an armament of nine 6in guns, four smaller quick-firing guns and two torpedo tubes, as well as the similar *Caledon*, *Calliope* and *Canning*. In addition 9 battleships, 2 light cruisers,

2 battlecruisers and 3 destroyers were earmarked to be equipped with winches.

The balloons towed by naval vessels, especially on Atlantic patrols, faced unique problems. One of the main ones for the crews was boredom, since their work lacked the sustained risk that kept their Army brethren alert. The lack of sightings for perhaps weeks on end generated slackness. In addition there were physical problems caused by the effects of salt air and the chafing of rigging and lines brought about by the motion of the vessel. Handling brought its own hazards, since it had to be carried out within the severe restrictions of the vessel's deck area.

The RFC also operated balloon aprons which were intended to protect important targets against aerial raiders. The British version was apparently adopted from the barrage of balloons flown at some 10,000ft over Venice in 1916 and inspected by a senior British officer in the same year. The idea was by no means new, having been generally discussed in several quarters before the war. It was formally proposed almost simultaneously in July 1916 by Lieutenant-General Jan Smuts and Major-General E.B. Ashmore, Commander of the London Air Defence Area. Edgar Booth, an engineer from Halifax, had published a 27-page document making similar proposals at the beginning of the previous year.

A balloon used in the Eastern Mediterranean is seen here stored in its protective naval vessel in 1915. (Bruce Robertson collection)

The British balloon barrage took the form of an 'apron', individual balloons not being used unless the deployment of an apron was impossible. This apron was made up of a number of Caquot balloons, some 500 yards apart, linked together by cables, from which were suspended weighted steel wires, 1,000ft long, at 25 yard intervals. The whole barrage was flown at 7,000ft, although this height was later raised to 9,500ft. The first trial of an apron took place at the Balloon Training Depot in Richmond Park, Surrey. It was noon on a blustery Friday, 21 September 1917, by the time the four linked balloons were ready. Flight Sergeant John Gardner was in charge of the handling parties and Second Lieutenant Andrew Edward Lowrie was in overall command. The whistle was about to sound the 'Let up' signal for the forty-eight men on the first balloon, eighteen of them hanging on to the handling guys, when a sudden gust of wind drove the three adjacent Caquots against the first, snapping the main cable 'with a terrible bang'.

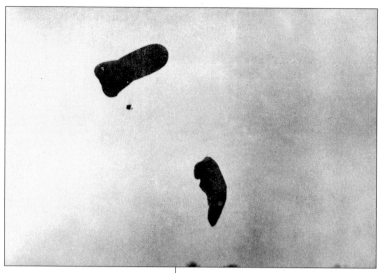

An accident involving a pair of observation balloons at Lydd in January 1918. The cable of the upper one fouled the fabric of the lower, which has begun to fall having ripped itself in consequence. The two observers concerned parachuted to safety three minutes before the photograph was taken. (P. Lamb collection via Author [381])

'Stand clear and let go, everybody!' bawled Sergeant Gardner. Forty-six of his men obeyed instantly, as the balloon, hauling the other three with it, shot up into the air. But two of the handling crew, Air Mechanics Henry Edward James, aged forty-six, and William John Peggs, aged twenty-eight, were still hanging on with both hands. It seemed that Peggs had got caught up in the guy rope. The balloon had reached an altitude of about 900ft and had travelled some 500 yards across the park when James lost his grip. He plummeted to earth, landing only a few yards from the officer; although he was immediately taken by motor ambulance to Richmond Military Hospital, he was pronounced dead on arrival, having suffered a broken neck and fractured skull in addition to internal injuries. Air Mechanic James, a married man from Leicester, had been a sailmaker in civilian life and had only joined the RFC on 14 July, being posted to London a little over a fortnight later, believing the move to be a preliminary to service in France. Meanwhile, Peggs had somehow managed to climb into the rigging of the balloon, despite, according to one report, being partially caught by one leg. The wind now drove the balloon swiftly south-eastwards as Peggs strength slowly ebbed. Nearing Croydon, the exhausted Peggs finally lost his grip and fell from the balloon. Leonard Gibbs, a gardener at Falklands Park in South Norwood, was looking up at the unfamiliar sight of the balloons overhead when he saw the figure falling, turning over and over as he did so. With the help of another gardener, William Davis, a search was made for the body. It was eventually discovered in a shrubbery, from which it had to be dug out, having been partially buried by the impact after a fall from some 2,000ft. Dr William Thomas Talbot ASC was called and pronounced life extinct. Peggs's back, jaw and legs were broken, beside other injuries, and his face was described as 'black'. Air Mechanic Peggs was a married man who lived with his wife Daisy Maud at Bell Hill, High Barnet. He had previously served in the Army, but had left and before the outbreak of war had been a milk roundsman. Anxious to serve his country again he had been accepted by the RFC in July despite having little sight in his right eye, so his medical category was B2. He is remembered on the war memorial inside St John's Church, Whetstone, some 2½ miles south of Barnet. The four run-away balloons were subsequently shot down by anti-aircraft fire.

The results of the first test indicated that under certain conditions more than three balloons supporting an obstructive apron were unmanageable but despite this disaster the first barrages of this type were introduced as part of London's defences in early October 1917. A total of twenty aprons was envisaged, but in fact only half that number materialised; effective as the device was officially judged to be, it suffered from the fact that the

A Caquot kite balloon with several Leyland 3-ton lorries in attendance in France. (IWM Q11873 via Bruce Robertson)

weight of the cables between the balloons tended to draw them together over a period of time. Deployment ran due east for about 7 miles from the Twickenham area before turning northwards a little to the west of Hainault. From this point the aprons extended as far as Enfield, the greatest length of the barrage being 51 miles. Projected explosive charges slung from the intermediate 1,000ft wires were never adopted but the slim cables of the kite balloons were a considerable danger to aeroplane pilots, a fact generally ignored by historians.

An illustration of their effectiveness was the case of Captain Stephen Reginald Parke Walter. Posted to 32 Squadron on 14 March 1917 after service in the Queen's Royal Regiment, he had taken off from his base at Droglandt on 31 July at 6.05a.m. in driving rain to take part with four others in a concentrated ground attack. The cloud base was no more than 1,000ft. Just north of Vlamertinghe Walter's DH5, no. B369, collided with an unseen balloon cable which sheared off the wings on the port side, sending the machine plummeting down and killing the pilot. He was buried at Lijssenthoek Military Cemetery near the village of Poperinghe, Belgium.

CHAPTER FIVE

AIRSHIPS: SHADOWS IN THE CLOUDS

The Army airship Gamma I *was launched in 1909. It had a capacity of 75,000cu.ft of gas and a single 80hp Green engine which drove twin swivelling propellers. (Author's collection)*

The Royal Naval Air Service (a title that was unofficially applied to the Naval Wing of the Royal Flying Corps much earlier) officially appeared on 1 July 1914, just over a month before the outbreak of war. However, the Royal Navy had taken over all airships six months earlier as well as the Army's non-rigid airships including *Beta*, a 1910 Balloon Factory design that survived until May 1916, *Delta*, another Balloon Factory non-rigid airship completed a year later and destined to be deleted at the same time as *Beta*, and *Gamma*, which was built in Paris. All now became the Navy's

Our Aerial Defence Series   H.M. Airship, The 'Gamma'   39266.   Pub. by: John Drew Aldershot & Farnborough

responsibility and were added to the airship force already under RN control. Conscious of their original 'owners', operational documents referred to these vessels as 'previously operated by the Royal Engineers'. Huge teams of men were required for the ground-crews. Their days started at 7a.m. with a wash in a 5-gallon petrol can heated over a coal burner, but men had to be alert for vessels returning at any time of the day or, occasionally, night.

As the airship came in to dock, her crew would drop a landing line from about 100ft to the men on the ground. The first few would seize the line and haul down the airship until more men could join in as the altitude decreased and more rope became available. The lines had wooden toggles at intervals to assist with grip. Even with the ground crew divided equally to port and starboard, the job was still demanding, especially in windy conditions. If a cross-wind caught the vessel, there was every chance of the ground crew being lifted off their feet. Inevitably this caused some men to let go. If too many did so the airship would rise higher, taking with it the hardier souls still hanging on, most likely to their deaths when their strength failed.

Once safely down, the dirigible's main line would be attached to a Burrell steam engine while the

"ARMY AIRSHIP · DIRIGIBLE NO. 1."

Nulli Secundus II, also known as Army Airship no. 1, was the second version of the airship seen in its original form in Chapter I (page 8). It was launched on 24 July 1908 and had a gas capacity increased from 56,000 to 85,000cu.ft but was broken up within the year. It could be identified by its twin rudders. (Author's collection)

ground party, hanging on to the additional ropes, and under the direction of the shed-master, 'walked' it into a hangar where the lines were secured to concrete blocks and the envelope, if it was to be deflated, was suspended from the roof. (This practice explains the emergence of the term 'hangar' for any aviation shed.) The hangar's massive doors were then closed with the aid of an unarmed Army tank. Wind was always a problem when handling airships in the open and in an attempt to minimise the dangers it posed, enormous screens were erected to protect the vessels.

However, the airships could prove even more uncontrollable if they were not properly ballasted. To do this, the vessel was prepared as for any other flight, being 'walked' out of the hangar after the strength and

Gamma II was rebuilt from the earlier vessel and had twin 45hp Iris motors and an increased gas capacity (101,000cu.ft). It emerged on 10 September 1912 and supported the 'Red Army' against the 'Blue Army' in that year's Army Manoeuvres. (A further difference between the two versions was the long, fabric-covered gondola of the second.) Absorbed into the RNAS on 1 January 1914, it became Naval Airship no. 18 and was decommissioned in 1916. (Copyright Hampshire County Library)

direction of the wind had been assessed from a study of the windsock (or on stations not boasting this useful accessory, a glance at Warrant Officer's handkerchief as he held it aloft for the purpose!). The vessel would be turned by the handling party to head into the wind. Then the airship would seem to take on a life of its own, bucking and straining at the ropes as the forces of lift from the envelope, forward thrust from the motors and the wind playing on the enormous frontal area combined to fight the human effort to hold it down! About eight men would be in the car as the airship was taken on a trip around the limits of the airfield while adjustments were made, the crew moving around as directed to act as mobile ballast.

With the exception of the 'AP' (airship-plane) series, the Navy's airship force was utilised to hunt enemy submarines in coastal waters, and to this end they carried a cargo of bombs. On sighting their quarry, the crew would perhaps attempt to destroy it from about 1,000ft by dropping hand-held bombs. Several crew members remember an alternative tactic: the airship would descend to a sufficiently low altitude where the downwash from its propellers would set up sufficient turbulence round the submarine as to render it uncontrollable. In addition to the necessary equipment for these tasks, an RNAS airship might also carry defensive armament according to type. Often they took a basket containing two carrier pigeons, the basket being divided into compartments to prevent the birds fighting, and emergency rations in the form of Horlicks tablets, which were recalled as being 'very sustaining'. Similar provisions for the unexpected were also carried by naval flying boats.

It seemed to many people entirely appropriate that the RNAS should be responsible for powered lighter-than-air craft since the Royal Navy had taken the earliest steps into the realms of rigid airship construction back in 1908. It was proposed that a 512ft rigid airship with a lifting capacity of 44,800lb should be constructed as a means of evaluating such vessels as weapons of war, and as a result a civilian/-naval team was assembled; none had much knowledge of the work entailed, although strangely some submarine experts were included. Consequently an order for HMA (His Majesty's Airship) *No. 1* was

The Armstrong car of SS42A, showing the Green engine, grapnel, trail rope and (forward) bomb underneath. It is seen at Pembroke in August 1916. (Sydney E. Taylor via Author [373])

placed with Vickers at Barrow-in-Furness. Work began using the new duraluminium alloy for the structure, this being a compromise between those who insisted on steel and the champions of timber. R1 ('Rigid No. 1'), now increasingly known as *Mayfly*, was ready for tests of her twin 160hp Wolseley motors on 13 February 1911, and it was hoped that the new craft would be ready to make its debut at the Coronation Review of the Fleet by King George V later that year. In fact, the first flight was delayed owing to political arguments as to which country should produce the necessary hydrogen gas, since the quantity required was beyond the output of British industry at the time. This problem overcome, R1 was ready on 24 May to be towed from its 'garage', and moored, with the help of a number of tugs, in Cavendish Dock. It proved to have novel features such as planing bottoms to its gondolas since it was intended to be operated from water; there was also provision for it to be moored to a short mast on a naval vessel, an entirely new idea at the time.

Mayfly seems to have made an earlier appearance since some reports mention the airship riding out, unharmed, winds gusting to 45mph. This time, however, ill-luck saw the airship damaged when she struck into one of the shed's uprights while being manoeuvred by a hauling party of three hundred sailors. While repairs were being carried out, the chance was taken to lighten R1 since the accident had been due partly to its excessive weight, which had proved to be considerably greater than estimated. It was not until 22 September that it was again taken outdoors after a 10½-hour inflation.

Unfortunately the weather was now deteriorating with the onset of autumn and at the very moment that the hauling party began to turn the vessel's head into the wind, a sudden squall struck. *Mayfly* heeled over to the accompaniment of a loud crashing from inside, indicating that her back was breaking. Acting on orders, the flight crew immediately jumped overboard and the lightened rear end rose up almost to the vertical before the doomed airship collapsed into the water. She never flew and was subsequently broken up.

Despite this inauspicious start airships, all at first non-rigids, were to form a significant part of the strength of the RNAS and before the end of the First World War the Royal Navy had established no fewer than twenty-seven bases in the British Isles (five of them with additional landing grounds), as well as a number abroad. The British bases, including a Stores Depot, were as follows. Commissioning dates are given where known:

Anglesey	Kirkleatham, Yorkshire
Auldbar, Angus	Laira, Devon
Ballyliffin, Donegal	Larne, Antrim
Bridport, Dorset	Longside, Aberdeen 3/16
Bude, Cornwall	Lowthorpe, Yorkshire
Capel, Kent	Luce Bay, Wigtownshire
Chathill, Northumberland	Mullion, Cornwall 6/16
Cramlington (SD), Northumberland 5/18	Pembroke, Pembrokeshire 1/16
	Polegate, Sussex
Cranwell, Lincolnshire	Pulham, Norfolk 2/16
East Fortune, E. Lothian 6/16	Ramsay, Isle of Man
Godmersham Park, Kent	Slindon, Sussex
Howden, Yorkshire 3/16	Upton, Dorset
Killeagh, County Cork	West Mersham, Kent
Kingsnorth, Kent	

In 1929 Cramlington briefly became a centre for trials investigating the advertising potential of airships for civil use. It later became an industrial site. In 1932 the first tenant of the main shed was William E. Appleby Ltd, model aircraft manufacturers, formerly of Newcastle-on-Tyne, and part of the former accommodation being used as offices. Despite its lowly status, being officially graded as a Stores Depot (SD), both 507 and 508 Flights had formed here on 23 May 1918 (but without vessels), while 509 Flight became their 252 Squadron on 2 June.

Additionally there was a preliminary school for the instruction of officers in handling both 'blimps' and captive balloons, at Wormwood Scrubs. There were also the RNAS stations which catered for both airships and heavier-than-air craft, one example being Dover/Marine. This had been founded in 1913 to accommodate the Royal Seaplane Patrol and the Training School in the following year. Towards the end of 1915 it was committed to anti-submarine patrols in the Channel for which it was equipped in November that year with 8 non-rigids and 48 seaplanes, the majority of these being Short Type 184s.

One serviceman remembered Cranwell vividly:

At the further side of the north aerodrome at Cranwell was a complex of buildings with a hydrogen-producing plant like a small town gasworks in the foreground and completely dominated by a huge hangar nearly 100ft high, its length trebled by corrugated-iron 'wind screens' extending from each end.

This was the Lighter-than-Air Section, a self-contained unit operating three types of craft. The small SS ones used for submarine spotting over

Amethyst tows SS25 off the coast of Anglesey. (Sydney E. Taylor via Author [369])

the North Sea were non-rigids with small engines and a primitive gondola slung underneath that would have delighted the heart of Santos Dumont. Next in size was the North Sea type, another non-rigid with a more powerful engine and better accommodation for the crew, Cranwell's example being the NS11.

Occupying the large shed [naval parlance for hangar] was an airship of the 'R.23 Class', which looked in all respects like a Zeppelin except for its red, white and blue roundel on the nose as it stood in the gloom of its 'home', stowed in a state of partial buoyancy on high trestles and anchored down to bags of ballast and ring-bolts in the floor, awaiting the large ground party necessary to winkle it out and haul it clear of the wind screens before flight. For this the small regular staff of the Lighter-than-Air Section was augmented by men of the Duty Watch from the main station, HMS *Daedalus* – a bleak, hutted establishment in those days – and some of the lads from the Boys' Wing in East Camp.

Small parties were detailed to hang on to the sprays of handling lines attached to heavy cables paid out from fore and aft of the ship and half-a-dozen kept their shoulders under each of the gondolas to prevent the others from pulling it to the ground. The anchoring lines were released and the delicate operation of getting it out began; the whole controlled by one of the ship's officers bawling orders to the widely scattered groups of men by megaphone from the open windows of the control car.

When clear of the hangar and headed into the wind, the engines were started, the handling lines cast off, the nose lifted and it rose effortlessly into the air before the sand and/or water ballast was jettisoned, to the delight of those not standing directly underneath.

To avoid having to valve off too much gas to reduce the buoyancy, the ship usually returned in the evening when the air was cool, the ground party having hung around for quite lengthy periods in readiness.

The BE2-type car of Sea Scout non-rigid airship no. 15. It was wrecked at sea on June 1917. (Sydney E. Taylor via Author [377])

With the propellers of two of the engines swung through 90° to the horizontal to help pull it down and the rest turning over slowly to keep it in position against the wind, the ground party took over and the engines were shut down. Coaxing the ship back into the nest must have put a few wrinkles on the forehead of the officer in charge. There was little room to spare either above or at the sides and once its great length was levelled off at the right height and lined up with the hangar, it was slowly 'walked' home and anchored down. Finally a couple of the small SS types were stowed alongside under the bulge of the envelope, looking like sparrow's eggs under a goose.

To those more accustomed to aeroplanes, the lighter-than-air craft seemed very quiet and gentlemanly and it made quite a change to handle something that had to be forcibly held down to prevent it from becoming airborne.

The Cranwell intake of trainees was about 25–30 men every four to six months. They were divided into battalions, each named after an admiral.

At the outbreak of war on 4 August 1914 the first necessity was to transfer the men and equipment of the British Army to France. One writer of the time pointed out that: 'During the first two months of war the Third Arm [ie aircraft] was used in an extraordinarily wide variety of ways, and thoroughly established itself. The first problem was the safe transport of the British Expeditionary Force. Conveying by warship is useful, but is limited by the fact that a warship travels on the same plane, and is practically subjected to the same restricted range of vision, as the transports it is meant to shield.' This is clearly a reference to the use of airships to protect the cross-Channel passage of the BEF, a use that caught the public's imagination a little later when an incident involving one of the dirigibles was made public. The Secretary of the Admiralty's report ran as follows: 'On one occasion it became necessary to change a propeller blade. The captain feared he would have to descend for this purpose, but two of the crew volunteered to carry out this difficult task in the air, and climbing out on to the bracket carrying the propeller shafting, they completed the hazardous work two thousand feet above the sea.'

EARLY NON-RIGID AIRSHIPS

Two types of RNAS non-rigids, Naval Airships no. 3 and no. 4, are known to have been used to provide an aerial escort to the British troops crossing the Channel. No. 3, the Astra-Torres, was the only one of the Navy's airships of the time to be armed. It was a non-rigid of tri-lobe design with a clover-leaf cross-section. It had originally been ordered from France in 1912 for experimental use and was delivered in the following year. Its envelope had a gas capacity of 229,450cu.ft and the twin 210hp Chenu motors made possible an endurance of roughly twelve hours. Its normal base was at Kingsnorth, the first RNAS airship station to be established. Its armament consisted of a Hotchkiss machine-gun, a weapon of French design, with the ammunition carried in either a belt or a 25-round tray. Although successfully used early in the war, in general the gun proved difficult to reload and was later turned over to use on the ground. Naval Airship no. 3, together with its companion no. 4, was used for war service from 10 August 1914 but was later relegated to training duties. It was withdrawn from service in 1916.

The Parseval, a German-designed vessel known to the manufacturers as PL 18, was ordered by the Admiralty in 1912 and delivered in June the following year, becoming Naval Airship no. 4. Powered by a pair of 170hp Maybach engines, this non-rigid was 308ft 4.8in long and had a diameter of 50ft 10.2in; the envelope capacity was 330,000cu.ft. It had a maximum speed of 45mph and an endurance of eleven hours, giving a maximum range of 621 miles. Combined with its theoretical ability to carry a 1,301lb bomb-load, this made it an ideal, if ironical, choice to

How a contemporary artist imagined the incident when an airscrew blade was changed in mid-air. A Parseval was the vessel involved since it had dismountable, steel variable-pitch airscrew blades (unusual at the time). Here the artist erroneously shows a complete wooden propeller being removed. Known as Naval Airship no. 4, the Parseval made the first airship flight of the war on 5 August 1914. (Author's collection [700])

A later Parseval (Naval Airship no. 6) which was Vickers-built and used for training. (Sydney E. Taylor via Author [370])

patrol the Thames Estuary on 5/6 August 1914, the day after the declaration of war on Germany. It was used again on 10 August, flying from Kingsnorth, when it was joined by the Astra-Torres. It was used to provide aerial escort for troopships plying between Dover and Calais during the first few months of the war, but since it carried no armament, unlike its companion, its defensive capability was nil and its ability as a submarine hunter purely psychological. Three other Parsevals which had been ordered for the RNAS were not delivered after war was declared so Vickers constructed near-copies (they differed mainly in the design of the car) which became Naval Airships nos 5, 6 and 7. All were used for training, as was no. 4 after the first months of war, being broken up in July 1917.

THE SS TYPES

Considerably shorter than the Parseval, measuring only 143ft in length and with a diameter of only 32ft, the prototype of the non-rigid SS Type was created by combining the envelope of the former Naval Airship no. 2 (which had in turn been known as the Willows no. 4) with the fuselage of a BE2c to act as a car. The SS Type was first tested in March 1915, with a dorsal fin. Lift was 6.615lb and the maximum speed was 50mph. It was designated 'Sea Scout' (or more usually 'Submarine Scout'), indicating the type's intended use for convoy protection, operating chiefly in the Dover Straits and Irish Narrows. Only two months later, on 8 May, the first example was posted to Capel (later to be joined by two more), the second arriving at Polegate on 6 July. It was the first of five there.

Although there were BE-type cars on the majority (SS1, SS2 and SS3, SS8, SS9, SS10, SS10A, SS11 and SS12 to SS20, plus SS23, SS24 and

SS25), eleven had Armstrong Whitworth FK3 cars and twelve others Maurice Farman fuselages. There was even a pair of 'SSPs' with pusher cars and six 'SSTs' powered by twin motors, but neither were built in larger numbers. Gas capacity was 70,000cu.ft and engines could be a 70 or 75hp Renault or a Rolls-Royce Hawk in the Maurice Farman cars, with 100hp Greens in the FK8s. Interestingly all carried a Lewis gun and a bomb-load. A few had twin ventral fins. Trials were made with a complete aircraft suspended underneath in order to investigate the possibility of lifting an interceptor to an operational altitude to intercept Zeppelins.

Bringing in SS13 at Polegate in high winds on 5 April 1917. The vessel became SS14A in October and was struck off charge in October 1919. This airship was originally based at Folkestone. (JMB/GSL collection)

SS40 had an enlarged envelope and black finish for planned night espionage work. An RFC unit equipped with BE2cs had been established for this purpose in April 1915; it was known as the Special Duty Flight but its first two sorties in September were failures. Training these agents was not the responsibility of the corps. (Sir Victor Goddard via Author [372])

Coxswain L.M. Bird on the rear of SSZ17's car, showing the engine and pipe to the hand-blower. This vessel was the first Barrow-built airship to fly successfully and on 15 July 1915 it was sent by rail to Stranraer. (Sydney E. Taylor via Author [379])

SS40 was unusual in being doped entirely black; it was intended to be used to introduce agents into enemy territory but was in fact never used for this purpose, being pressed into service for night reconnaissance instead. It differed from standard in having an enlarged fin.

The SSZ was regarded as the ultimate development of the SS Type. The first of the new model was assembled at Capel during June in time to be flown to Dunkirk (St Pol) on 21 September 1916. Powered by a 75hp Rolls-Royce Hawk, the new version boasted an identical specification to the earlier one, except that the envelope was 3ft longer and cars replaced the earlier aeroplane fuselages. The first sixteen examples of Sea Scout Zeros (from the total production batch of seventy-seven) were delivered in July 1917. All were exclusively employed for sea patrols; it had originally been intended that they be used by the Belgian coast patrol to assist in gunnery spotting. For this purpose, they would be towed by monitors, proceeding under their own power only after release.

Patrols took an average of twelve hours, although a 'long patrol' could double that time. However, the record is said to have been held by SSZ39 which remained airborne for fifty hours in the summer of 1918 when the type was still in production. Forty-nine submarines are recorded as having been spotted by this type, twenty-seven of which were claimed to have been destroyed.

COASTAL TYPE AIRSHIPS

Similar to the Astra Torres, the Coastal Type was of clover-leaf section. The first of these non-rigids, with length of 190ft, a diameter of 39ft 6in and a gas capacity of 140,000cu.ft, was ordered from Kingsnorth in 1915, flying for the first time from that station on 9 June the following year. It differed in having a gunner's position mounting a pair of Lewis guns above the envelope, the prototype having a shorter envelope (by 10ft) than that of the twenty-six subsequent versions. C1 also had a smaller gas capacity (by 30,000cu.ft). The twin engines were one tractor and one pusher, the motors ranging from 150hp to 220hp; Sunbeams were the most common type. Where two motors of dissimilar power were used, the greater was always aft of the gondola, although overheating of this motor

The bow of airship C1 at Kingsnorth in 1916. (Sydney E. Taylor via Author [376])

presented early problems and the nose of the envelope also had to be strengthened. Maximum speed was 50mph and a twelve-hour flight was possible. The first of the operational versions was issued to the Pembroke RNAS station in June 1916, others going a little later to East Fortune, Howden, Longside, Mullion and Pulham. In September of the same year one vessel of this type, numbered C1, was involved in trials to look into the possibility of refuelling airships from surface vessels, these trials being carried out offshore with the light cruiser HMS *Canterbury*. Coastal Class dirigibles offered improved accommodation for the four members of the crew who remained in the car; the fifth member of the crew was the gunner who had to ascend to his position above the envelope via an internal climbing tube.

The Coastal Star Type, marked on the envelope with a five-pointed star between the letter C and the individual number, was a perfected edition of the earlier Coastal Type, introduced in January 1918. Only ten were constructed, single examples of these being issued in numerical order to the airship stations. Vessels of this class measured 210ft in length and had a gas capacity of 210,000cu.ft; their power units were a combination of a 110hp Berliet and a 240hp Fiat (with the exception of C*1 which was finally powered by a 220hp Renault and a 240hp Fiat).

NORTH SEA TYPE AIRSHIPS

The last of the RNAS airships, the North Sea Type was a non-rigid with a 360,000cu.ft capacity envelope of clover-leaf trefoil configuration. Engines were at first two 250hp Rolls-Royce Eagles, but these were replaced by 240hp Fiats (or in the case of NS11 a pair of 300hp Fiats). Only twelve were used by Britain, although a number were held in reserve, and the number thirteen may not have been allocated. They were ordered in

NS6 made its first flight in January 1918. It was mostly commanded by Captain Struthers and made a notable flight from Kingsnorth to East Fortune on 31 May 1918. It was struck off charge on 8 February 1919. (Sydney E. Taylor via Author [375])

January 1916, the first being delivered to Pulham in the following February. Teething difficulties were experienced with the 10ft long engine shafts and transmission. The construction method permitted a V-form of internal rigging which enabled the car and engines to be brought much closer to the envelope so that drag was reduced. However, early models were distinguished by a number of external fuel tanks along the envelope. Later these were carried internally, but on the lower port side all had the prominent pressure distribution duct (which maintained the internal pressure, and therefore the aerodynamic shape) between the six internal ballonets.

More than one type of car existed, some with an unfaired connection to the motors, but the forward part was well equipped with bunks for the off duty half of the ten-man crew and even a chart table. Armament consisted of four Lewis guns, one mounted on the top of the envelope, and a 400lb bomb-load. Useful lift was 8,400lb, top speed was 55mph and the range 3,000 miles. All were used for ocean patrols, mostly operating from East Fortune over the North Sea; although the original concept of the design was that they should be used in cooperation with surface vessels on convoy protection duties, the North Sea Type was never put to this use.

BOMBER AIRSHIPS

Late in the First World War the RNAS looked into using airships for strategic bombing. Since a suitable dirigible seemed already to exist in Italy, a single example of the semi-rigid M Class was ordered by the Admiralty for trials in 1918. It was delivered on 28 October. This vessel was 275ft 3.7in long and 55ft in diameter; its gas capacity was 441,434cu.ft, giving a useful lift of 8,378lb, and power differed from that

Wheeled aircraft were regarded as 'too dangerous' for deck landings late in 1918, but SSZ59 was successfully used for trials aboard HMS Furious. *(JMG/GSL collection)*

of the Italian versions, coming from a pair of 220hp Italia D.2 engines mounted on outriggers and requiring complex linkage, and a single 200hp SPA 6.A motor. The propellers had variable pitch and were also reversible. In addition to its 2,205lb bomb-load the SR.1 (Semi-Rigid no. 1, as it was known in the Navy) was armed with a single Lewis gun mounted above the envelope; its potential for bombing sorties lay in its high service ceiling if it was to be used against well-defended targets such as rail heads and docks as was originally envisaged. From a structural viewpoint, the type was interesting in that the keel supported both tailplane and bows, wires from this connecting its canvas girdles and bands round the circumference of the envelope to suspend the gondola. Internally, the envelope was divided into six chambers, thus reducing leakage, and entry of air to maintain the aerodynamic shape was through a shuttered valve in the heavily reinforced nose. However, the war situation at the time the SR.1 was accepted for trials, in competition with British non-rigids, and the fact that these were proving costly, meant that the tests were never completed and the type remained the Navy's sole example of a semi-rigid airship, albeit a non-operational one.

Despite the Navy's unfortunate experience with the *Mayfly* before the war, an attempt was made to reintroduce rigid types from 1916 and a programme of shed construction for their accommodation was begun at a number of RNAS stations. One was completed in December at Howden, at Pulham in February 1917, at Longside in March, East Fortune in April and Cranwell in June, and before the war ended eleven naval rigid airships had been constructed. All used chiefly for training or experimental purposes. They were:

Type	Class	Allocation
R.9	—	Howden, 4 April 1917
R.23	R.23	Pulham, 15 September 1917
R.24	R.23	E. Fortune, 28 October 1917
R.25	R.23	Howden, 15 October 1917

Type	Class	Allocation
R.26	R.23	
R.27	R.23X	
R.29	R.23X	
R.31*	—	
R.32*	—	
R.33	R.33	E. Fortune and Howden
R.34	R.33	E. Fortune

*R.31 and R.32 were based on the German SL design.

Described at the time as an 'enormous airship', R.23 was constructed from metal and covered with two layers of rubber-coated fabric and one of rubber. Measuring some 535ft long and with a gas capacity of 942,000cu.ft in eighteen cells, it was capable of a maximum speed of 52mph and had a ceiling of 3,000ft. It was first used in trials for air-launching a pair of Sopwith 2F.1 Camels from 212 Squadron in June 1918; both were successfully launched in the last week of the First World War and flew back to Pulham. The R.23 carried a crew of seventeen, with four 100lb bombs; at one time it was armed with a 2lb quick-firing gun above the envelope, it being recalled that the vessel 'had almost to stand up' for this to be fired. In charge of these tests was a youthful Vickers employee named Neville Barnes Wallis, who later invented the famous bouncing bomb.

FIXED WING AIRCRAFT

'FRAIL THINGS OF STICKS AND STRING'

Although to modern eyes the machines of the RFC and RAF seem tremendously fragile, the ordinary, fixed wing machines which both services flew were in fact immensely strong. They were largely constructed of fabric-covered timber, the resultant structure being wire-braced. It is interesting to reflect on the fact that both services were constituted only six years after the Wright brothers first flew at Kittyhawk in the United States of America and just three years after the English Channel had first been crossed by air. In a comparatively short time a large number of aircraft types were created, and many found their way into service with both the RFC and the RNAS. This chapter looks at some of the better known types and is a selected list.

A DH9A after a heavy landing. This incident was said to involve Lieutenant Tryggve Gran, a Norwegian serving with the RFC. (via Dr J. Cunbrae-Stuart)

ARMSTRONG WHITWORTH FK8

This two-seat reconnaissance-bomber was developed from the earlier FK7, itself a modification of the earlier FK3. The first examples went into action with 35 Squadron RFC at the end of January 1917. Described at the time as 'a rugged, sturdy machine', attempts to introduce an oleo undercarriage caused problems, especially on the rough landing fields of France. With its 160hp Beardmore engine giving a maximum speed of some 98mph, the FK8 is best remembered as the type flown by Lieutenant Mcleod when he won the Victoria Cross. The crew of another FK8 were responsible for bringing down a Gotha on 7 July 1917 during an intended attack on the British Isles. The FK8s of 2 Squadron were heavily involved in the Battle of Messines in June 1917. It was popularly known among its pilots by the curious nickname 'Big Ack-W'.

AVRO 504

Popularly dismissed as a trainer, this biplane, best remembered in its Avro 504K version, caused something of a stir in aviation circles when the prototype first appeared at Hendon late in 1913. In the following April the War Office ordered twelve for the new Royal Flying Corps, itself created only in the previous year. Generally a two-seater, although a few 504Ds were produced in single-seat form, its use in action was limited. However, on 21 November 1914 four Avros, nos 179, 873, 874 and 875, led by Squadron-Commander E.F. Briggs RNAS attacked the Zeppelin airship works at Friedrichshafen.

In the main, four versions of this aircraft existed, all based on the earlier Avro Type 'E' and 'Es' of which a number were ordered for the RFC in 1913 for exclusive use as trainers. The basic 504 was powered by an 80hp Gnome, Le Rhone or Clerget engine, the former rotary type also being used for the 504D. The later 504J, powered by a 100hp Gnome Monosoupape engine, was the version adopted for instruction at the Central Flying School, while the best-remembered of all, the Avro 504K, was powered by a variety of motors, such as the 130hp Clerget, the 110hp Le Rhone or 100hp Monosoupape. The Le Rhone engine produced the best performance, with a maximum speed of 95mph. There also existed single-seat versions, some of which were used as night interceptors; one such Avro 504K was involved in an incident while monitoring the surrender of 150 U-boats at Harwich on 20 November 1918.*

BEARDMORE WBIII

Operated by the RNAS toward the end of the First World War, this aircraft has been largely forgotten. It was based on the Sopwith Pup but bore little or no resemblance to that aircraft. Like the Pup, the WBIII was a single-seater produced exclusively for aircraft-carrier operations. Its wings were unstaggered and the 25ft wingspan could fold down to a mere 10ft 4in for stowage between decks; the undercarriage could also be folded up to further conserve space. The undercarriage was of unusually

---

*This aircraft was E4253, a night-fighter version which had two-colour roundels and a rudder equally divided into red and blue. On this the serial number appeared in black on the upper half under a slightly smaller letter 'E', all in a style similar to that now known as 'Fortune Bold'. This aircraft came down into the water owing to engine trouble and was salvaged by HMS *Seymour*, the crew being rescued by a whaler from the same vessel. Other aircraft engaged in surveillance of the U-boats on 20 November were the rigid airship R.26 and the dirigible NS8.

Beardmore WBIII N6100 on the foredeck of HMS Furious. This was the first of the initial production batch. There were two types of this machine, the SB3D and the SB3F, the suffix letters indicating an undercarriage capable of being 'ditched' and one that could be folded for stowage respectively. This view shows the unusually narrow track of the undercarriage and the box-line directional runners for the wheels to assist take-off. (T. Smale collection)

narrow wheel track, and during take-off the wheels ran in a pair of lengthened 'troughs' for guidance. The wheels also could be jettisoned in the event of an emergency landing.

Other novel design features included the absence of conventional centre-section struts, these being replaced by an extra bay of interplane struts set at the wing roots adjacent to the fuselage sides, while another unusual feature was the use of struts connecting upper and lower ailerons. These were of especially sturdy appearance on the early variants but slimmed down on subsequent versions. Records show that eight days before the Armistice, the RNAS had on its strength fifty-five Beardmores, eighteen of which were with the Grand Fleet. Powered by either an 80hp Le Rhone or Clerget rotary engine, it had a maximum speed of 103mph.

BLERIOT MONOPLANE

The RFC had several of these aircraft, which were similar to the historic aeroplane in which Louis Bleriot first flew across the Channel. One of the first to be sent to the Military Wing had been used for publicity purposes by the International Correspondence Schools until 28 January 1913 when it became number 216. The Naval Wing adopted its own Bleriot Monoplane, the two-seat Type XI-2, in February of the same year. These aircraft were powered by either 50hp or 80hp Gnome rotary engines, although both the RFC and RNAS subsequently acquired a few that were powered by Anzani motors. Although Anzani had also built the engine for Bleriot's historic machine, the later engines were of far greater power. In general, the Type XI was used for general military purposes, while the XI-2, being capable of taking an observer, was generally intended for

A school's Bristol Boxkite biplane. Those with extended upper wing-tips were regarded as the 'military' version. One such, numbered F4, was on the strength of the Air Battalion of the Royal Engineers during the summer of 1911. (Author's collection [L16])

reconnaissance, a duty made more hazardous by the aircraft's slow top speed of 70mph. It was in an aircraft of this type, no. 389, that Captain (later Air Chief Marshal Sir Philip) de la Ferte undertook the first reconnaissance flight ever made by the Royal Flying Corps on 19 August 1914. Less than a month later the first reconnaissance flights were made over enemy territory during the Battle of the Aisne.

The Bleriot XI and XI-2 were not the only aircraft from the famous French 'stable' to be absorbed on to the strength of the fledgling Flying Corps. Others included the Type XXI, a side-by-side two-seater resembling the Type XI with a 70hp Gnome motor giving a maximum speed of nearly 60mph. Only one of these entered service, seeing action with 2 Aeroplane Company of the Royal Engineers and later with 3 Squadron RFC. Mention must also be made of the high-wing Bleriot Parasol, of which the Military Wing had fourteen. Most were used for instruction, although tentative arrangements were made for delivering bombs at the then-noteworthy speed of almost 70mph. One Parasol, no. 616, is known to have flown in action, Air Mechanic J.T.B. McCudden recording in his memoirs that this aircraft was used to bomb Laon railway station with 'sixteen hand grenades, two Shrapnel bombs . . . in a rack on the outside of the fuselage [from thence having to be thrown by hand] and a Melinite bomb'. The latter was tied on with string which had to be cut in order to drop the bomb with the aid of a determined push!

BRISTOL BOXKITES

Pre-dating the French monoplanes, these British & Colonial Aircraft Company products were first ordered as trainers for the Air Battalion of the Royal Engineers on 14 March 1911. Four were ordered, and the first was delivered on 18 May 1911. Of 'open girder' construction, these biplanes were powered either by 50hp Gnome or 60hp Renault motors, giving a maximum speed of about 40mph. This aircraft clearly illustrates the swift progress of military thinking in the formative years of aviation, since one version with extended upper wings was designated as a military version, several of which were sent to Czarist Russia for this very purpose.

BRISTOL SCOUT

The Scout was based on the design of Lord Carbery's sporting biplane, which was lost in the Channel only twenty-three days before the First World War engulfed the civilised world. The Scout Type B was one of the first aircraft to be armed; this was achieved by means of a rifle pointing forward at an angle at which it missed the airscrew arc when fired. There was also provision for the pilot to drop by hand five rifle grenades carried on a device resembling a pipe-rack on the outside of the fuselage, on the starboard side. These grenades had their standard rods removed and replaced by a bundle of cloth rags to act as tails. One machine from 5 Squadron augmented this fearsome armoury with a Mauser pistol in a holster on the outside of the fuselage within the pilot's reach!

As development of the type went on, the 'C' and 'D' variants were introduced, and it was in one of the latter, no. 1611, that on 25 July 1915 Captain Lanoe G. Hawker of 6 Squadron fought the action for which he was awarded the Victoria Cross. The Type 'D' also earned its place in RFC history when no. A1761 was experimentally fitted with a Vickers Challenger interrupter gear, offset to port and aimed in the direction of flight. This device pre-dated the later synchronisation gear for fixed aircraft armament.

Bristol 'D' Scout A1747. (IWM Q55987)

Regarded as the best of its type, the Bristol Scout 'C', powered by an 80hp Le Rhone rotary motor, was capable of a maximum speed of nearly 93mph. Nineteen squadrons on the Western Front alone had 'C' Types, although no unit was equipped entirely with them, in the manner of military air organisation of 1915 and 1916. The type was also used by the RNAS on many fronts as well as at home coastal stations, and aboard HMS *Vindex*, which operated in the North Sea. It was from the short deck of this seaplane-carrier that on 3 November 1915 Flight Sub-Lieutenant H.F. Towler made the first take-off in an aircraft with a wheeled undercarriage from a British naval vessel. Two Bristols could be accommodated in this carrier, dismantled to save space. They could not land back on this carrier, instead flotation bags were fitted so the aircraft could touch down in the sea alongside the ship and then be hoisted aboard.

BRISTOL F2A AND F2B

It was not until May 1917 that the next Bristol design entered service with the RFC. The new aircraft was a two-seat reconnaissance machine powered by a 120hp Beardmore engine, and was unusual in having the engine mounted mid-way between the upper and lower wings. This was an attempt to minimise the degree to which the upper mainplane obscured the pilot's field of view, and although tests proved satisfactory, the decision was taken to fit the 120hp Rolls-Royce Falcon liquid-cooled engine as an alternative. At the same time the designation changed to that of a fighter-reconnaissance machine, and it was not long before Bristol F2As began to equip 48 Squadron which was to leave for France on 8 March. However, operational use was delayed and it was not until the opening of the Battle of Arras that the type was first operationally used. It was hoped by this to achieve an element of surprise, but in the event the type proved rather a failure.

A Bristol F2B is positioned by the ground crew at Marske. This particular machine appears to have a camera-gun above the upper centre-section and a Rolls-Royce Falcon motor driving a four-bladed propeller. (JMB/GSL collection)

On 5 April a formation of Bristol F2As made their first offensive patrol over enemy territory. The patrol was led by the national hero Captain W.L. Robinson, who had won the Victoria Cross following the destruction of Airship S.L.11 on the night of 3 September 1916. Sadly, this time three of the four F2As were swiftly dispatched by Manfred von Richthofen and his unit, Robinson being taken prisoner. The reason for this débâcle was in no way due to Robinson's leadership, but was largely the result of trying to use the Bristol like a conventional two-seater; it was not until the adoption of the bold new tactic of flying the Bristol in the manner of a single-seater enhanced by the availability of a second, manned gun, that the F2A was pronounced a success.

Lessons learned with the F2A were incorporated in its successor, the F2B. This aircraft proved a great success and was soon affectionately dubbed the 'Biff' ('Brisfit' came later). A number of engine trials ensued, including the fitting of the 230hp BHP motor; however, this had to be discarded because it would be too high powered to act as an escort fighter. Instead, some were powered by Falcon engines, giving a top speed of 113mph, and others by the 200hp Sunbeam Arab, giving 104mph. Bristol fighters of this genre continued in one form or another until 1928, long after the disappearance of the RFC.

BRISTOL M.1

This monoplane was the centre of a series of rumours that circulated in aviation circles on the Western Front at the beginning of 1917. This single-seater was expected to appear in large numbers, while its performance was confidently expected to exceed anything which the enemy could put into the air. Great was the disappointment therefore as time went by and no such aircraft appeared. In fact none was ever issued to squadrons in France, although they did appear in Palestine and the East, but their numbers were never large enough to make an impact on the war situation. This was a direct reflection of the official attitude to the type: just 125 were ordered from Filton in the late summer of 1917, although the reason for this official lack of enthusiasm for the type has never been conclusively established. Suggestions range from a residual echo of the monoplane ban of several years earlier to the rumour that their endurance was allegedly limited. Whatever the reason, production ceased in March 1918.

Three versions of the Bristol M.1 existed, differing chiefly in engine installation, the final variant being powered by a 110hp Le Rhone rotary engine giving a maximum speed of 111mph. Armament was a single Vickers machine-gun synchronised to fire through the airscrew arc.

CURTISS FLYING BOATS

At the other end of the scale there existed from as early as November 1914 the first of the Curtiss H.4 Small America Flying Boats. The first pair were tried out for ocean reconnaissance duties from Felixstowe before a further sixty-two were specially constructed in Britain. Despite their span of 72ft, they were dubbed 'small' after the introduction of the 92ft span H.12 Large America Flying Boats. First operated from Great Yarmouth from mid-April 1917, a total of seventy-one of these aircraft eventually served on the strength of the RNAS. Crews of these aircraft were credited with the destruction of UC-36, UB-20, UC-72 and UC-6, but of the total strength only eighteen survived to the end of October 1918. Six were of the improved type, which were almost indistinguishable from the Felixstowe F.2A boats, which served exclusively from home stations while the F.3s went to the Mediterranean.

DE HAVILLAND DH1

Although the organisation headed by Geoffrey de Havilland was trading under the name of Airco when its products were being supplied to the RFC/RNAS, they were usually known under the more familiar name of de Havilland. The first type appeared in January 1915. This was the two-seat pusher known as the DH1. Although today the appearance of open-girder construction is unusual, this was not so at the time. The DH1 also had a crew nacelle, at the rear of which was the engine driving a 'pusher' airscrew. This was quite conventional, and offered the advantage from a fighting viewpoint that forward-firing guns did not have to fire through the revolving propeller blades.

Although by the standards of the time, the DH1 was an acceptable warplane, delivery was slow. This was partly because of the limited availability of the most suitable engine, the liquid-cooled 120hp Beardmore. The early stages of this engine's development were plagued with unforeseen difficulties to such an extent that only two, then known as Astro-Daimlers, were available in August 1914. Other DH1s were powered by 70hp Renault engines, and these went mostly to training units. However, the Beardmore engine was specified for the second version of the aircraft, the DH1A, giving a quoted maximum speed of 90mph.

Although officially described as a fighter-reconnaissance type, this designation does little more than emphasise the vague ideas of aircraft use at the time, the retention of the term 'reconnaissance' doing no more than perpetuate the idea that flying machines could fulfil the role of the cavalry in earlier wars. In practice the six DH1As sent to equip 14 Squadron RFC in Palestine were to see limited use as escort-fighters. Armament consisted of a single Lewis machine-gun on a flexible pillar mounting in the front cockpit. A number were allocated for home defence, while the remainder were pressed into service with instructional units, including those specialising in night-flying tuition.

DH2

This was the RFC's first real single-seat fighting scout, a machine that was both fast and robust. Initially unpopular owing to its limited speed and sensitive controls, it required careful handling to avoid the spinning accidents which claimed the lives of a number of its pilots in training.

Nevertheless the arrival of the type on the Western Front was greeted with a swift adoption for active service with 24 Squadron. The new aircraft began flying regular patrols over the front during the opening phases of the Battle of the Somme, in the process going some way towards securing air supremacy from the Fokker monoplanes which had previously created serious problems for the Allies. However, there is no truth in the once widely held belief that the de Havilland machine was designed specifically to wrest control of the air back from the Fokkers. Now, due to their achievement, slower reconnaissance machines were able to go about their work in greater safety.

The DH2 was not on the scene for long. By mid-September enemy units were re-equipping with Albatros scouts which the de Havillands could not match. Even so, there was no better type available in numbers, so operational use of the DH2 had to continue as before. Among the pilots associated with the type during this period were Sergeant (later Major) James McCudden and Major Lanoe Hawker, both of whom were later awarded the Victoria Cross for gallantry.

The DH2 was powered variously by rotary engines such as the 100hp Gnome Monosoupape or the 110hp Le Rhone, both giving a maximum speed in the region of 93mph. The armament consisted of a single Vickers gun in the front of the nacelle on a flexible mounting (although these became unofficially 'fixed' in service).

DH4

Despite its reputation for catching fire in the air (for which it was dubbed the 'flaming coffin' in RFC messes), this de Havilland two-seat bomber was one of the best aircraft of the First World War. It was able to defend itself against interceptors, although the crew were too far apart for easy communication, which sometimes caused problems, especially in a fight. The prototype first flew in the middle of August 1916, with a second appearing later. Although a production order was anticipated, considerable problems were encountered in finding a source of suitable engines. Only a small percentage of the first production batch was powered by early Rolls-Royce Eagle motors, and the first aircraft issued for active service went to 55 Squadron for use as fighter-reconnaissance machines. In all the DH4 formed the equipment of six squadrons on the Western Front and two in Mesopotamia, plus 51 Home Defence Squadron, while a large number went to training units of various types. Some of those committed to France became early components of the Independent Air Force.

The type was also used by the RNAS. The first squadron so equipped was 2 (Naval) Squadron based at St Pol, in March 1917, but four others in France and at Port Victoria subsequently flew the DH4, in addition to units at Mudros, Stavros, Thasos, Mitylene and Andrano. At all of these venues, the aircraft were pressed into service on anti-Zeppelin patrols, as well as anti-submarine patrols; for the latter the standard load of 460lb of bombs was replaced by depth-charges. Armament consisted of a single Lewis gun on a Scarff mounting aft, and a synchronised Vickers firing forward. Maximum speed with the Rolls-Royce engine was 119mph.

DH5

This little Airco scout was of unusual construction and owed much of its visual appeal to the negative stagger to the wings. This was an attempt to improve the pilot's view, and it attracted much attention when the first example flew late in 1916. Despite its looks, this has been called the least successful of de Havilland's designs of the First World War. Such an opinion is probably based on the fact that the type only saw operational service for a period of eight months, but in the minds of many it proved to be a useful, if not exactly inspired production. The prototype (A5172) of this particular machine made its first flight in December 1916, being sent to France later in the same month for service trials, possibly with 24 Squadron. By this time it had undergone a number of changes, such as the fitting of a synchronised Vickers gun, offset to port above the front fuselage, and the introduction of a new fin and rudder. The original more rounded design was replaced by one that conformed more closely to an outline that was later regarded as 'typical' of Airco. Since no alterations were deemed necessary on the prototype's return in November, a production order was placed for fifty.

In fact the first of these was only received, by 24 Squadron, in May 1917. It was followed by a second on the next day. Delays were due to changes to the aileron balance system, installing cable for balance instead of bungee, and fitting external stiffeners on the cowling. In fact, the type had been dogged by problems from the start, when excessive vibration from the French-built 110hp Le Rhone engines caused the instruments to become unreadable!

Described as 'DH5s at Wyton in 1917', these aircraft are probably from 65 Squadron which was working up here at the time, having been formed on 1 August 1916. (Captain G. Olley via Dr J. Cunbrae-Stuart)

The mainstay of the RFC's attack potential through the greater part of its existence was the light 20lb bomb, four of which are seen here under the wing of a DH9A. (Author [520])

In RFC use the DH5 was not particularly popular, partly because pilots distrusted the unconventional wing arrangement and were over-cautious when landing, since by then the aircraft had gained a reputation for being difficult to put down safely. Some pilots even said it was generally inferior to the DH2. Whatever the truth of these allegations, when 41 Squadron began to re-equip with the SE5a in October 1917, many felt their criticism of the little de Havilland justified, there being no comparison with its successor. Five squadrons had flown the DH5 on the Western Front, with a further three working up at the same time; the remainder were with training schools. Maximum speed with the 110hp Le Rhone engine was 102mph.

DH6

This slightly unconventional-looking two-seater, the later version of which had wings rigged with moderate negative stagger like its predecessor, was over-docile and therefore not ideal for the training duties to which it was put. Nevertheless, a number of these two-seaters made up the thirty-two flights used for coastal patrol over home waters by the RNAS. For this work it was necessary to dispense with the second crew member in order to make room for the 100lb bomb-load it carried in case the pilot spotted a U-boat. The notoriously unreliable 90hp Curtiss OX-5 engine fitted to some examples resulted in a number of emergency landings at sea; fortunately the DH6 floated for a considerable time. Its almost bizarre appearance with wings said to be manufactured by the mile and cut off by the yard, gained it a number of soubriquets including 'clutching hand' and 'the skyhook'. With the 90hp Royal Aircraft Factory 1a motor (one of three commonly fitted), it was capable of a maximum speed of 66mph at 6,500ft, an altitude it took twenty-nine minutes to reach.

Evidently a presentation aircraft, this DH9, D3259, is marked 'Rigger Parish No. 4' in white on the grey nose. (JMB/GSL collection)

DH9

This well-remembered single-motor, two-seat bomber owed much to the DH4 but the crew were seated closer together. Unfortunately, however, it was again powered by a BHP (Beardmore-Halford-Pullinger) engine, despite which the type was soon committed to bombing enemy industrial targets from April. None saw service with the RFC.

THE FAIREY CAMPANIA F22

Two-seat floatplanes of this type were the first in British naval aviation to be specifically designed for operations from a carrier. They joined the carrier *Campania* in 1917, taking their name from this vessel. They lacked wheels and took off with the aid of a mobile trolley, which was discarded as the machine became airborne. Immediately before the end of hostilities in 1918, forty-two were still in service. Powered by a 250hp Sunbeam Maori II, their maximum speed was 85mph.

HANDLEY PAGE O/100 AND O/400

As military aviation progressed and new strategies evolved, the warring nations developed the heavy bomber. Britain's sole examples of this concept before the RFC vanished into history were the impressive Handley Page O/100 and O/400. It is not readily appreciated that the creation of a long-distance bomber force for Britain was due more to the Admiralty than to the War Office, the first specification for such a type being issued as early as December 1914. The resultant bomber, known as the O/100, appeared in November 1916. Powered by a pair of 250hp Rolls-Royce Eagle IIs, it was capable of carrying a 1,800lb bomb-load and a crew of four. Production versions serving with the 3rd Wing at Luxeuil and the 5th at Dunkirk were within striking range of targets in industrial Germany (although the original idea was that the bombers would be used for attacks on U-boat bases).

However, the strategy proved sound, thus making possible the foundation of the Independent Air Force. The introduction of the improved version, the O/400, powered by a pair of 284hp or 375hp Rolls-Royce Eagle engines, was able to deliver the new 1,650lb bomb. The new bomber had a maximum speed of almost 98mph, compared with an estimated 85mph for the earlier machine. In time the O/400 was further developed into the Handley Page O/1500, with four motors mounted in tandem. These were introduced too late to see service in the war, but were operated by the new Royal Air Force.

NIEUPORT SCOUTS

The Nieuport single-seaters were only the second scouts of French origin to be operated by the early British air arms (the Spad 7s, 12s and 13s were the other). The RNAS placed an order for some 170, of both Types 10 and 12, followed by a further sixty, probably of the same design, later. The naval machines entered service during 1915. A further 150 may have been

This Nieuport wears British insignia but is unusual in having non-standard provision for twin machine-guns above the upper centre-section. (JMB/GSL collection)

No. 1 Squadron at Bailleul in 1917. Among these assorted scouts may be made out A6721, B3459 (probably '2') and B3630, all Nieuport 17s. (Captain G. Olley via Dr J. Cunbrae-Stuart)

Seen at Chingford in January 1918, this Nieuport 17bis carries the serial number N5875 on the rudder. (JMB/GSL collection)

ordered at a later date. Twenty-one Nieuports were transferred to the RFC from the Navy (and there may have been others). However, these were to see action only briefly, being relegated to training purposes when the Nieuport 17 appeared. Together with some Nieuport 24s, identified by the slab-sided fuselages of the earlier models being now stringered and rounded, four Nieuport 17s from Eastchurch were lent to the RFC for the protection of artillery observation machines in France in March 1916. In the following June two flights of Nieuport Scouts are recorded as being detached from No. 1 Wing and sent to Furness, there to become the famous A Squadron RNAS.

Armed with a single Vickers gun above the cowling (replacing the earlier Lewis gun firing over the upper centre-section) and on occasion with eight Le Prieur rockets for attacks on balloons, the Nieuport 17c1 was powered by a 110hp Le Rhone engine which gave a maximum speed of 107mph.

ROYAL AIRCRAFT FACTORY BE TYPES

Notwithstanding the limited intakes of foreign types such as Spads and Nieuports, the Royal Aircraft Factory's machines continued to figure prominently among British service aircraft. The first BE biplanes were issued to 2, 4 and 6 Squadrons of the RFC during early 1913, those for 2 Squadron making the trip from the south of England to Montrose in thirteen days despite unreliable engines.

These aircraft were followed by the BE2b, which differed from the earlier model in having more substantial decking round the cockpits in addition to a revised control layout and new fuel system. It was in a BE2b, no. 687, that Lieutenant W.B. Rhodes Moorhouse carried out the action for which he won the Victoria Cross.

This was followed by the BE2c, a design that introduced a fin for the first time. More were produced of this version than of any other. Like its predecessors it enjoyed inherent stability, a feature desirable in a trainer, but not in a warplane, where manoeuvrability was crucial. The colourful MP of the day, Noel Pemberton Billing, who was rather given to emotive language, claimed in the House of Commons that crews killed in these machines had been 'murdered rather than killed'. Pressed into use in a variety of roles in the days when aircraft specialisation was still controversial, the BE2c became very unpopular. The RNAS was the first to use the type overseas. The maximum speed of the BE2c with a 90hp Royal Aircraft Factory 1a motor was 72mph, and a bomb-load of 224lb could be carried if flown solo.

There were other variants. The BE2d boasted a rounded fin and dual controls; the BE2e had shortened lower wings; the BE2f was a redesignation of the modified BE2c; while the BE2g was a rebuilt BE2d. Most of these had no distinguishing external features, the unequal span wings being perpetuated in the subsequent BE12 and 12a.

A rare view of a BE2c in flight. This aircraft is known to have operated with No. 2 Wing RFC in March 1916. (JMB/GSL collection)

ROYAL AIRCRAFT FACTORY RE8

A two-seater reconnaissance aircraft, the RE8 also had wings of sesquiplane pattern. (RE stood for 'Reconnaissance Experimental'.) A development of the RE5 and RE7, the RE8 was intended to replace the much-maligned BE2c for corps-reconnaissance. Despite their reputation as dangerous to fly, with a tendency to spin and break up in a dive, they were affectionately known as 'Harry Tates'. Riggers too, disliked the type, claiming that as well as normal dihedral, it also had lateral dihedral — an allusion to the 'nose-high' appearance in side elevation. The purpose of this was to shorten the landing run, but in practice it caused the aircraft to 'buck' on landing. This was extremely dangerous, since it forced the hot engine back into the fuel tanks. One RFC member summed up the type with the succinct dismissal, 'She was no good!'

The first examples reached 52 Squadron in November 1916, but after a series of accidents they were exchanged for BE2es in the following January! But despite its faults, the RE8 did a tremendous quantity of good work in artillery observation, often in the face of determined anti-aircraft fire, although the necessarily slow work of checking on artillery shoots inevitably meant heavy casualties. The RE8 was powered by a 140hp RAF4a engine and had a maximum speed of 98mph and was due for replacement by Bristol F2A fighters, with Sunbeam Arab motors, but the war ended before the exchange could take place.

This preserved RE8, at one time displayed in the Imperial War Museum, London, is seen here with part of the fuselage fabric removed to show the structure. This aircraft amassed only thirty minutes flying time in France on 31 October 1918 before being crated and returned to store in Britain. (Peter Low)

ROYAL AIRCRAFT FACTORY SE5 AND SE5A

The chief qualities that made this fighting scout into an outstanding war machine centred on its vice-free handling qualities, robust construction and ability to achieve a good ceiling. All these qualities were apparent in the Fifth Scouting Experimental (hence 'SE5') design with which 56 Squadron was equipped in April 1917. These aircraft even had such advanced features as an extended windshield, an early form of transparent cockpit hood. In practice, this feature was disliked by the pilots and the windshields were promptly removed. The aircraft was powered by a 150hp Hispano-Suiza engine which gave it a maximum speed of 120mph and was armed with a fixed, synchronised Vickers gun on the engine cowling and a Lewis gun on the upper centre-section. The Lewis gun was carried on a form of trapeze enabling it to be drawn down to change the ammunition drum in flight.

Although it lacked the agility enjoyed by single-seaters powered by rotary motors, the new design proved more than satisfactory and so plans went ahead to evolve an improved version. This was the SE5a, powered at first by a 200hp geared Hispano-Suiza engine. However, when these motors proved troublesome, causing delays in the production of the new type, they were exchanged for 200hp Wolseley Vipers, giving a maximum speed of 138mph, but it was not until well into 1918 that the SE5a was to be seen in the numbers originally planned. Even so, it quickly became associated with such men as Bishop, Mannock and McCudden, all of whom were to earn the Victoria Cross while flying an SE5a.

A variety of aircraft types could be found at RFC aircraft depots. This scene at Depot No. 2, Rang du Fliers, just south of Etaples, where the workshops occupied a disused sugar factory, shows DH9 D1720 which was to go to 98 Squadron and later to Russia, and SE5a B8424 which was to join 24 Squadron on 13 April 1918. The Russian caption to this picture reads: 'A Novelty. A bicycle wheel is used by an English airman as the base for a telescope.' The captain in the centre wears the ribbon of the Military Cross. (Author's collection)

НОВИНКА
Велосипедное колесо служитъ англійскому авіатору основаніемъ для подзорной трубы

SOPWITH CAMEL

The first version of this splendid aircraft, the F1, flew for the first time in December 1916, and the first example was allocated for squadron trials on 15 June 1917. Unfortunately, this aircraft was damaged in transit and another had to be sent out four days later. Meanwhile another had gone to the RNAS in May for operational trials.

The Camel quickly acquired an evil reputation among pilots for its handling. The greatest weight was concentrated in the nose, and the Camel tended to drop its nose during a right hand turn, and raise it during a left turn, both movements being due to the gyroscopic effect of the Clerget motor with which it was powered. A spin could quickly develop if the turn was not corrected with the rudder sufficiently swiftly. Another problem was that it would stall and spin into the ground if the mixture was not weakened immediately after take-off. However, in skilled hands the Camel was a formidable warplane.

The aircraft's name was derived from the 'hump' over the twin synchronised forward-firing guns, and the first unit to be fully equipped with the F1 Camel was 70 Squadron in July 1917. In all, a total of 5,490 were built, including the night-fighter version armed with twin Lewis guns on the upper centre-section. Most F1 versions were powered with Clerget motors, although some had Le Rhones or Gnome Monosoupapes of varying power. Those powered with the BR1 engine achieved the fastest speeds – 124mph compared with around 113mph for the lesser rotaries.

The 150hp BR1 engine also powered the majority of 2F1 Camels, a type particularly associated with naval use. The fuselage was constructed

A Sopwith 2F1 aboard HMS Furious. The markings resemble those of the F1 Camels of 210 Squadron in France, although here they are carried over the tail and there are no rudder stripes, while the wheels are turned with the conical side inwards to gain a track extended by some 11in. Strutter A6971 in front is a former RFC machine modified to RNAS standards at the Isle of Grain; it has the call-sign 'JD7' on the side. (T. Smale collection)

The RFC's ubiquitous Sopwith F1 Camel. D6458 is seen here at No. 3 AAP, Norwich, where it was tested by P. Wilson, ferry pilot, on 22 March 1918. The next day it had to be force-landed at Wye, en route for Lympne. (Captain G. Olley via Dr J. Cunbrae-Stuart)

with a removable rear section to facilitate storage on carriers. Its armament differed, too, consisting of a single, synchronised Vickers gun, with a Lewis gun mounted above the upper centre-section. It was an aircraft of this type, launched from a destroyer-towed lighter of the Harwich Force, that successfully intercepted and destroyed Zeppelin L.53 on 10 August. The pilot was Lieutenant S.D. Culley, and his victim was the last airship to be destroyed in combat. Other 2F1s were carrier-based, but some were Clerget-powered.

SOPWITH 1½ STRUTTER

This two-seater design, so-named from its peculiar strut arrangement, was perhaps the first British military aircraft to be conceived from the start as being armed with a synchronised gun, although the observer was also equipped with the traditional Lewis gun. It was a multi-role aircraft and could carry two 65lb bombs in an internal rack behind the pilot. The first examples reached No. 5 Wing RNAS on 24 April 1916, while those that later equipped No. 3 Wing are considered by historians to be the first British strategic bombers after their attacks on enemy industrial centres in the same year. A single-seat version of the 1½ Strutter also existed. Known as a Ship Strutter (or officially as the Type 9700), this was capable of taking twice the bomb-load of the two-seater. Night-fighting versions of the Strutter also existed.

Although traditionally associated with the Royal Navy, the type was not scorned by the RFC. In the late spring of 1916, 70 Squadron began to receive the type, although delivery was slow, taking place one flight at a time. C Flight was finally equipped by means of the transfer of a number of RNAS machines. This process was accomplished in time for participation in the first Battle of the Somme. For a time, C Flight's

A Sopwith Ship Strutter taking off from a platform rigged on the forward guns of a warship. (T. Smale collection)

aircraft were the only ones with No. 2 Scarff rings in the rear positions, these mountings having been replaced by Nieuport and Scarff pillar-mountings. Maximum speed of the type with the 110hp Clerget 9Z motor was 106mph.

SOPWITH CUCKOO

Thoughtfully named after the cuckoo's habit of laying its eggs in the nests of other birds, this Sopwith designed torpedo-carrier first appeared in June 1917 following a suggestion from Commodore Murray Sueter, who reasoned that aircraft with this torpedo armament should be able to operate without the handicap of floats and in almost any weather conditions. (Floatplanes in general could operate only in the calmest conditions.) The prototype was powered by the 200hp Hispano-Suiza, and after trials at the Isle of Grain an order for a hundred Cuckoos was placed in September 1917. Another hundred were ordered in the following February.

   The production models were powered by 200hp Sunbeam Arab engines which gave a maximum speed of 103mph, although the MkII, produced in small numbers with a Wolseley Viper engine, may have proved slightly superior. However, none was produced before the amalgamation of the RFC with the RNAS. The earliest Cuckoos, which joined the Fleet in early October 1918, were the last Sopwith aircraft supplied to the Navy. Subsequently, the units equipped with them on the three carriers were designated 'RAF, attached RN'.

Protected against the elements, a group of Sopwith Cuckoos are picketed down, probably on the deck of HMS Furious. *The divided undercarriage, designed to straddle an 18in Mk.IX torpedo, may just be made out. (T. Smale collection)*

SOPWITH SCHNEIDER

Descended directly from the Sopwith Tabloid floatplane which won the Schneider Trophy contest in 1914, production of what might be termed the 'military version' commenced in November of the same year. Twelve were built, similarly powered by a 100hp Gnome Monosoupape rotary engine. The first examples had a triangular fin and wing warping, but on the later machines these features were replaced by a fin of greater area and ailerons. Attempts were made in 1915 to use Schneiders to intercept enemy airships, but they were frustrated by an inability to take off in heavy seas. Trolleys that would enable the Schneiders to take off from the short decks of seaplane carriers were tried, the first successful attempt taking place on 6 August 1915 from HMS *Campania*. Maximum speed was about 90mph.

Sopwith Schneider floatplane no. 3788 is hoisted aboard a seaplane carrier attached to No. 2 Wing RNAS, somewhere in the Mediterranean. (JMB/GSL collection)

MEN AND MACHINES

A very early artist's impression of the Christmas Day attack on Cuxhaven in 1914 – the world's first carrier air strike. In reality the machines employed by the RNAS were Short Type 74s and Short Folder floatplanes. (Courtesy Dr R. Suchett-Kaye)

Records and memories of the early days of the RFC have tended to be eclipsed by later recollections so the complete picture is seldom seen and the public interest that was aroused in the doings of the new breed of fighting men – flyers – is lost. One action early in the war that was greeted as a significant victory was the destruction of the German 3,350-ton protected cruiser *Konigsberg*. Armed with ten 103mm quick-firing guns and two torpedo tubes, and with a complement of 322 officers and men, she was launched in 1905 and completed two years later. Her maximum speed was 24 knots. Some time earlier, the 2,200-ton British Pelorus class protected cruiser *Pegasus* had bombarded Dar-es-Salaam before putting in to Zanzibar for attention to her boilers; while in port she became a sitting target for the *Konigsberg* which was able to remain beyond the range of the British guns while inflicting so much damage to *Pegasus* that she was never to put to sea again. The date was 20 September 1914. Six weeks later the German vessel, still patrolling the Indian Ocean coast, was discovered by HMS *Chatham* sheltering in the Rufiji River of German East Africa. The British captain promptly sank an enemy liner in the mouth of the river to prevent the cruiser escaping, then shelled his target from long range. He also sent in the collier *Newbridge* as an additional blockship. Meanwhile the German seamen had established a shore position at Pemba, the better to defend themselves.

With *Konigsberg* trapped, the two monitors *Severn* and *Mersey*, together with an RNAS force, were despatched to the area, and a headquarters set up at Mafia. From here aircraft were dispatched to assess the situation. A reconnaissance sortie on 25 April by Lieutenant-Commander Coll and his observer finally discovered the precise whereabouts of the enemy warship, although Coll had to fly at only 700ft through anti-aircraft fire in order to do so. The Germans had camouflaged the ship by laying tree trunks on her decks to blend her outline into the surrounding jungle.

On 6 July two aircraft took off from Mafia to attack the *Konigsberg*. The first, piloted by Lieutenant-Commander Harold E.M. Watkins, with a volunteer, Assistant-Paymaster Harold G. Badger, from HMS *Hyacinth* acting as observer, took off at 5.25p.m., with the second, crewed by Lieutenant-Commander Coll and Flight Sub-Lieutenant H.J. Arnold, being away fifteen minutes later. Meanwhile the two monitors took up firing positions further down the river and the cruiser HMS *Weymouth* moved to cover the enemy shore installation. Firing commenced at 6.30p.m.

After six hours or so, the cruiser was only slightly damaged although she had been bombed as intended by the two aircraft. At 3.50p.m. engine trouble forced one aircraft to abandon the attack, while the crew of the other remained on station to observe the fall of shot from the monitors.

On 11 July the attack began again, with both aircraft once again taking part. Realising that one aircraft was spotting for the guns, the Germans remaining on their ship, who had been able to get one of their guns working, concentrated on the aircraft circling overhead while their colleagues manning the shore fort at Pemba dealt with the *Mersey*, using their five guns with such deadly accuracy that the monitor was soon hit twice. One shell killed four men and left another four wounded.

The *Konigsberg* was now on fire again. However, accurate shooting by the Germans hit Commander Coll's machine at an altitude of 3,200ft; his engine out of action, Coll was unable to return to Mafia, 30 miles distant, and it was clear he would have to touch down on the water. For fifteen minutes, while Coll fought to keep the aircraft aloft, his observer Arnold continued to direct the gunners below, but he was obliged to give up when the aircraft was hit again and became difficult to control. It alighted close to the *Mersey* and a boat was quickly launched from the monitor. Lieutenant Arnold had already swum clear, when he realised that his pilot was tangled in the machine and was in danger of drowning; regardless of his own safety he swam to Coll's assistance, extricated him and supported him in the water until help arrived.

The time was now 12.50p.m. and it was clear that the *Konigsberg* was doomed as the fire aboard her reached unmanageable proportions. Her sinking marked the end of an operation which, in the words of a contemporary writer, 'proved in a remarkable way the value of the newest arm in warfare'.

A Nieuport 17c Scout. (Author's collection)

As late as January 1918 the Commander-in-Chief of the Grand Fleet requested additional aircraft for fresh coastal patrols in the Tyne and Tees area. A flight of FE2bs of 36 (H.D.) Squadron and two flights of DH6 trainers were made temporarily available to the Admiralty to patrol off the Tyne, with another flight of FEs ordered to patrol off the Northumbrian coast. In addition, the RFC, finding itself with a surplus of three hundred de Havillands, offered the Admiralty a total of 192 of these. They could carry either an observer or bombs, but not both. Five flights of these aircraft were allocated to patrol between the Humber and the Tees, and four more between the Tees and St Abbs Head. The remaining aircraft, despite being able to make only feint attacks, were distributed to various other coastal areas.

It would be wrong to give the impression that the RNAS was totally concerned with shipping in one way or another; as other chapters show this branch of the Royal Navy made significant contributions to the development of air interception and strategic bombing, among other things. Even so, the maintenance of security patrols to discover and sink U-boats occupied the service throughout the war.

In May 1918, a month after the RNAS had officially ceased to exist, having amalgamated with the Military Wing of the RFC to form the RAF, Captain Henry Kendall was transferred to Houton Bay, Scapa Flow. Not one of his anti-submarine patrols from Scapa had been rewarded by so much as a glimpse of a U-boat. With the war dragging to an end, the five hundred men and thirty officers stationed here loafed about, killing time at a posting without any form of entertainments or amusements. This was too much of a challenge to Kendall's thespian interests and he immediately began to organise a concert party.

Kendall's introduction to the service had been typical of many. He joined the 3rd Battalion of the Honourable Artillery Company as a private in April 1916 and he had the good luck to be accepted as a Probationary Flying Officer in the RNAS thanks to the influence of Ivor Novello, a week after an interview by 'an impressive gathering of very senior naval officers'. Kendall found himself at Crystal Palace to learn the elements of naval discipline before going to Chingford to be instructed in the art of flying. The approach to Chingford aerodrome was dominated by a reservoir and a sewage farm.

By the spring of 1918 21-year-old flying-boat pilot Kendall had amassed a goodly total of hours in the air, but his heart still lay in the entertainment world after an attempt to promote theatricals at Chingford. This May afternoon found him at Scapa in charge of the final dress rehearsal for his most ambitious production to date. Great was his chagrin, when, in the middle of his theatrical activities, the station received a signal from the C-in-C: 'Enemy submarine sighted 50 miles south-south-west of Shetland. Proceed Immediately! Attack, Attack! Kendall, as duty pilot, had to abandon his production and depart immediately with his three crewmen in their Short seaplane.

Flight-Lieutenant Henry Kendall carried out an attack on a U-boat nine days before the end of the First World War. Here he wears the uniform of the RAF, which had been formed only some seven months before. (Author's collection)

About an hour later the plane arrived over the spot where the submarine had been reported. The crew were astonished to see below them a U-boat on the surface, stalking a convoy of Danish trawlers just visible to the north-east. Kendall, unable to believe his luck, shouted to his observer that he was about to attack, putting down the nose of the machine as he did so. Almost at once the enemy submarine attempted a crash-dive and Kendall's first bomb fell short. The second, however, was a direct hit and the enemy vanished in a huge upheaval of water and foam, marking the victorious end of Henry Kendall's only sighting of a U-boat. Some time later he was rewarded for this exploit with the recently instituted (3 June 1918) Air Force Cross, an award identified at the time by horizontal stripes on its ribbon. Kendall later observed that he found 'nothing heroic in sending forty young Germans to their deaths'.

Operational areas for this type of work were the responsibility of groups of coastal patrol stations, those making up the Portsmouth Group on 2 December 1917 being typical, constituting the Group Headquarters, land and seaplane bases, an airship station and instructional units:

Calshot	Headquarters (and Seaplane School)
Bembridge	
Cherbourg	Operations commenced 26 July
Lee-on-Solent	Seaplane School (Flying commenced 5 October 1917)
Newhaven	Operations commenced 11 May
Polegate	Airship station (Transferred to Group on 23 July)
Portland	

An unidentified artist's impression of a floatplane encountering a U-boat, which is about to crash-dive to escape the aircraft's attack. (Courtesy Dr R. Suchett-Kaye)

A number of soldiers joined the RFC. Typical of many were Captain A.E. Borton, formerly of the Black Watch, and Captain Anthony Marshall, formerly of the 28th Light Cavalry Brigade. On 7 July 1915 both these men won the DSO for their bravery in an incident that took place over the front lines. They were carrying out a reconnaissance in the neighbourhood of Staden, with Borton at the controls, when their aircraft was attacked by a hostile two-seater, the enemy gunner getting in a burst of fire which riddled the RFC machine, severely wounding the pilot in the head and neck. He was losing blood very quickly, and Marshall realised that he needed to take immediate action to prevent his pilot from losing consciousness. He began to improvise bandages, with which, assisted by the wounded man, he managed to staunch the flow of blood, all the time firing repeated bursts from his Lewis gun to keep the enemy aircraft at bay. The German pilot seemed intent on attacking them, perhaps trying to force them to land behind enemy lines where they would be captured.

While Captain Borton continued to evade the enemy attacks as best he could, his observer took copious notes of the installations below, filling several pages of his notebook, until with a tap on the wounded man's shoulder, he signalled the work complete. To the surprise of the German crew, the RFC machine then banked sharply

A Felixstowe F2A flying boat on patrol over the North Sea. On its nose are the bizarre stripes that indicated operations from that port. (Real Photographs)

How a contemporary artist portrayed a dog fight. The RFC machines resemble Royal Aircraft Factory FE2bs. (Courtesy Dr R. Suchett-Kaye)

and ran for the British lines. As the British trenches came into sight the German pilot gave up the chase. Marshall, now less busy in the rear seat, realised Borton was almost at the end of his tether, driving himself to the limits in an effort to remain conscious and control their machine. Still he managed to make a safe, if rough, landing before he was immediately removed to a field dressing station for treatment. Marshall handed in his notes; these were afterwards described as 'detailed and complete for the last as for the first part of the reconnaissance'.

Captain Roger Henry Garside Neville was commissioned into the Duke of Cornwall's Light Infantry on 14 July 1915 and transferred to the RFC on 5 December the same year. He joined 21 Squadron as a BE12 pilot early in 1916, but it was many months before he claimed his first victory on 14 July, winning the Military Cross in the process.

The weather had not been good when he took off on his patrol in no. 6563, but soon conditions had

A6601, a Morane-Saulnier Type P, pictured at Turnhill. These two-seaters were flown by 1 and 3 Squadrons RFC on the Western Front for reconnaissance duties, powered by an 80hp Le Rhone engine giving a maximum speed of 100mph. A Lewis or Vickers gun was carried in addition to a small load of bombs. (F.A.W. Mann)

deteriorated sharply with gale force winds and heavy rain. Neville was concentrating so hard on controlling his machine that he failed to notice the approach of a large German LVG aircraft, its wing span about 7ft greater than the BE12's. As the aircraft passed, Neville flung his aircraft into a sharp turn and closed on the enemy's rear quarter, raking him with gunfire. This attack was unsuccessful and the LVG pilot merely turned for home. Neville latched on to his tail and a chase developed, although he could see little with the rain obscuring his goggles. After a while the increasing anti-aircraft fire indicated that they had crossed enemy lines. Reports of the time frequently refer to one type of anti-aircraft fire as 'flaming onions', a name indicative of the shape of the exploding shells. They were defined by one witness as 'a kind of incendiary rocket fired by special batteries'. Neville fired intermittently at the enemy aircraft as the range closed. Eventually his quarry began to lose height, and it soon became clear that he was approaching his base as hangars and tents could be made out ahead. While the enemy gunner did his best to drive Neville off, the latter returned fire, and this time he was successful, and the LVG crashed about half a mile from its base.

Six days later Captain Neville was wounded in combat and spent some time in hospital. When he was fit again he joined 23 Squadron now equipped with Spads. He went on to become a flight commander with this unit.

The following is a select list of men who served in the RFC or the RNAS as junior officers, and continued to serve in the RAF between the wars. Many saw service again in the Second World War:

Babington, John T. Born in 1891, he joined the Royal Navy in 1908, being attached to the RNAS in 1913. Later he took part in the attack on the Friedrichshaven airship sheds in November 1914. After the war he became a member of the Aeronautical Commission of Control in

Opposite: *History best remembers Second Lieutenant L.A. Strange for his escape from death by hanging on to a jammed ammunition drum over Menin on 10 May 1915 but this is how contemporary artist W. Avis imagined the action over the railway junction at Courtrai which won Strange a Military Cross. (Author's collection)*

A 'Fee' – otherwise an FE2d – a variant powered by a Rolls-Royce Eagle motor instead of the earlier Beardmore. It is marked A6389. (Real Photographs via Author)

Germany, taking a course at the RAF Staff College in 1924. He was later posted to Iraq and in 1929 became Air Representative to the League of Nations. In December 1935 he took command of RAF Halton. Six years later, as Air Marshal Sir John Babington, he became Air Officer-in-Chief, Technical Training Command.

Babington, Philip. Born in 1894, he served in the Hampshire Regiment before joining the RFC. He commanded 46 and 141 Squadrons before being granted a permanent commission in 1919. Later, as a squadron leader, he served in the Middle East on both operational and staff duties. He subsequently commanded 19 Squadron in England and later No. 5 Flying Training School. As Air Marshal Sir Philip Babington he became AOC Training Command in the middle years of the Second World War.

Balfour, Harold H. Born in 1897, he first entered the Royal Naval College, Osborne, later joining the 60th Rifles and then the RFC, gaining pilot's certificate no. 1399 in July 1915. Rising to the rank of major, he was wounded when serving with 43 Squadron and returned to England in 1917. He was later posted to the Central Flying School and the School of Special Flying, Gosport, and in the following November joined 43 Squadron. In 1921 he became a flying instructor at Cranwell, carrying out similar work for HQ Inland Area from November 1922 to April 1923. In 1929 Captain (later Lord) Balfour became an MP and was appointed as Secretary of State for Air in May 1938. Aircraft types with which he was familiar during his RFC career included the Morane Type N, of which he said 'I loved her dearly.'

Barratt, Arthur S. Born in 1891, he joined the Royal Artillery in 1910, later becoming a pupil at the Central Flying School. He left the CFS in 1914 to join 3 Squadron as a captain in France; the squadron's duties including Army Cooperation and spotting for the artillery, to which work he is recorded as having made a 'valuable contribution'. During 1918 and 1919 he was attached to HQ RAF Cologne, later joining the Air Ministry as a squadron leader. He then went as an instructor to the RAF Staff

A Maurice Farman MF11 Shorthorn. (Author's collection)

College, becoming its second-in-command. He then went to India to command No. 1 Group. In September 1939 Sir Arthur became the Principal Liaison Officer in France and after the British evacuation from Dunkirk returned to Army Cooperation Command.

Brooke-Popham, Robert. Born in 1878, he joined the Oxford Light Infantry in 1898 but qualified as a pilot in 1911 and joined the Air Battalion of the Royal Engineers. On the formation of the RFC he joined as an instructor before becoming a temporary lieutenant-colonel commanding a Wing from 1915 to 1918. He became the first commandant of the RAF Staff College in 1921 and C-in-C Air Defence of Great Britain in 1933. Sir Robert retired in 1937 but rejoined the RAF in 1939 becoming C-in-C Far East in November 1940. In the face of ignorant interference from London he fought doggedly for improved resources and was unjustly relieved from his command as a result.

Caldwell, Keith L. Born in Wellington, New Zealand, in 1895 he joined the NZ Territorial Infantry in 1914, learning to fly the next year. He joined the RFC in 1916 and went to France with 8 Squadron in July. In November he was posted to 60 Squadron, later joining the School of Special Flying, Gosport, for two tours of duty, before being posted to 74 Squadron in France in April 1918. He was something of an 'ace', scoring a total of twenty-four victories in the air. After the end of the war 'Grid' Caldwell returned home and took up farming but in the Second World War he joined the RNZAF in which he held a number of training posts until 1945 when he became AOC RNZAF HQ in London. He later returned to farming.

Collishaw, Raymond. Born in 1893 in British Columbia, Canada, he joined the Merchant Navy. In 1916 he joined the RNAS, being posted to

No. 3 Wing, serving first with 3 (Naval) Squadron and later 10 (Naval) Squadron. In May 1917 he was posted with 10 (Naval) Squadron to No. 11 Wing RFC, then operating in the Western Desert. Returning to France in 1918, he rejoined 3 (Naval) Squadron. He remained in the RAF after 1918, and led 47 Squadron's Fighter Flight (later known as A Squadron) in South Russia. He commanded No. 201 Group in the Western Desert during 1940 and 1941 and then No. 12 Group, Fighter Command, in England.

Coningham, Arthur. Born in 1895 in Brisbane, Australia, he joined the New Zealand Expeditionary Force in 1915. The following year he came to England and joined the RFC, going to France with 32 Squadron in 1917. He later took command of 92 Squadron. During the Second World War he commanded the Desert Air Force between 1941 and 1943 and later, as Sir Arthur, he commanded British and US air forces in the First Allied Tactical Command; he subsequently served as AOC of the 2nd Tactical Air Force which covered the invasion of Normandy. He was known as 'Mary' Cunningham by his men – this was no insult but rather a corruption of an earlier nickname 'Maori'.

Douglas, Sholto. Born in 1893, he entered the Royal Field Artillery in August 1914 and was posted to France in the following January as an observer to 2 Squadron, RFC. He later commanded 43 and 84 Squadrons, rising to the rank of lieutenant-colonel. He was granted a permanent commission as a squadron leader in 1920, eventually becoming station commander of RAF North Weald in 1928 before being posted to the Middle East. In 1936 he was appointed Director of Staff Duties at the Air Ministry and Deputy Chief of Air Staff in 1940. As Sir Sholto he was briefly AOC Fighter Command, in succession to Dowding, before becoming C-in-C Middle East two years later. In 1943 he took over Coastal Command where he was responsible for measures to defeat the U-boat.

Dowding, Lord Hugh. Born in 1882, he joined the Royal Artillery in 1900 and the RFC fourteen years later. In the course of his service he

Aircraft specialisation for the RFC, slowly being realised in 1917, saw the introduction of such aircraft as this BAT FK23 designed in the same year, but the seven Bantams built never saw service except as racers. Here F1657, constructed in May 1918, is about to participate in a Saturday afternoon pylon race at Hendon in 1919/20. (Real Photographs/Author's collection)

commanded 16 Squadron. He became known as 'the Starched Shirt' owing to his rather shy manner which made him seem rather aloof, and later as 'Stuffy', perhaps a reference to his asthma. He was appointed Air Council Member for Research and Development, and his experiences made him the perfect choice to be the first commander of the newly created Fighter Command in 1936. One of his tasks was overseeing the creation of electronic fighter control, known at the time as radio location and later radar. A shrewd commander who refused to be drained of his resources to support an already doomed France in 1940, he had great regard for the men who served him. (On one occasion he ordered a hot meal and coffee from the Officers' Mess to be sent out to Sergeant Stanford who had been on guard duty for twelve hours in the cold without nourishment at Fighter Command Headquarters.)

Freeman, Wilfred R. Originally a member of the Manchester Regiment, in which he was promoted to second lieutenant in 1908 at the age of twenty, he became a first lieutenant four years later. He won the Military Cross for service in 2 Squadron, RFC. He was spotting for the guns with the aid of wireless communications when anti-aircraft fire caused grave damage to the mainplanes and propeller of his aircraft. He subsequently became a brevet major, commanding Nos 9 and 10 Wings at different times, and a lieutenant-colonel in 1918 having responsibility for No. 2 Training Group in south-east England. In 1940, as Sir Wilfred Freeman, he was the Vice-Chief of Air Staff and of his work during (and before) this period Lord Hives of Rolls-Royce was to say: 'it was the expansion which was carried out under his direction in 1937–9 which enabled the Battle of Britain to be won'.

Harris, Arthur T. Born in 1892, he joined the 1st Rhodesian Regiment as a bugler in October 1914. He joined the RFC in the following year and served in France where he rose rapidly through the ranks, becoming a major by April 1918. He was granted a permanent commission the next year, eventually serving in Iraq, the Middle East and at home where, as an Air Commodore, he commanded No. 4 Group from 1937, thus strengthening his connection with bombers. This was continued with his appointment to command No. 5 Group in September 1939, having

This Sopwith Scout served with No. 3 TDS, Edinburgh. It was numbered D4031. (Frank Yeoman collection via Author)

French-built Morane–Saulnier BBs, powered by 80 or 110hp Le Rhone engines, were flown by 1, 3 and 60 Squadrons RFC and by 4 Squadron RNAS for reconnaissance late in 1915. Armament was a single Lewis gun, occasionally augmented by another over the centre-section, a small load of bombs also being possible. The distinctive 'casserole' spinner was sometimes discarded to assist engine cooling. Maximum speed was about 80mph. (Cross & Cockade International)

returned from leading an RAF delegation to Canada and the United States. He was appointed AOC Bomber Command in February 1942. It has been stated that in his final years 'Bomber' Harris was greatly troubled by the tremendous loss of life on both sides that resulted from his implementation of the orders of the War Cabinet.

Hill, Roderic M. Born in 1894, he enlisted in the Royal Fusiliers in October 1914 and was granted a commission in the following month. He joined the RFC in 1916, serving both in France and at home. He rose to the rank of major (afterwards squadron leader) in the new RAF, taking command of 45 (Bomber) Squadron in Iraq during 1924. On his return he became an instructor at the RAF Staff College and was Air ADC to King George V in 1934. After a period in Palestine and Transjordan he became Director of Technical Development at the Air Ministry in 1938, and was the assistant to that department's director-general from September 1940, later becoming the director-general.

Joubert de la Ferte, Philip B. Born in 1887, he served for six years in the Royal Artillery before joining the RFC in 1913. He saw action in France and held the distinction of making the service's first reconnaissance flight on 19 August 1914, flying his Bleriot Monoplane, no. 389, over the Nivelles–Genappe area to discover the whereabouts of Belgian forces. He was in company with Lieutenant Gilbert Mapplebeck in a BE2b, whose orders were to seek out the cavalry at Gembloux. Later Joubert served in Egypt and Italy, being mentioned in dispatches seven times; he was granted a permanent commission in the new RAF in 1919. He was a special duty instructor at the Imperial Defence College from 1926 to 1929 and Commandant of the RAF Staff College in the following year. After a period as AOC HQ Fighting Area from 1934, he took charge of Coastal Command in 1936, returning to this duty in June 1941 after a period as AOC India. He was appointed Inspector General of the RAF in 1942 and commanded the air defence of the British Isles during the preparations for the Allied invasion of Europe. He is especially remembered for his life-long interest in the younger generation's enthusiasm for aviation.

A general RFC New Year card of about 1917. The drawing at bottom centre shows a Farman 11 with Union Flags used as the national marking. This was the RFC Military Wing's first distinguishing sign, introduced three years earlier. (Courtesy W. Wood)

Leigh-Mallory, Trafford. Born in 1892, he served with distinction in the RFC, winning the DSO and being mentioned in dispatches. He was granted a permanent commission in the new RAF in 1919, later becoming commandant of the Army Cooperation School between 1927 and 1930, when he became an instructor at Camberley Staff College. After the outbreak of war in 1939, he took command of No. 12 Group, Fighter Command, and during the Battle of Britain seemed to engage in a battle over tactics with Air Marshal Park, commander of the adjacent No. 11 Group. When he took over from Park in December 1940, his 'big wing' measures were experimentally introduced, but met with only limited success. A forceful character who eventually rose to lead Fighter Command in November 1942, his critics claimed that he could be unprofessional, although there is no doubt that he was a brilliant organiser, overseeing aerial protection for the Allied invasion of Europe.

Park, Keith R. Born in 1892 near Auckland, New Zealand, he served with the NZ Artillery in Egypt and Gallipoli. Having been commissioned in July 1915, he transferred to the Royal Artillery with whom he served in France. In December 1916 he joined the RFC and such was his talent for flying that he was almost immediately made an instructor before being posted to 48 Squadron in July 1917. He was shot down twice but accounted for twenty enemy aircraft. He remained in command of 48 Squadron between the wars, also commanding 25 and 111 Squadrons. He found immense strength from his deeply held Christian convictions, especially during the critical days of the Battle of Britain when he commanded No. 11 Group which bore the brunt of the fighting. He later assumed air command of the Middle East and his similar appointment in South-East Asia largely enabled the successful retaking of Burma.

Portal, Charles F.A. Born in 1893, he joined the Royal Artillery as a despatch rider in August 1914; later commissioned he was seconded to the

Air Chief Marshal Sir Keith Park pictured when he commanded No. 11 Group, Fighter Command, during the Second World War. (Author's collection)

RFC as an observer in 1915. The following year he qualified as a pilot at the Central Flying School. On active service he later encountered the German 'ace' Immelmann whom he engaged with a rifle. Rising to the rank of colonel, and later a squadron leader in the RAF, he was appointed to command No. 59 Wing at Cranwell and later 7 Squadron before being posted to Aden. Several other appointments followed until in March 1940 he became AOC of Bomber Command and later Chief of Air Staff. Air Chief Marshal First Viscount Portal of Hungerford is remembered as a man of quiet demeanour, immensely likeable and absolutely honest.

Tedder, Arthur W. Born in 1890, he entered the Army in 1913, joining the Dorset Regiment where he was commissioned in the same year. Rising to the rank of captain in March 1916, he transferred to the RFC three months later, eventually commanding several units serving in France and Egypt. He was twice mentioned in dispatches. Remaining in the RAF, he served at Constantinople in 1922 before taking command of No. 2 Flying Training School in 1924 and later the Air Armament School, becoming AOC Far East Command in 1936 and Director General of Research and Development two years later. After the outbreak of the Second World War he was appointed Commander-in-Chief Middle East. Working closely with Generals Alexander, Auchinleck and Wavell, he evolved the 'Tedder Carpet', an obliteration tactic establishing 'safe' corridors for the infantry into enemy-held areas. After further service in the Mediterranean theatre he returned to Europe, becoming deputy to the supreme commander Eisenhower. He possessed an exceptionally clear grasp of strategic issues combined with a democratic attitude to all ranks. He seldom lectured those who served under him. He preferred to meet small numbers of them, and sitting on the grass in their midst he would ask 'What do you want to know?' After the end of the Second World War he retired to his home in Banstead in Surrey.

These former RFC and RNAS officers are among the best known of those who continued to serve their country and the commonwealth into the

'The Dell' was a civilian billet for pilots under training at 17 Reserve Squadron, based at Beddington Aerodrome (Croydon) in Surrey between February and June 1917. Other personnel were housed in a former theatre about half a mile distant. (Frank Cheesman collection via Author)

Second World War; but there were many others – a casual selection reveals at least forty-six – who also rose to senior rank. Men like Ronald Adam (see Afterword) of 18/12 (Reserve), 44 (Home Defence) and 73 Squadrons, who was recalled to the RAF in 1940 as a squadron leader, becoming the Sector Controller at Hornchurch, and Sergeant Alfred Jessop of 56 Squadron RFC, who in the Second World War twenty-one years later became a rigger in 615 Squadron of the (later Royal) Auxiliary Air Force. All these men, with others of similar spirit, were endowed with talent, bravery and a measure of genius.

C H A P T E R   E I G H T

SIGNIFICANT ACTIONS

The first significant action of the RFC was a logistic one. In the summer of 1914 a 'Concentration Camp' was held – in effect it was a trial mobilisation in the light of the deteriorating political atmosphere in Europe. This camp brought together all the squadrons of the service – nos 2, 3, 4, 5 and 6, together with detachments from nos 1 and 7 – at Netheravon in Wiltshire in early June. Such were the hazards of flying in those days that 2 Squadron, flying down in stages from Montrose, lost three aircraft in forced landings and another damaged in thick fog during the trip. One mishap claimed the lives of Lieutenant Empson and Air Mechanic Cudmore, both of whom were buried at Northallerton. The journey for 2 Squadron was the longest, with assembly taking place at Edinburgh on 25 May, although a fifth machine, Lieutenant Waldron's Maurice Farman, had to be brought from Berwick.

A programme had been devised for each day at Netheravon. The mornings were devoted to flying experiments and trials, with the

BE2Cs of 13 Squadron RFC at Gosport, about to leave for France in October 1914. Nearest the camera are nos 2017, 4084, 4079 and 2043. (JMB/GSL collection)

afternoons given over to discussions and lectures. The subjects to be covered included:

(a) Tactical exercises; reconnaissance (at 2,000ft) of areas for transport and troops; searching for a free balloon; photography with hand cameras; changing landing grounds;

(b) Speed, climb and short landing (over a tape) tests;

(c) Motorised transport movements (described as 'novel' as the Army was still using horse transport);

(d) Committee meetings to work out establishments for stores and personnel.

To these subjects Major Burke, the Commanding Officer of 2 Squadron, contributed his 'Notes on Aviation', and the personnel of all units present took part in tactical, reconnaissance, photography, balloon handling and 'co-operation with other arms' exercises until the end of the month. Camp was struck on 2 July and the squadrons dispersed. The propaganda value of a gathering of five squadrons was great, but in fact no more than thirty aircraft were ever airworthy at any one time. At the Camp the chief topic of conversation was the likelihood of war.

The outbreak of war saw another concentration of the RFC's strength, this time on the windswept Swingate Downs above Dover. Here 2, 3, 4 and 5 Squadrons gathered, the aircraft guarded by armed troops, before crossing the Channel to Amiens between 13 and 15 August 1914. The aircraft carried no armament (and were ordered to ram any enemy aircraft encountered) and the pilots 'wore' inner tubes from motor tyres in case they had to ditch into the Channel.

Air Mechanic James McCudden remembered being 'busily engaged' preparing Bleriot 389, 'putting in maps [at a scale of 6 miles to the inch] and bags; also a rack for a

The granite memorial on Swingate Downs, Dover, marks the makeshift aerodrome from which the first RFC squadrons left for France in 1914. (Author [172])

The plaque on the Swingate memorial. (Author [172])

The ROYAL FLYING CORPS contingent of the 1914 BRITISH EXPEDITIONARY FORCE consisting of No's 2, 3, 4, and 5, Squadrons flew from this field to AMIENS between 13 and 15 August 1914.

B.

Certificate No. *104*

ROYAL FLYING CORPS.

(Flying Certificate—Warrant, Petty and Non-Commissioned Officers, and Men.)

CENTRAL FLYING SCHOOL,

UPAVON,

4th May 191*6*

THIS IS TO CERTIFY that *No. 892. Flight Sergt. J.B. McCudden*

Royal Flying Corps

has graduated at the Central Flying School, and is qualified as a* *Second*
class flyer in the Royal Flying Corps.

C.J. Burke

Lt. Col
Commandant.

* Here insert " First " or " Second."

W 2557—2015 500 8/12 H W V G. 12
                                    664

RFC pilots were graded First or Second class. This example was awarded to 892 Flight Sergeant J.B. McCudden on 7 May 1916. Some two years later he had risen to the rank of major and had been awarded the Victoria Cross. (Author's collection)

rifle and an ammunition sack'. No. 2 Squadron was finally away on the morning of 12 August, taking off at about 3.30a.m. An 80hp Bleriot Monoplane, one of four in C Flight, took off an hour later, flown by Second Lieutenant R.B. Skene with Air Mechanic R. Keith Barlow as passenger., but landed again for an engine adjustment. The aircraft looked tail-heavy as it took off for the second time, and soon it crashed from an altitude of only some 80ft, falling into a small copse of firs about a mile away at about 6.30a.m. Both occupants were killed. In the meantime Lieutenant Harvey-Kelly had set course for France flying BE2a no. 472. This was a new aircraft, issued to him on 5 August. His previous aircraft, no. 347, issued in June, had been damaged in a forced landing at Kettering.

On 6 October 6 Squadron left Farnborough for Bruges. This unit's departure had been delayed because all its original aircraft had been used to bring the other units up to strength. In November, Headquarters RFC took over control of 4 Squadron, the Wireless Unit and the Aircraft Acceptance Park at St Omer. Meanwhile 2 Squadron was allocated to IV Army Corps, 3 Squadron (later) to the Indian Corps, 5 Squadron to III Corps and 6 Squadron to II Corps. On 22 August 1914, 6 Squadron suffered the first of the RFC's wartime casualties: an Avro 504 brought down by 'friendly' rifle fire while engaged on reconnaissance. It was brought down over Belgium, killing the pilot Lieutenant V. Waterfall and his observer Lieutenant C.G.G. Bayly.

Representative list of pilots and aircraft which flew to France:
6 Squadron

Maj. J.H.W. Becke	BE2a, no. 667	(Commanding Officer)
Capt. F.J.L. Cogan	BE2b, no. 646	(Flight Commander)
Capt. A.C.E. Marsh	BE2b, no. 492	(Flight Commander)
Capt. C.L.N. Newall	BE2b, no. 488	(Flight Commander)
Capt. G.H. Cox	BE8, no. 636	
Capt. A. Ross-Hume	Henry Farman F.20, no. 440	
Capt. W. Lawrence	Henry Farman F.20, no. 680	
Lt P. Rawson-Shaw	BE	
Lt J.B.T. Leighton	BE8, no. 632	
Lt H.G. Hawker	Henry Farman 653	
Lt C.Y. McDonald	Henry Farman F.20, no. 669	
Sgt C. Gallie	BE2a, no. 470	

(The remainder of this unit's aircraft went to France by sea, the fuselages having first been towed behind the squadron's lorries to Gosport. (During the journey the wheel bearings on the aircraft began to seize up so that the trip had to be completed with a mechanic riding on each, armed with an oil can.)

It was not until 25 August 1914 that the RFC scored its first victory. A little after 11a.m. a German Rumpler Taube aircraft was discovered taking photographs of British defences; it was forced down by three aircraft of 2 Squadron, the leader being crewed by Lieutenants H.D. Harvey-Kelly and W.H.C. Mansfield. The German machine made a good landing in a field not far from Merville, and its crew of two, a sergeant and a sergeant observer managed to avoid capture and escaped into a wood. The British machine landed nearby later in the morning, now with Sergeant-Major Street aboard in place of Lieutenant Mansfield, so that the prize might be flown back to base. However, in the meantime a party of retreating British infantrymen had set the Taube on fire and destroyed it.

Means of arming aircraft at the time were still at the experimental stage, and strict standardisation of equipment was yet to come. No. 5 Squadron was typical of the many attempts made to discover the best solution to the problem. When it left England for Boulogne and then Amiens on 12 August this unit consisted of three flights. A Flight had four 80hp Gnome Avros, while B and C Flights each had four 80hp Henry Farmans. However, once in France, it was the squadron's sole Bristol Scout, no. 648, that was selected to carry the first makeshift offensive array. The armament consisted of a Lee-Enfield rifle, with its stock sawn off, set on the starboard upper longeron at an angle to the line of flight in order to fire outside the airscrew arc. In addition the pilot carried a Mauser pistol and on the starboard side had at his disposal an array of rifle grenades, each with its rod discarded but with rags attached to act as a tail. The pilot was expected to remove the priming pin from each grenade with his teeth before dropping them over the side by hand.

Much favoured by RFC men as a gift for the ladies in their lives were 'sweetheart' brooches such as this. With blue enamel wings, a white centre and red within the crown, it measured 1⅛in (41mm) across. (Author's collection [700])

Two days after the Taube was forced down, the RNAS arrived at Ostend in the form of its Eastchurch Squadron, commanded by the redoubtable Commander C.R. Samson (who in 1912 had been the first British pilot to take off from a ship). Their equipment consisted of a pair of Sopwith Tabloids, three BEs, two Bleriots, a Short floatplane, a Bristol biplane and a Farman, plus the Astra Torres (Naval Airship no. 3). The latter was the only armed craft and shortly after arrival it made the first RNAS reconnaissance of the war along the Belgian coast in support of a brigade of the Royal Marines. This was the first air operation of the conflict carried out by the Royal Navy.

The dispatch of an RNAS contingent to Dunkirk gave birth to the new concept of related land and air warfare, from the plan that the service should form its own armoured aircraft recovery service. This sprang from a series of minutes drafted in September 1914 by Winston Churchill in his capacity as First Lord of the Admiralty ordering that an aeroplane force consisting of three squadrons with twelve machines each, comprising the 1st Wing, should be stationed on the French coast to attack enemy airship bases from which London and the south-east could be targeted; these RNAS stations would enjoy the protection of a force of about sixty armoured cars, served by 200–300 officers and men, their chief responsibility being to prevent Uhlan patrols (German light cavalry) approaching within 50 miles of the air stations.

The Eastchurch squadron was subsequently sent to Dunkirk under the command of the multi-talented Commander Charles Samson, who introduced the motorised patrols, using at first armoured Rolls-Royce 'Alpine' Silver Ghosts. These differed little from the standard cars, except that they had protective plating for the engine and body, and were armed with a machine-gun operated from the rear seat. At least one of the five cars first introduced in September 1914 had a pair of French guns as additional armament. Samson himself led some of the patrols in a 35hp

Bronze collar badge of Samson's armoured car unit. (Author's collection [700])

Mercedes tourer (the car on which the first experimental modifications had been carried out). First encounters with the enemy proved successful and permission was obtained for additional vehicles to be modified for the purpose in France. Meanwhile the squadron moved to new headquarters at Hazebrouck on 19 September.

The use of armoured road vehicles for the RNAS was rapidly developed and four London General Omnibus Company B Type chassis were converted for the purpose and sent to France with a detachment of 200 Royal Marines, supporting the RNAS vehicles from 8 September. The buses were protected by armour all round, with loopholes for the twelve riflemen carried. However, in practice these heavy monsters were unable to keep up with the faster armoured cars and they were eventually relegated to guard duties. The idea was not completely abandoned, however, with another pair of similar vehicles being converted from lorry platforms of the same type. Each was armed with a 3lb Vickers semi-automatic gun and carried ninety-six rounds of ammunition. This pair saw regular use from 16 October onwards, being finally defeated by the atrocious road conditions encountered as November drew towards its close. In an attempt to solve the problem of moving heavy vehicles, Samson ordered the experimental fitting of a 3lb Hotchkiss gun on to a two-wheeled trailer.

The spring of 1915 brought better weather and a consequent improvement in mobility for armoured cars. A number of variants soon appeared, including vehicles employing chassis of Lanchester, Talbot and Wolseley design. Their potential was enhanced by the fitting of (mostly Admiralty pattern) rotating turrets housing a machine-gun, while another excursion into the 'heavy' field was marked by the adoption of the mighty Seabrook car based on a five-ton truck and originally armed with a 3lb Vickers and machine-guns. The first of these, protected by 8mm armour plate and powered by a 32hp engine, was delivered on 16 October 1915 and saw action the next day supporting the 3rd Cavalry Division of the 2nd Life Guards.

In France at least, the period when the RNAS could use armoured cars with such success was moving towards its close, partly because of the prevailing weather conditions and partly because of the adoption of trench warfare. As a result, Samson's forces were withdrawn from France and redeployed in Africa, the Aegean, the Dardanelles and, eventually, Russia, where the former 15 Armoured Car Squadron (now divided into the newly created 1 to 3 Squadrons) supported the White Russian forces. These squadrons were the last to remain under RNAS control after the formation of the RFC.

At their peak, there were no fewer than twenty such RNAS squadrons, although not all were actually equipped with armoured cars. The final squadron was non-operational, being devoted to experimental and development work in the United Kingdom.

On 24 December 1914 the RNAS mounted an historic attack on the enemy base at Cuxhaven. This was the first attack of the kind to use seaplanes. Nine aircraft were earmarked for the raid, all coming from the seaplane carriers *Egandine*, *Riviera* and *Empress*, but only four actually took part. Ten bombs were dropped in all, but only the three from

Lieutenant Edmond's Short 74 seaplane, no. 811, from *Riviera*, did any real military damage, hitting the cruisers *Graudenz* and *Stralsund*. The other attacking aircraft were two Short 74s, nos 814 and 815, from *Empress*, and a Short Folder, no. 119, from *Egandine*.

After the harsh winter of 1914/15, plans were laid to open an attack at Neuve Chapelle with the object of capturing the Aubers Ridge, which ran along the eastern edge of the valley, and had been lost to the enemy in the previous October. Although only some four miles in length and nowhere more than 50ft in height, the ridge offered exciting possibilities to the French and English commanders. The approach would involve advances across open fields that had been turned into a series of swamps by the winter rains, the men and horses being forced to cross the morass loaded with vast quantities of equipment.

The first contact patrols were flown in connection with this offensive, which opened in March 1915. In trials of this new tactic of cooperation with the Army special missions were flown in order to determine how far the infantry had advanced. This system was later extended and improved in the light of experience gained at Aubers Ridge, and the ground troops were issued with large strips of white cloth with which to signal to patrolling aircraft. Meanwhile normal collaboration with ground troops had to be maintained, despite one of the wettest springs on record.

Cloud base was down to 500ft when Second Lieutenant A.A. Benjamin Thompson, formerly of the Royal Warwickshire Regiment, was ordered to commence spotting for a heavy gun. The weather conditions were so bad that after a while he and his observer became disorientated and lost in the cloud which the pilot had deliberately entered to escape from exceptionally heavy anti-aircraft fire. Fearful that he would not have enough fuel to reach base, he resorted to the desperate stratagem of emerging from cover, losing altitude almost down to trench level and, despite a hail of small arms fire, making for home across the German trenches above which he had unknowingly been flying. This action earned him a Military Cross, the citation explaining that, before becoming lost, his careful work had enabled the gunners to achieve ten hits on their target in addition to a small number of near misses.

Second Lieutenant Malcolm Henderson, late of the 4th Ross Highlanders, was engaged on a different type of operation, when a

Entitled 'The RNAS at Work', this is how artist G.H. Davis portrayed the sinking of an enemy seaplane off the Belgian coast early in the war. The floatplane is a Short 225 of 1916. Davis was to become renowned for his illustrations in the Second World War. (Courtesy Dr R. Suchett-Kaye)

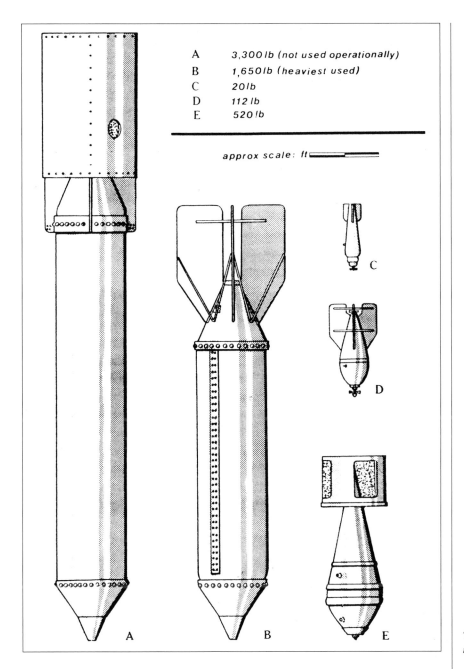

A	3,300 lb (not used operationally)
B	1,650 lb (heaviest used)
C	20 lb
D	112 lb
E	520 lb

approx scale: ft

The RAF/RFC's armoury of bombs in 1919. (Author)

dry day found him attempting to photograph enemy installations in weather that called for lower-altitude work than normal if the plates were to be of any value. His height was therefore such that his machine was an easy target for ground fire, one hit throwing the BE temporarily out of control and taking off one of the pilot's legs below the knee. Sick with shock, loss of blood and pain, he climbed to 7,000ft and set course for friendly lines; although still pursued by heavy fire from the ground, he managed to make good his escape.

September 1915 saw the RFC engaged in bombing operations against rail and communication centres ahead of the offensive launched at Loos in Belgium. Both high explosive and incendiary bombs were used. In addition, interdiction operations were carried out in support of the ground forces, but in total only 5½ tons of bombs were dropped.

After months of preparation, the Somme offensive was opened on 1 July 1916. The first aircraft took off at 4a.m. and flew through the closing hours of the most withering bombardment ever laid down. Three and a half hours later the guns fell silent and the assaulting infantrymen waited for the whistles that would order them forward, hopefully without opposition, into the enemy trenches. Contact patrols had now been developed, based on information gathered during other offensives, but in the heat of the battle which followed the observers above the battlefield saw few signs of the expected ground signals, and fewer still of the red flares which troops had been ordered to light to indicate their position. The reluctance of infantry to use these flares was understandable since their use gave away their exact position to the enemy. At Loos, the enemy troops had survived the artillery barrage by taking shelter in deep underground fortifications and in the natural shelters and caverns with which the area abounded; as the British troops advanced, they emerged from their dug-outs and poured murderous fire across the ground between.

The difficulties faced by the contact patrols had been foreseen, and in the south each man of the 30th Division on the ground had been issued with a small polished metal triangle to be worn on the back-pack or suspended apex downward on the back of the tunic collar. The idea was that these would reflect the light and be easily seen by the aircraft. In point of fact, these were of little use so that the RFC pilots were forced to resort to the dangerous practice of flying low over the battlefield, despite making themselves easy targets by doing so, in order to see the colour of the uniforms. A frustrated Cecil Lewis, flying a BE2c, remarked in one of his reports that the attempts to keep watch and ward over the men on the ground was nothing more than 'an entire failure'.

Had they been in a better position to assess the situation below, pilots would have witnessed a wholesale slaughter, for not only had the enemy emerged in strength, but they were able to do hideous execution among the men in khaki since the 'mighty bombardment' that had preceded the offensive had made little difference to the barbed wire through which great gaps should have been cut, and the soldiers were trapped helplessly in the open. The German defence was best organised in the northern sector of the battlefield, but even there 4 Squadron was able to report that the enemy had been forced to evacuate several batteries in the Schwaben Redoubt in the Grandcourt Village sector, although any real successes that marked the opening of the Somme offensive were those gained in the south which was less well defended. Here 3 and 9 Squadrons were able to report advances of up to a mile.

Meanwhile artillery observation continued, both from aircraft and captive balloons, although distinguishing between shell burst and other explosions was often impossible. Naturally, front line activity was heavily dependent on the ability of both sides to keep the men supplied and bring up reinforcements, so that in addition to reconnaissance flights which, weather permitting, went on almost continuously for the four months that the First Battle of the Somme lasted, the RFC's pilots were engaged on bombing operations. Typical sorties were those carried out jointly by I, II and III Brigades with the 9th Wing when squadrons from these units bombed rail centres in the rear areas, their BE2s using 112lb bombs, although they were only capable of carrying a pair each.

By 9 November 1916 it seemed that a new push by the Allies might still secure a significant victory. The main part of this thrust was concentrated to the north-west of Bapaume, in the direction of Vaulx-Vraucourt. It was here that the RFC proved its value. From an historical viewpoint the attack was important since it saw a force of no fewer than thirty aircraft heading for the military depots which abounded in the vicinity. The bombers and their escorts were intercepted a few miles short of the target by some forty enemy machines, according to contemporary reports, and the largest air battle ever seen then ensued. Six German aircraft were shot down, and four British machines. A contemporary reporter described the battle: 'Such a large number of aeroplanes, of various types, engaged in a fight to the death at an average height of 5,000 feet, makes an impressive sight. . . . a battle royal [such] as the world had never seen before.' But whatever the accuracy of the figures and however emotive the phraseology, it is clear that in the struggle for the Somme valley the new fighting service had proved its worth.

Although the Royal Flying Corps is generally considered to have 'won its spurs' at the First Battle of the Somme in 1916, its military coming of age was 'Bloody April' 1917, a month that brought heavy losses to its components in France. In the second week of the month Communique no. 83 recorded the loss of fifty-eight machines, its crews being either killed or taken prisoner, although losses in the following week were less severe, amounting to sixteen.

The year 1916 seemed to vindicate the activities of the RNAS at sea, in its fight against surface vessels, and May of that year saw the first use of aircraft by the Royal Navy to assist warships in action. British and German fleets were committed to the convergent courses that would ultimately lead to the Battle of Jutland. Among the vessels was HMS *Egandine* which had been ordered to sail with the Grand Fleet, commanded by Admiral Beatty to engage the enemy in the North Sea on 30 May. On the following day at 2.47p.m. the admiral had ordered the seaplane carrier to send up her Short 184 floatplane, no. 8359, to reconnoitre the enemy position. The crew consisted of Lieutenant Rutland as pilot with Assistant-Paymaster Trewin as observer. The weather was cloudy but after just ten minutes the aircraft had reached an altitude of 1,000ft and the German Fleet was sighted although Rutland had to close to 1½ miles to make certain identification, simultaneously attracting the attention of enemy anti-aircraft gunners.

Once observer Trewin had counted the vessels and was making his report, Rutland began to shadow the fleet at a distance of 3 miles; the weather cleared slightly so that he could also see the British Fleet, and the sight so impressed him that he later commented: 'The picture from the air of the battlecruisers and the Queen Elizabeth Class battleships . . . all rushing forward to cut off the enemy was [one] that can never be forgotten.' However, his attention was suddenly distracted when a petrol line broke at 3.45p.m. and he was obliged to land. Having repaired the defect with a length of rubber tube, he reported his readiness to go up again but was instead ordered to come alongside and be hoisted in. Eight weeks and one day later, the RNAS achieved another 'first' when a Bristol Scout took off from the deck of HMS *Vindex* and intercepted a Zeppelin over the sea but the pilot did not engage it.

Meanwhile the presence of the enemy over Britain was giving rise to public concern. Since the earliest days of the war German air activity had become a fact of everyday life. It varied in intensity, on occasion being little more than a token presence, but for two weeks in June and July 1917 the War Office had seen fit to withdraw 56 Squadron, equipped with SE5s, to augment the home defences, while on 24 July 44 Squadron RFC was formed specifically for home defence. This unit was initially equipped with Sopwith 1½ Strutters, but these were replaced within the month with aircraft better able to combat Gotha attacks on London.

At first 56 Squadron was described as a day-fighting unit, 'Camels' being generally regarded as unsuitable for night-fighting. But the commanding officer, Major T. O'Brian Hubbard, generally regarded as the Corps' first experimenter with aircraft armament, and later the Station Commander of RAF Hinaidi in 1930, had other ideas and Camels were used for night flights from September; that they were able to do so was testimony to the great improvements that had taken place in interception techniques since mid-August 1914, when Lieutenant W.R. Read of B Flight, 3 Squadron, had been sent aloft armed with three bombs (to

Circumstances had forced the RFC to address the question of night defence, sometimes using types such as this FE2b D9741, which was built from spares. The unusually small roundels have their white rings overpainted, while the white discs mark the location of Holt flare brackets in order that ground crews might locate them in the dark. The date is the second half of 1918. The dope scheme is entirely black. (via Dr J. Cunbrae-Stuart)

No. 100 Squadron RFC was formed for Home Defence in February 1917 and received four BE2 aircraft, including this BE2e A1855, with Holt flares under its lower wing tips. (JMB/GSL collection)

drop, by hand, on the enemy) and a revolver (for air fighting) to tackle a Zeppelin over France.

Meanwhile, after protracted preparations, a new offensive began on 20 August 1917. The opening of the Third Battle of Ypres was the first ground operation to be supported by a large number of aircraft, although the arrangements were considerably less bizarre than those preceding projected advances at Vaire Wood and Hamil, when a 'noise barrage' was set up, with aircraft repeatedly overflying the area so that the roar of their motors would drown out all sounds of the preparations. Probably the last time such a tactic was used was in August 1918, when an offensive along the southern edge of the Lys battlefield between Festubert and Rebecq was overflown by squadrons attached to the 4th Army, covering all tell-tale sounds as well as providing air cover to the troops and denying air space to the enemy.

However, a month before the Armistice was signed, the RFC and RNAS, already seven months united into the RAF, might well have staged the most significant action ever seen, and visitors to the Firth of Tay were greeted by the astonishing sight of a vast assembly of maritime air strength, for here were gathered examples of every conceivable type of seaplane and flying boat. The object of this concentration was to deliver a massive bombing attack on the German homeland, in collaboration with almost every airworthy machine that could be mustered in France. The flying boats would be unable to carry enough fuel to make the return flight from Berlin, the principal target, so it was decided that they should be taken to within 10 miles of the Dutch coast by night with the aid of lighters, and from here they would be launched to rendezvous with the French-based machines before the mighty assembly set course for the target area.

However, the planned operation was suddenly cancelled. Contemporary rumours attributed this to a request from President Wilson of the United

Almost forgotten among the First World War's potential fighting scouts is the Martinsyde F4. Four similar F3s were allocated to Home Defence. This F4 is pictured at Brooklands, probably after the emergence of the RAF. (F.A.W. Mann via Author)

States on humanitarian grounds. Thus the assault by the largest air fleet of the time remained no more than 'the operation that never was'.

Another early candidate for the title 'greatest air fleet of all time' dated from 1915 and was described by the officer who suggested it as 'a looting raid on a German aerodrome near St Quentin'. Lieutenant A.J. Insall* was then serving as an observer with a squadron based north of the Somme.

He went on:

The operation would certainly have succeeded, had it been tried. A BE2c squadron was to land spare pilots who would have flown a number of the enemy's machines back. Engine fitters were to be landed to start up the engines of the LVGs, Aviatiks, and other aeroplanes known to be kept at the aerodrome selected, and these mechanics, and the spare pilots, were to receive training on previously captured specimens of these types.

A fighter squadron was to land machine-gunners armed with tripod guns, and the German squadron was to be completely 'written off' – either removed by air, or burnt. Prisoners were to be flown back, handcuffed.

Photographs of the German aerodromes were available in the Royal Flying Corps, and a close study of the layout of the chosen ground had

*After the war Insall was one of those responsible for the creation of the Imperial War Museum, at the same time being concerned with the official air history while serving on the staff of the Air Ministry, and was soon to become well-known as an author and translator of aviation books as well as writing widely for the technical press. During the Second World War he was engaged on special work for the War Office and Admiralty, joining the Shell Petroleum Company's research department in 1945 before retiring to Radnorshire 'to pursue trout'.

shown how easy the affair would have been. On a bad flying morning, the whole German squadron would have been present on the ground, and nothing could have prevented an overwhelming success. Retaliatory raids were to be provided against for several weeks after, but it was essentially an operation to be conducted once, and once only. Alas it was never tried!

Vickers FB26 Vampire B1484, seen here in its revised form with new wings, wide centre-section, side radiators and Eeman triple gun mounting, was still on trial as an armoured trench-fighter when it was pressed into service on two occasions for Home Defence, flying from 198 Depot Squadron's base at Rochford during July 1917. On the second occasion, Lieutenant Moore found it impossible to replace an inaccessible ammunition drum after having exhausted all his ammunition. (Author's collection)

THE NEW ARM
IS DEVELOPED

BOMBING

Perhaps surprisingly, the evolution of the RAF in to a mighty bombing force, some twenty or more years after the Royal Flying Corps had officially ceased to exist, was influenced to a degree by the Royal Navy, whose officers had taken an interest in the question of bomb-dropping from aeroplanes as early as 1912. Indeed Lieutenant H.A. Williamson submitted a paper to the Admiralty in January that year making the somewhat radical suggestion that heavier-than-air craft should be operated from ships for the detection of submarines; a slightly later paper took this idea a stage further, proposing that such vessels be attacked with delayed-action bombs. It was hoped that the delay would enable the attacking aircraft to get clear of the area of the explosion in order to minimise the risk of damage. Later in the year the redoubtable Commander Samson experimentally dropped a 100lb bomb, enormous by the standards of the day, from a Short pusher biplane to investigate the effects this would have on the aircraft's trim. Development of delayed-action bombs was slow, the Royal Arsenal at Woolwich producing only limited numbers. (This highly dangerous missile was equally hazardous to its users since it was not fitted with any type of safety device.)

Trials investigating the dropping of high-explosive bombs continued into the next year, and in March Lieutenant R.H. Clark Hall, a gunnery expert, was appointed to take up armament duties with the Naval Wing of the RFC. His influence brought about new trials in December intended to determine the minimum altitude from which a high-explosive bomb could be dropped from an aircraft without inflicting damage on the machine. To augment the small range of bombs then available, moored floats were used, each with a different charge, varying between 2¼ and 40lb; these were detonated by remote control from an attendant destroyer while a Maurice Farman seaplane was flown over each target float at varying heights.

The standard bomb of the time, introduced in 1913, was the 20lb Hale, but even at the outbreak of war the Navy possessed only twenty-six of these. Despite their description, they weighed only 18½lb and contained a mere 4½lb of Amatol explosive, a mixture of Trinitrotoluene (TNT) and ammonium nitrate. Introduced specifically for the Naval Wing by

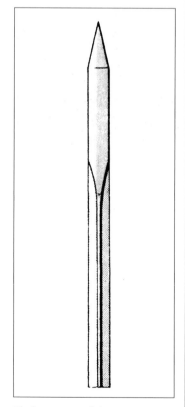

Flechettes or steel darts were scattered from special canisters against troops with no head cover or against lighter-than-air craft. The type shown was 5in long and 5/16in in diameter with the rear milled out to make a cruciform shape; an alternative version had a tubular brass tail pressed on to the steel shank. (Author)

F. Martin Hale, an expert in explosives, they were manufactured by the Cotton Powder Company of Faversham, Kent, and were armed by a small propelled device aft of the tail fins rotated by wind pressure during the fall.

Meanwhile other experimental bombs were being produced by the Woolwich Royal Laboratory, including a 100lb weapon with a thin skin and a high blast effect for use against 'soft' targets. The first bombs of this weight were much simpler, being converted from 6in shells (mainly by the addition of four tail-fins), but only a very few of these had been manufactured by the outbreak of war. Work was also under way to develop a bomb weighing 112lb.

There existed in 1915 no effective means of coping with the angle at which bombs should be aimed to allow for a cross-wind, despite the existence of sighting devices. Both the RFC and RNAS employed a bomb-sight that had been devised by Lieutenants R.B.

The mainstay of the RFC's early days was the 20lb Hales bomb. This actually weighed 18½lb, of which only 4½lb was Amatol. Its length was 23¼in, the greatest diameter 5in. (Author's collection)

Bourdillon and L.A. Strange of the Central Flying School's Experimental Flight. It was based on a similar instrument perfected in the United States by Lieutenant Riley Scott. Known as the CFS 4B sight, it incorporated a timing scale with which a pilot using a stopwatch could measure his groundspeed by taking two sightings of a chosen datum-point on the ground. The movable foresight was then adjusted to the difference between the two readings and the correct angle at which the bomb should be released was read off; in 1916, however, the Royal Aircraft Factory was able to announce the development of its own periscopic bomb-sight.

The Naval Wing had also turned its attention to incendiary bombs, and only a few days after war was declared, successful trials were conducted with such a weapon, invented by another naval officer, Lieutenant C.R. Finch-Noyes. Bombs of this type were essentially simple, consisting of no more than a thin-skinned container filled with two gallons of petrol which was ignited by the detonation of a small cartridge.

All this is ample evidence of the fact that credit for this form of attack must go to the Navy, since it is possible to trace its beginnings to the activities of No. 3 Wing of the RNAS, the Admiralty being aware of the necessity of targeting Germany's naval, military and industrial centres, particularly the steel-producing works in the Sarr Valley on which warship production was dependent. This is no reflection on the military outlook of

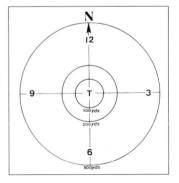

The 'clock face' system for bounding the target of a destructive artillery shoot, '12' being the reference point orientated on True North. An 'inner' hit on this system was regarded as within 50 yards of the target. (Author)

the War Office, but rather emphasises the fact that the RFC was essentially made up of soldiers, who in those days thought in terms of a restricted battle area, while the Navy viewed warfare in terms of huge, if not yet global, areas – and applied this thinking to the Naval Wing of the Royal Flying Corps.

However, Admiralty ambitions in this direction were ahead of aeronautical progress until the appearance of the Sopwith 1½ Strutter in early 1916. In its single-seater version this aircraft was capable of delivering four bombs, each weighing 56lb, and in May of that year Captain W.L. Elder RN was posted to France to prepare for the arrival by 1 July of twenty aircraft of this type together with fifteen Short bombers. These aircraft were to constitute a new bombing unit, to be known as No. 3 Wing. The chosen date was unfortunate and some people have criticised the lack of communication between the various services, since the date selected for the opening of No. 3 Wing's bombing campaign would also see the beginning of the Battle of the Somme.

The Somme illustrated the woeful shortage of aircraft in the RFC's Military Wing. The War Office appealed to the Admiralty for reinforcements with the result that by mid-September 1916 a total of sixty-two Naval Sopwith 1½ Strutters had been transferred to the RFC. This meant a serious diminution of No. 3 Wing's operational strength so that it was not until October that the RNAS was able to initiate the planned attacks with any significant numbers of aircraft.

Public opinion and strategic considerations led to the renewal of a long-postponed idea when, early in October 1917, Major-General Trenchard set about forming the RFC's new 41st Bombing Wing. Based at Ochey near Nancy, this unit was commanded by (then) Lieutenant-Colonel C.L.N. Newall,* who had been awarded the Albert Medal after extinguishing a fire in an RFC bomb store.

The new Wing consisted of 55 Squadron flying DH4s, 100 Squadron with FE2bs, and A Squadron RNAS, formed from a flight of 7 Squadron. Later known as 16 (Naval) Squadron and still later as 216 Squadron RAF, this unit flew Handley Page O/100s throughout the war and specialised in night attacks. On 24 December 1917, 55 Squadron attacked Mannheim; this was followed up with raids on Mainz on 9 March and Coblenz on the 12th. Both 100 and A Squadrons paid particular attention to enemy airfields.

This bombing force was soon to develop into the RAF, but in its brief existence the RFC's 41st Wing bombed Cologne, Kaiserslautern, Saarbrucken, Stuttgart and Volklingen, as well as the targets listed above. Official establishment of a headquarters for the new force took place on 11 October 1917 at Bainville-sur-Madon, although the three flying squadrons were actually based at Ochey.

The RFC Military Wing was still regarded as a tactical force, and this affected early attempts to expand the force since proper bombing tactics had been evolved only a little over two years earlier, during the summer of

---

*Later Marshal of the Royal Air Force Sir Cyril Newall, he was Chief of Air Staff from 1937 to 1940 when he became Governor-General of New Zealand.

1915. These had been developed by the French and once proven had been adopted and modified by the RFC. The first machine to take off was always that of the commander, who would act as leader throughout. He was quickly joined by the rest of the aircraft, guided in by flares fired by the leader, and the force formed up well behind the lines out of sight of the enemy. In close formation, the machines would then head off towards enemy territory, flying at the maximum cruising speed of the aircraft employed. Once the target was reached, the formation would deliver its attack downwind, thus shortening the time each aircraft spent over the target; attacks were delivered from varying altitudes thus forcing gunners on the ground to constantly alter their range.

In February 1918 the RFC's specialist Bombing Wing was reorganised as the VIII Brigade. At the same time it was augmented by the addition of two squadrons, nos 99 and 104, equipped with DH9s. No. 99 Squadron did not actually arrive until May, the severe winter of 1917/18 preventing their flight from England although it had been officially attached to the Wing since April. This comparatively small bombing force carried out fifty-seven sorties, by both night and day, the last attack being made on 5 June 1918. Targets included both industrial centres, such as those at Coblenz, Cologne, Mainz, Mannheim and Stuttgart, and the enemy's lines of communication to the battle-zones via Charleroi, Liege and Namur.

The amalgamation of the RFC and the RNAS, with effect from 1 April 1918, made no immediate difference to the personnel concerned, nor did it alter the service's contribution to the war for a time. One of the first obvious changes resulted from a proposal put forward in May 1918 that an Independent Air Force should be created within the RAF. (This was largely based on the experience of the RFC's 41st Bombing Wing.) This was created on 6 June, with Major-General Sir Hugh Trenchard taking tactical command on the previous day and complete control ten days later. The ground had been prepared for Trenchard by the 41st Wing's commander, Lieutenant-Commander C.L.N. Newall, whose responsibilities had included overseeing the construction of fresh airfields.

The new force was to attack the enemy quite independently of naval or military requirements, its striking potential reaching a peak in late 1918 when it comprised two Wings, with five squadrons each. (Additional squadrons joined the IAF in August/September 1918.)

41st Wing
45 Squadron	Sopwith F.1 Camels
55 Squadron	DH4s
99 Squadron	DH9s
104 Squadron	DH9s
110 Squadron	DH9As

83rd Wing
97 Squadron	Handley Page O/400s
100 Squadron	Handley Page O/400s
115 Squadron	Handley Page O/400s
215 Squadron	Handley Page O/100 and O/400s
216 Squadron	Handley Page O/100 and O/400s

The arrival of such 'giant' aircraft as this Handley Page O/400 attracted much attention even in 1919 when this photograph was taken. The bomb-load of this aircraft was 2,000lb and the armament up to five 0.303 Lewis guns. (Dr A.G. Wilson MC)

As early as 1916 the Canadian-designed twin-boom Curtiss 'C' had been the subject of examination at CFS, Upavon, only to be rejected three months later, it proving inferior to the Handley Page O/100 about to be adopted by the RNAS. (B.J. Gray collection via Author)

The Sopwith Camels had been intended for escort duties but it was decided that they should not be used operationally. The squadron was subsequently re-equipped with the long-range version of the Sopwith 7F1 Snipe. Since these were not forthcoming before hostilities had ceased, 45 Squadron never saw operational service with the IAF.

The Handley Page O/400s dominated the 83rd Wing. This was the 'bloody paralyser of an aircraft' requested by the redoubtable Commodore Murray F. Sueter when he was Director of the Admiralty's Air Department. It was developed from the Handley Page O/100, the RNAS specification for which had been submitted to the industry as early as December 1914. The normal crew of this heavy night-bomber was three; its maximum speed was 97mph and its load of eight 250lb (or sixteen 112lb) bombs was stowed internally.

Supporting the IAF's operational squadrons, there had also to be created or enlarged a number of aircraft parks and depots, with a Port Detachment at Cherbourg. Forward planning saw the formation and attachment of two further Wings, nos 85 and 88, while American Handley Page squadrons were also provided with training facilities at Ford, Sussex, Rustington, Southbourne and Tangmere aerodromes. Also being formed in the autumn of 1918 was a fresh Group, to be known as no. 27, and consisting of the 86th and 87th Wings. This new Group was to be equipped with the Handley Page V/1500, a twin-engined bomber capable of a greater bomb-load and range. It was suggested that some might operate from Prague.

After the war Major-General Trenchard was in a position to make public detailed information about his comprehensive bombing force. His report included the following:

Total Bombs Dropped, 6 June–10 November 1918
During daylight: 160 tons; at night: 390 tons.
Total: 550 tons.
Of this total, 220.25 tons were dropped on enemy aerodromes.
Targets Attacked

Baalon	Frankfurt	Landau	Pastatt	Worms
Baden	Forbach	Lahre	Rombas	Voelkinen
Black Forest	Hagendingen	Lumes	Rottweil	Wadgassen
Bonn	Heidelburg	Luxembourg	Salingen	Zweibrucken
Cologne	Hagenau	Oberndorf	Saarburg	
Coblenz	Kaiserslautern	Offenburgg	Saarbrucken	
Darmstadt	Karthaus	Oberndorf	Stuttgart	
Duren	Karlsruhe	Pforzheim	Treves	
Dillingnhen	Ludwigshafen	Pirmaisens	Wiesbaden	

The Handley Page O/400 bombers of 216 Squadron were a potent addition to the IAF. Based at Ochey in the Moselle region since leaving Manston in October 1917, the unit was subjected to a series of attacks by enemy aircraft. This was not surprising since the station had been a peace-time aerodrome and former French base, and was all too conspicuous with its permanent hangars. A change of station was imperative since 216 Squadron was to play an important role in the new attacking force, and in the summer of 1918 the unit moved to the American station at Autreville, about 10 miles south of Ochey, despite the fact that it was still only partly completed. Attempts to minimise German interest in Ochey airfield had gone to some lengths, and in March 1918 the accommodation huts and canvas hangars were moved from one end of the airfield to the other where a wood provided natural camouflage. At first this proved

Technical support for the RFC was supplied by the Armament Experimental Station at Orfordness, one of the aircraft there being this FE2b A5771, which is seen with a hand-wheeled refueller nearby. In the background a Bessonneau hangar is being erected. (Author's collection)

successful, with enemy attacks continuing to be made on the much-punished permanent buildings. To enhance the deception, decoy bonfires were set alight, using plenty of oily waste, during an attack. But the ruse was to be only temporarily successful, and soon after the departure of 216 Squadron, the enemy realised they had been deceived and Ochey was heavily and determinedly bombed.

The personnel of 216 Squadron had made themselves comfortable at

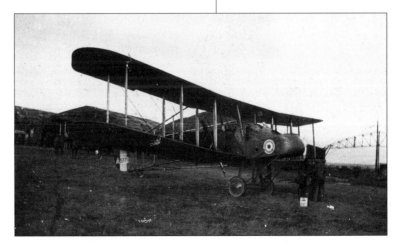

Also at the AE Station was this unidentified Sopwith Pup. The additional cooling slots in the leading edge of the cowling may point to its being powered by a 110hp Gnome Monosoupape rather than an 80hp Le Rhone. (Author's collection)

The wing-tips in the right foreground may be those of a captured enemy aircraft, thus further indicating that this is Orfordness. Sopwith Triplane N5430 has been wrongly remarked A5430. This was the only example of the type in RFC service and in addition to being used for combat and armament trials it was used for Home Defence on five occasions. The armament is mounted higher than usual. (Author's collection)

their first French station, enjoying the facilities such as a medicine-ball court on a stretch of level ground outside the wood, near the Officers' Mess. The base was identified by a homing beacon flashing the letter 'Z' in Morse code: this was always a welcome sight to returning crews in their Handley Page bombers which carried no wireless. The only reliable landing aids were wing-tip flares, and flares on the ground alongside the runways, although several veterans have recalled the use of hand-dropped 'doctored' flares that ignited at low level, throwing the ground into sharply defined areas of light and shade.

Situated behind the French lines, prepared to move forward as advances were made, these bomber crews have been described as 'ignoring rank; just a bunch of friends doing a job together'. They were certainly aware of the way in which their French equivalents were treated: O/400 crewman recalled 'There was always a hot meal ready for us after a trip, whereas our allies seemed to be expected to scratch what they could.'

Before the First World War there existed no specialist military aircraft, since aeroplanes were largely regarded as aerial versions of the cavalry horse. One result of this was that small, fast single-seaters were described as 'scouts'. The first fighters were modified two-seat reconnaissance machines armed with a machine-gun for protection; this was fired by the observer who usually occupied the rear seat. This was far from ideal, since it was soon clear that the pilot required armament that could be aimed ahead; the path to achieving this was long and difficult, and included such unsatisfactory arrangements as a weapon mounted on an upper longeron at an angle to the line of flight in order to avoid hitting the aircraft's airscrew. A further attempt to solve the problem saw a gun mounted above the propeller arc, while an alternative school of thought favoured deflective wedges on the propeller. An answer seemed to have been found in the evolution of the pusher aircraft, with the engine and propeller aft, giving the pilot a clear field of fire ahead of him. The RFC's first true purpose-built fighter, the manoeuvrable DH2, entered service with 24 Squadron in France during 1916, and proved a match for enemy monoplanes when the first of the squadron's victories was achieved on 2 April. This type was hampered at first by official insistence that the forward gun be 'flexibly' mounted. Later a complete solution to the problem was found using interrupter gear and, later, gun synchronisation.

The key factors for fighter design were conceived as ease of control, manoeuvrability, speed and rate of climb. A parallel development saw the development of larger two-seaters with greater range; these included such designs as the Bristol F2B, the first examples of which were received by 48 Squadron in February 1917, though it took some time for tactics to be evolved that were applicable to the new design. Other types of scout were also being evolved, such as the 'Trench Fighter'. This was basically a modified twin-gun single-seater, capable of carrying light bombs and suitably armoured against the hazards of low-altitude attacks. One type, the Sopwith Salamander, incorporated these ideals but appeared only in October 1918. Its potency lay in the prodigious armament of six Lewis guns, with one pair firing forward through the airscrew arc, two others on a special mounting above the wing centre-section and a further pair angled downwards at 45°.

PHOTOGRAPHY

During the war, some 650,000 prints of aerial views were made on the Western Front alone, the vast majority for reconnaissance purposes, primarily to assist commanders of ground forces in the field. For example, those taken of the salient before the battle of Neuve Chapelle showed how the enemy trenches stretched so far back that they simply

Photographic work being conducted outdoors in France with a mobile darkroom in the background. (Author's collection [700])

The observer in the front seat of a BE2-type aircraft demonstrates the method of handling a Type 'A' camera. For oblique pictures the Type 'C' semi-automatic camera would have been set externally, generally on the starboard side of the fuselage on a Type 'L' mounting inclined at a slight angle to ensure even overlap of the frames. (Author's collection)

could not be captured in the first assault. Other photographs provided the raw material for mapmakers, a forgotten adjunct to Army organisation which enabled every officer, however junior, to know exactly what lay ahead. Each officer was further equipped during major offensives with prints of trench systems issued via the printing section of the appropriate Army Headquarters.

Certainly the Army had long ago realised the importance of aerial observation, with balloon observers being required to make sketches. The value of photographs was shown in 1914 when in a single day the whole of the Isle of Wight had been photographed from an altitude of 5,600ft, the negatives being processed in the air so that they were ready for printing immediately on landing. The results of this procedure were described as promising, but it was decided that under war conditions it was not likely to be practical. Much of this pioneering work had been carried out by the Army's Experimental Photographic Section under the direction of Lieutenant J.T.C. Moore-Brabazon (later Lord Brabazon of Tara) who, together with D.C.M. Campbell, was responsible for the design of the A Type camera in 1915. This was manufactured for the RFC by the Thompson-Pickard Company.

The A Type camera required ten distinct operations per exposure, and it was not long before the C Type was evolved. This resembled the earlier design except for its high plate magazine at the rear which housed its semi-automatic plate feed. This was the first of the RFC's cameras to be carried on an external cradle on the fuselage side. These new mountings were designed by Corporal Parton in 1917, tilting the camera at an angle of 23° to ensure an adequate degree of overlap for the creation of mosaic maps. Hand-held instruments continued to be used but on a reduced scale as smaller and lighter models capable of focusing from higher altitudes were introduced. New designs by the Williamson Manufacturing Company included:

Photo interpretation at 7 Squadron. A pencil, magnifying glass, variable calipers and parallel rulers are on the desk. Note that this man's tunic lacks an RFC shoulder title. (Dr A.G. Wilson MC)

Description	Date	Features
F.1	1916	Known as the 'Aerocam', this was introduced for use in Mesopotamia and Palestine, being the RFC's first fully automatic camera using roll film. Power was provided by a windmill device set in the aircraft's slipstream.
P.6 and P.7	1917	Also known as Types L and L.B, these were fully automatic plate cameras.
F.2	1918	Identified by a long nose-cone, this L.F camera produced a larger picture.

Picture quality improved with the new cameras, but many of the techniques on which the RFC's photographic sorties relied, stemmed from the experience gathered by 3 Squadron, which in turn relied on earlier trials from airships.

For some reason, perhaps the conservative attitudes of military authorities, stereoscopy was not used to its full potential, although during 1917 alone some 2,695,750 views were made. RFC personnel were lectured on the subject. Cameras for normal and mosaic exposures used 5 by 4in glass plates; this was a laborious process, often carried out under fire. The operator first had to activate a lever to set the shutter, then depress a plunger to time the exposure. Illustrated instructions were issued, setting out the procedure for preparing the prints:

STEREOSCOPY
A diagram, showing how to obtain stereoscopic effect, from two prints, taken from different negs of the same area. First select two negs of portion of photo required for stereo, with shadows in the same

The countryside round the Yser Canal, as seen from an RE8 of 7 Squadron. (Dr A.G. Wilson MC)

direction in each case; make print from each. Both same scale as in Illustration.

Superimpose one over the other and mark then left and right according to margin. Imagine a line drawn through the centre of each: this is termed line of flight and indicates course of machine. Cut portions required, being sure the top or bottom is parallel with the line of flight.

Mount on black card seven inches long, width according to prints, the centres of each print to be not more than three inches apart.

Stereoscopic photographs were much more useful compared with 'single' views, but they still lacked detail. This was tolerated in the early days when reconnaisance photography was of greatest use to local commanders and most pictures were taken from fairly low level. In contrast, maps assembled for the use of strategic bombing attacks were invariably built up from pictures taken at higher altitude and augmented from intelligence sources.

Although the value of photographs had been realised in military circles long before the First World War, the Western Front's clear, fogless weather made it possible, for the first time in the history of warfare, for troops to move forwards with advance knowledge of the enemy concentrations and ground contours.

However, the slow-flying camera aircraft were tempting targets for both ground gunners and enemy pilots, and observers were obliged to operate in freezing conditions. (The opposite problem affected plates exposed in the Mediterranean theatres, where the excessive heat caused the emulsion to deteriorate, rendering reconnaissance of this type on any but the smallest scale virtually impossible.)

Early in the war all photographs were developed at Wing level, but by 1916 the demands proved too great, resulting in delays. From then on, responsibility for this was transferred to the individual squadrons and a School of Photography was set up at Farnborough on 1 January 1917 to train more personnel.

WIRELESS

The ability to communicate with (and from) aircraft in flight had occupied men's minds almost since the dawn of powered flight; indeed, wireless transmission had been established between England and France four years before the Wright brothers' first flight, and during the 1912 Army Manoeuvres reconnaissance reports had been transmitted to the ground from the Army airship *Gamma*, with the aid of wireless telegraphy (wireless telephony was to come later). As early as 1898 the redoubtable Murray F. Sueter RN had delivered the first-ever lecture on wireless telegraphy to the crew of the torpedo training ship, HMS *Vernon*. Even this, however, had been anticipated when Army balloons crewed by Lieutenant C.J. Aston and Sergeant G.R. Johnson, both wireless enthusiasts, made airborne radio trials. Aston and Johnson were members of the Royal Engineers Wireless Company commanded by Captain Llewelyn Evans, a unit that would contribute greatly to the later use of wireless under active service conditions.

An example of the thousands of photographs taken from RFC aircraft. This one, showing the moon-like surface created by shelling round Mallet Copse, was taken at 1.30a.m. on 6 December 1917 from an RE8 of 7 Squadron. (Dr A.G. Wilson MC)

Certainly the development of aircraft wireless owed much to the conviction that it could be used for ranging artillery shoots. This was largely due to Lieutenant Donald Swain Lewis of the Royal Engineers who had been seconded to the RFC. In June 1914 Lieutenant Lewis and his friend Lieutenant Baron Trevenan James RE flew two BEs from Netheravon to Bournemouth. Remaining some 10 miles apart all the way, they were able to communicate during the flight using suitable apparatus installed in the aircraft. James had carried out experiments in his own right in May 1913, when he had carried 'the first wireless experimental set' for trials from Jersey Brow using a silver-doped BE2a.

Since the wireless telegraphy system could only transmit signals in Morse Code, there was some question as to how this was to be done, since neither

Experiments with wireless had begun before the 1912 Army Manoeuvres, where this early BE2 was sent from Willian Camp, Cambridge, to support the 'Blue Army', by Captain Geoffrey de Havilland, seen in the rear cockpit. It had earlier been involved in radio trials. (JMB/GSL collection)

Away from the fighting areas, changes anticipating the end of the RFC included termination of the experimental wireless work at Woolwich and of the RNAS centre at Cranwell. In their place the Wireless Experimental Establishment (Lieutenant-Colonel L.F. Blady DSO commanding) was formed at Biggin Hill, its aircraft including the Bristol F2b C4611. Its airscrew is smaller than standard. (Author's collection)

was proficient in Morse. The answer seemed to lie in raising their standards of speed and efficiency, and after several weeks of intensive work the pair approached a friendly commander of a 9.2 Howitzer battery proposing practical trials. The new system was put to the test with Lewis flying and James in charge of equipment on the ground. Their success meant that the pair were immediately sent to France with orders to make further trials, and after a wasted month while further orders were awaited, the first trial took place. Three aircraft took part, each carrying a 300-watt Rouget set run off the crankshaft, while the receivers had Brown relays. Despite the need to economise on ammunition, since the assault on the Aubers Ridge was imminent, the tests were pronounced a success, the subsequent report ending 'one can generally hit a target with the first three shots'. The gunners were informed of their accuracy by means of a simple system in which the target was at the centre of an imaginary clock face, so that the fall of the shot could be easily communicated once range had been established.

The aerial lead-in and reel carried externally on Armstrong Whitworth FK8 C8576. (Author's collection)

Lieutenant Jones was shot down and killed by anti-aircraft fire on 13 July 1915 while ranging for artillery guns; Lewis was killed seven months later near Wytschaete.

Trials with wireless were carried out by 4 Squadron RFC. On 13 August A and B Flights flew to France, with C Flight following on the 20th. They took with them a wireless detachment capable of receiving W/T transmissions from aircraft in flight. Unfortunately this was destroyed in a road accident and was impossible to replace until the middle of September. Subsequently Morse code signals were used to direct artillery fire and the system proved so successful that the pioneer unit was redesignated the Headquarters Wireless Section on 27 September. It was elevated to squadron status and known as No. 9 on 8 December, with its own headquarters at St Omer, sending out detachments to collaborate with artillery units in the front line.

Pioneer wireless sets were carried in a variety of locations on aircraft. Some simply sat on an external 'shelf' on the fuselage side, but the Stirling set, adopted as standard in 1915, was carried internally with the aerial wound on to a hand-cranked drum and paid out via a fairlead in the bottom of the fuselage. Three 2.5 volt accumulators wired in series supplied the power. As

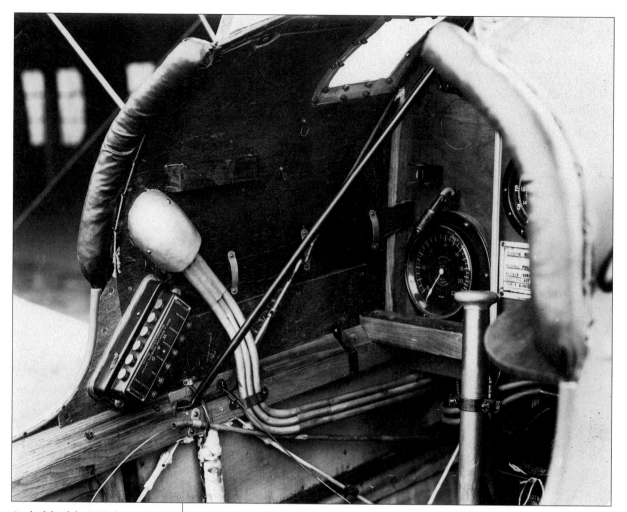

As the life of the RFC drew to its close, innovations included cockpit lighting such as this Mk.III Aeroplane Dashboard Lighting System with switches for the ASI, compass, anemometer, engine revolution counter, etc. These were manufactured by Worsnop & Co. Ltd of Halifax. (Author's collection)

with the reconnaissance cameras of the period, wireless sets were both heavy and bulky so that they had to be accommodated in the rear cockpit of two-seaters, with the observer having to be dispensed with. But in 1915/16 there was something of a breakthrough in transmitter design when a new one was introduced weighing a 'mere' 20lb. This was an improvement over the first type which could add an extra 110lb to the aircraft's load (or at best some 75lb).

Meanwhile the potential of wireless telegraphy was not lost on the Admiralty and 12 March 1915 was to see the first of a series of experiments being carried out at Eastleigh, with Lieutenant Basil Binyon RN (a cousin of the poet) acting as observer to test the practicability of spotting for the guns using this method. During the following month these test were repeated, this time at Shoeburyness in collaboration with the old battleship HMS *Revenge*.

On the Western Front, wireless was further developed for use by strategic bombers and also to allow for communication between aircraft in flight. Captain Charles Findlay of 88 Squadron remembered such exchanges made under battle conditions. Aware that the enemy could overhear their conversations Findlay and the other Bristol Fighter pilots deliberately included pungent comments on the enemy's characteristics and organisation – in a sense anticipating psychological warfare!

C H A P T E R T E N

WARS UNCEASING

THE AEGEAN THEATRE

It is all too easy to imagine that the first war in the air was fought exclusively over France and Italy, so any history of the RFC and RNAS must include a mention, however brief, of air fighting over Greek waters. Captain Augustine Francis Marlowe RNAS was stationed at Redcar when he received orders for his new Aegean posting on 25 July 1916. His diary entry for 24 August recorded: 'We arrived here at Mudros from Malta [and] have to be accommodated in tents alongside the aerodrome owing to congestion.' The following day he wrote: 'there was gunfire and I saw a German machine overhead, probably photographing one of our Blimps', and nine days later: 'Our cabins here are made from the original packing cases used for crating aeroplanes from England. Each has a wooden bed (or our own canvas camp bed), also a canvas table, chair, washstand. . . . Our Mess is a rough stone building fitted with a mixed assortment of chairs and settees and of course the inevitable gramophone. In the harbour a few miles from us there are wooden dummy warships to kid the enemy. We use an old Ford for our journeys there and back to collect mail, etc.'

DH9s of the RAF North Russian Expedition at Bereznik in 1919. (JMB/GSL collection)

This Armstrong Whitworth FK8 ('Ack-W'), C3558, was operated by 17 Squadron RFC in Macedonia. (Author's collection)

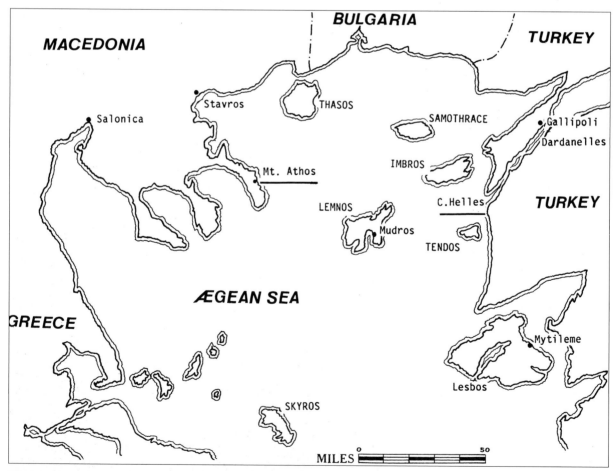

The Aegean area surrounding the RNAS base at Mudros. (Author)

Operated by the RNAS in the Aegean theatre, this Nieuport 12, no. 8905, was powered by a 100hp Clerget motor. Its defensive armament was on a Nieuport (not a Scarff) mounting and there is a rack for light bombs aft of the rear undercarriage legs. (F. Marlowe via Author)

Later, once he had settled down to the new life, a typical day was described as taken up with 'Routine flying – a bit of bombing, some spotting and the usual chasing the elusive Hun.' Two years later he was still there, and there is an interesting entry in his diary for 24 March 1918: 'A Paymaster from the *Ark Royal* arrived on the *Ena* (which brings our mail etc). He is on the way to Salonika to arrange matters concerning our proposed joining with the RFC to make a "Royal Air Force" which is to come about on 1 April.' In the main, his unit flew Nieuport 12s but by 21 January 1918 Marlowe was flying a DH4 nicknamed 'Blotto'. Ordered to a rest camp after his last operation on 30 August, Marlowe remained in the RAF until May 1939 when he was forty-two years of age – long enough to realise that the universal hopes for peace, centred around the 1918 Armistice, were just pipedreams.

It seemed to many that the Armistice of November 1918 had brought to a close the 'war to end all wars' but in practice the officers and men of the new British flying service experienced few differences in the day-to-day atmosphere in which they served. One commentator remarked: 'We were no longer soldiers and were not sailors, but something completely new and

different called airmen', but this was an unusual opinion, most of his fellows believing that the Royal Flying Corps had done no more than undergo a change of name. All this was played out against the political background that shapes every serviceman's life, and one of the most momentous events of the century took place while the RFC still had five months of life to run.

THE RUSSIAN EXPEDITION

In Russia, where Tsar Nicholas II had been forced to abdicate in March 1917, the unrest that had resulted from the First Revolution had seemed to be quietened in the summer by the accession to premiership of Alexander Kerensky; however, he was driven out of office in November by the Bolsheviks. In the meantime, the Army had become demoralised not only because of the lack of organisation and supplies but also because of its inept leadership. During the struggle that followed, the Reds, lacking experienced officers but enjoying a numerical superiority over the White Russian forces, were in control of an area south of Shenkursk on the River Dvina, as far west as a line from Narva to the Caucasus and from Perm, which lies west

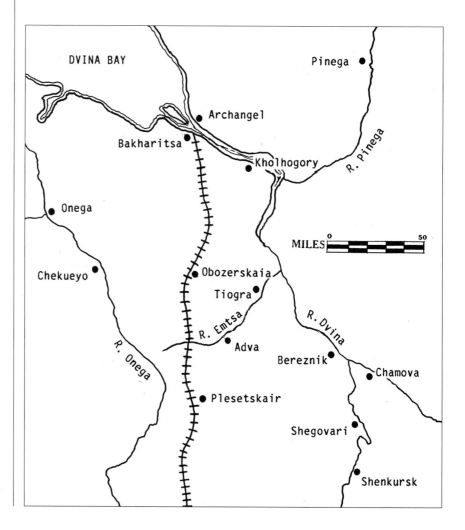

The area surrounding the RAF North Russian Expedition's base at Archangel, 1918–19. (Author)

of Kazon, into the Caspian Sea. Small wonder that by 1919 the Whites were in retreat on both the western and eastern fronts, with the exception of the areas around Kiev and Orenburg where advances had been made.

The signing of a peace treaty in March 1918 between Russia and the Kaiser's Germany triggered a series of events. Its terms permitted the German fleet to begin using the Arctic ports of Archangel and Murmansk as U-boat bases, and allowed access to the resources of Western Siberia. Moreover, the newly established and independent Czechoslovakia had over 90,000 troops in Russia and it was planned to take these out of the country via Vladivostock for eventual service on the Western Front. Since partial solution to these problems seemed to lie in the employment of aircraft, in May General Poole was dispatched to Russia with orders to set up his headquarters in Murmansk and set about the foundation of a North Russian Expeditionary Force. An indication of what was to come appeared in a short column in a British newspaper: 'News has been received in Copenhagen from Konigsberg that a surprisingly strong British fleet has passed in an easterly direction, and conjecture in well-informed circles has it that it is designed to take part in the Allies' general offensive against the Bolsheviks in North Russia.' The subsequent events are among the lesser-known of those which marked the early days of the new RAF. Two detachments were dispatched to assist the White Russian forces, 'Eklope' force being based at Archangel and 'Syren' at Murmansk, opposing the Bolsheviks and their allies in the south. The force consisted of de Havilland 4 bombers, together with Sopwith F1 Camels, five Fairey IIIC seaplanes and a pair of Sopwith Baby floatplanes, and its principal task was to support the Allied troops about 100 miles south of the main British airfield at Bereznik between August and September. Later these aircraft were augmented by a number of Fairey IIICs, Short 184s, DH9As and Sopwith 1½ Strutters, while some reports suggest that several Handley Page O/400 bombers were completed at Murmansk. The twelve floatplanes (six of each) had been delivered to Archangel together with

Having been lowered from Pegasus, *Fairey IIIC N9250 is about to be flown off by Captain Stanley. (Courtesy C. Webster)*

A Sopwith 1½ Strutter on the flight deck of HMS Pegasus. *(Courtesy C. Webster)*

A Fairey seaplane maintenance crew aboard Pegasus. *(Courtesy C. Webster)*

thirty-nine personnel (officers, NCOs and men), having departed from Tilbury aboard the seaplane carrier *Pegasus*.

It was felt in London that the deepening crisis in Eastern Europe presented a threat to the newly independent countries of Estonia and neighbouring Latvia. The arrival of HMS *Vindictive* in July 1919, charged with the task of preventing Bolshevik vessels leaving Kronstadt to carry out operations against Finland and elsewhere, was welcomed also for the aircraft she carried: Short Seaplanes, Sopwith Camels and 1½ Strutters. These were to be used chiefly for offensive patrols. The force was commanded by Squadron Leader D.G. Donald and was augmented in September by the arrival of HMS *Furious* bringing six additional Shorts, a pair of 1½ Strutters and twelve Camels, together with thirteen pilots and four observers. At least one Sopwith 7F1 Snipe is also known to have been with the RAF in Russia.

Initial tasks consisted largely of reconnaissance and anti-submarine patrols from Biorko, but on 30 July the Admiral in charge of the British

The light carrier Pegasus *(3,070 tons), formerly the Great Eastern steamer* Stockholm, *brought twelve aircraft (half of them Short floatplanes), plus thirty-nine officers, NCOs and men from Tilbury to Archangel. (Courtesy C. Webster)*

naval force ordered an attack by eleven aircraft on Kronstadt harbour, wherein lay the depot ship *Pamyat Azova*. There was also an important dry dock there. He hoped that this would prevent the Reds from attacking the ships under his command. The aircraft crews dropped sixteen bombs, ten of them 112-pounders, the remainder being 65-pounders. All aircraft returned safely to base despite heavy defensive fire over the target. They claimed five direct hits, starting two large fires.

The same port was the centre of a combined operation on the night of 17/18 August when eight aircraft made a diversionary bombing attack in conjunction with a raid by Royal Navy torpedo boats on ships in the harbour. That this was successful was revealed by subsequent reconnaissance, only a small number of destroyers remaining afloat while two battleships and the depot ship that had been the centre of the previous month's attack had been sent to the bottom.

Nevertheless, the task which the force faced, attempting to turn the weight of Communist support, was an impossible one, and as the year drew to its close it was decided that the northern campaign should be brought to an end by a tactical retreat, while the White Russian forces were to be sustained in the south. The extreme conditions under which air operations were carried out resulted in rapid deterioration in the machines. The ground staff began each day with attempts to start engines in which the oil had frozen solid overnight; even when fresh, warmed lubricant was poured in, this too would rapidly freeze. The severity of the conditions in which they battled to keep the machines airworthy is illustrated by the average temperature at Archangel between 1 October and the following 26 May, which was minus 53°F. Even in June temperatures might drop as low as 60° of frost.

The best known part of the new air arm's contribution to the support of the White Russian Forces in the south was supplied by 47 Squadron, which in October 1919 was redesignated A Squadron, RAF Mission, South Russia. It had formerly been stationed in Macedonia where it had dropped a total of 54 tons of bombs. On 16 April 1919 one flight left for Novorossisk, the Black Sea port with a rail connection to Ekaterinodar,

Fairey IIIC N9250 being lifted out from Pegasus. *(Courtesy C. Webster)*

this advance flight being joined by the remainder of the squadron by 28 May.

Once in Russia, the squadron's chief duties were low-level bombing and ground strafing, while the Sopwith F1 Camels of B Flight (identified with a horizontal white band on the cowling and the Imperial Russian national insignia) were pressed into service as dive-bombers.

During this period the squadron was commanded by Major R. Collishaw who had arrived at Ekaterinodar on 11 July. Although its headquarters remained at the base adjoining the racecourse there, a move was later made to Beketovka, with C Flight later moving up the Volga so its DH9s could commence operations in the skies over Tsaritsin. Later these machines were replaced by RE8s, with which Z Flight was also equipped.

During a raid on Tcherni-Yar in July, one of 47 Squadron's DH9s was shot down, though its pilot, Captain W. Elliott (later Air Chief Marshal Sir William Elliott, AOC of Fighter Command until 1954) managed to make a reasonable forced-landing. Seeing this, another pilot landed nearby and the two downed men scrambled into the cramped rear cockpit just before a group of Red cavalry arrived on the scene. The aircraft returned to base in this uncomfortable manner, with the displaced gunner standing on the lower wing to block the bullet holes in one of the fuel tanks. The *London Gazette* put some 'flesh' on the bare bones of this story when it announced the awards recognising the gallantry of the men involved:

His Majesty the King has been pleased to approve the award of the Distinguished Service Order in recognition of gallantry and distinguished service to Flight Lieutenant Walter Fraser Anderson and Observer Officer John Mitchell of C Flight, 47 Squadron.

On July 30, 1919, near Cherni Yar (Volga) these officers were pilot and observer respectively on a DH9 machine, which descended to 1,000 feet to take oblique photographs of the enemy's positions. A second machine of the same Flight was completely disabled by machine-gun fire and forced to land five miles behind the enemy's foremost troops. Parties of hostile cavalry which attempted to capture the pilot and observer were kept away by the observer's Lewis gun while the pilot burned the machine. Flt Lt Anderson, notwithstanding that his petrol tank had been pierced by a machine-gun bullet, landed alongside the wrecked aeroplane, picked up the pilot and observer and got safely home. . . . The difficult circumstances of the rescue will be fully appreciated when it is remembered that Observer-Officer Mitchell had to mount the port plane (wing) and stop the holes in the petrol tank with his thumbs for a period of fifty minutes flying on the return journey.

Another squadron associated with operations in the south was no. 221, which had been formed from D Squadron of No. 62 Wing, RNAS, on 1 April 1918 and based first at Baku and later at Petrovsk on the Caspian Sea, having arrived aboard HMS *Rivera* in January 1919 with two flights of DH9s and 9As for reconnaissance sorties over the Astrakhan area. The squadron also carried out bombing attacks, while the unit's sole Sopwith Camel was primarily used for escort work. Later this unit was joined by 266 Squadron which was equipped with floatplanes and flying boats and was committed to coastal patrol from Petrovsk.

General W. Ironside, who commanded British forces in Murmansk between October 1918 and October 1919, about to board Pegasus at Archangel. Fairey IIIC N9252 is in the distance. (Courtesy C. Webster)

The British Expeditionary Force to Russia was intended to support the counter-revolutionary armies commanded by General Denikin and Admiral Koltchak and their small air arm, the Volunteer Army Aviation Force. This was commanded by Colonel Kravleserlkts and consisted of four squadrons, with one assigned to each of the three Army Corps and the last sharing the aerodrome at Ekaterinodar with 47 Squadron RAF, supporting the Army Reserve. Kravleserlkts' force was not impressive: the total number of aircraft amounted to a mere thirty-eight, only ten of which were airworthy. Of the ninety 'mechanics' available to him, only seven were trained. Some twenty-five further aircraft were available for operations over the Don, Southern and Astrakhan fronts. In so vast a country, defeat of the White Russians was inevitable and after October 1919 the Red advance forced Denikin to withdraw his wings after his centre was pushed back following the fall of Kiev. By this time the RAF presence had already been withdrawn, the aircraft of at least one section

DH9 D2803 crashed at Petrovsk on the Caspian Sea, South Russia, killing Second Lieutenant Machin. The aircraft is marked I on the side and decking, and G on the horizontal tail unit. (JMB/GSL collection)

No. 47 Squadron in South Russia. Back row, left to right: Flight Lieutenant Smith, Jack Mitchell, 'Tommy' Thompson, 'Gus' Edwards, 'Sport' Menton, a Russian interpreter. Front row: Dr Murphy, 'Seedy' Broughall, S.M. Kinkead (later killed off Calshot in Supermarine S.5 N221 on 12 March 1928), an unidentified Russian, Walter Anderson, Dr Flood. (Author's collection [701])

being burnt to prevent them falling into enemy hands. The personnel returned home aboard the *Kildonan Castle*.

In its brief existence, some notable men served with the Russian Expedition, among them Squadron Leader J. Ira. T. Jones DSO, MC, DFC, MM, Russian Order of St George,* best remembered today as an early biographer of Mannock VC; and Flight Lieutenant S.M. Kinkhead DSO, DSC & bar, DFC & bar, who later piloted the Gloster IV floatplane in the 1926 Schneider

RMS Kildonan Castle. The men of the RAF North Russian Expedition came home on this ship in 1919 after the British withdrawal. (Courtesy C. Webster)

Trophy contest and the Supermarine S5 in 1927, only to be killed during an attempt on the World Absolute Speed Record the following year. Both these men had their first air service experience with the Royal Flying Corps while Lieutenant-Colonel Raymond Collishaw DSO & bar, DSC, DFC, C de G, had been a member of the Royal Naval Air Service. Other former RFC pilots who saw service in Russia included Majors J.O. Andrews, G. Bowman, Alan Jerrard VC and Keith Park.

After a peace treaty had been agreed between the Bolsheviks and Estonia, the RAF finally left the Baltic on 2 February 1920. By then, its crews had amassed a total of 837 operational hours and thirty-three aircraft had been lost. Nine were shot down, but the rest had simply deteriorated beyond repair on account of the climate. The last action of the second RAF detachment had been associated with the bitter fighting around Kharkov while supporting General Mai-Maevsky's White volunteers. When they were routed the RAF was ordered home from here also, the personnel destroying their aircraft before making their own way to Rostov from where they were evacuated in March 1920.

THE AFGHAN WAR

While these events were taking place in the still-evolving Soviet Union, the descendants of the Royal Flying Corps were active in warmer climes. In May 1919 RAF aircraft were involved in the opening stages of what was to become the Third Afghan War. Here the son of the hereditary ruler, Amir Ammanullah, whose father Habibullah Khan had been assassinated shortly before, was to make strenuous efforts to unite his divided people by launching an invasion of India.

The subsequent war lasted only four weeks, but during that period 31 Squadron and 114 Squadron, which had been formed at Lahore two

---

*The ribbon of this order was interesting in that it was slightly narrower than the majority, being 24mm wide; it was orange-yellow with three 4mm black, vertical stripes, the outer ones leaving a 2mm margin.

Ordered into production before the formation of the RAF, the Sopwith 7F.1 Snipe continued to be used after the war. H4884 seen here was flown by 1 Squadron RAF at Bangalore in 1920 and on 1 November Flying Officer Soden successfully force-landed it at Mysore. (JMB/GSL collection)

years earlier from a nucleus provided by the former, were flying in support of British troops in the vicinity of the latter's station at Quetta. The main air operations took the form of bombing attacks on rebel strongholds, together with a notable attack on Kabul on 25 May in the course of which four bombs from a Handley Page O/400 hit Amir Ammanullah's palace. Not surprisingly, he sued for peace soon afterwards, although the activities of anti-British Pathan tribesmen meant that attacks were resumed in November. However, after the first of these, the Mahsuds and Waziri proved to have an extraordinary ability to bring down aircraft merely with rifle fire. During a raid on 14 January 1920 three aircraft were accounted for in this way, while a similar number, although they struggled back to base, were so badly damaged that they had to be withdrawn from service. Finally the account against thse tribesmen had to be settled by ground forces, supported from the air. These missions called for flights over wild and desolate terrain where an emergency landing meant at best death from starvation and thirst, at worst capture by the primitive savages who were the enemy. However, success was achieved by May.

The aircraft having proved their worth in this new field of operations, the total number of squadrons in India was raised first to six, then to eight, with a pair in Iraq (then Mesopotamia) and seaplanes at Alexandria and Malta. Of the twenty-five operational squadrons then in existence, about half were based in the Middle East.

Also in 1919, the RAF took part in the struggle against the tribesmen in British Somaliland led by the anti-British Mohammed bin Abdulla Hassan, known to history as the Mad Mullah, who had extended his influence over the greater part of the country during the years of the First World War. The use of aircraft seemed to present a solution to this problem and as a result in December eight DH9s were sent aboard HMS *Ark Royal* to Berbera. These were soon joined by a further pair equipped as air

Former RFC/RAF men who served in the Middle East after the Armistice of November 1918 were largely forgotten. This BE2c had a bomb rack between the undercarriage legs and was usually flown by Lieutenant Steward-Dawson from 7 (Naval) Squadron's base at Dar-es-Salaam. (JMB/GSL collection)

This BE2e at Aboukir had a personal marking in the form of a Maltese Cross on the white rudder stripe. (JMB/GSL collection)

ambulances. The former went into action on 21 January, bombing the main enemy fortress at Medishe, and this successful attack was followed by a mopping-up operation by the Camel Corps. The following month the enemy leader fled to Abyssinia where he died.

The end of the First World War had brought with it the fragmentation of the Ottoman Empire, founded by Othman in the fourteenth century. Within eighteen months of the Armistice agreement in Europe, large sections of the Middle East, no longer under Turkish rule, were evolving into unstable, disorganised and penurious new nations. This state of affairs caused great concern to the League of Nations, a body designed to prevent the outbreak of future wars. One result of this was that a system was evolved whereby member countries were charged with maintaining the peace in one or several areas, with the United Kingdom being responsible for Mesopotamia (Iraq), Transjordan and Palestine.

In the first of these, the situation was especially difficult. The 120,000 British and Indian troops were supported by four RAF squadrons. After the Cairo conference, 8, 30, 55 and 84 Squadrons were deployed in the area, all flying ex-wartime DH9As. They were later joined by 6 Squadron with Bristol Fighters and 1 Squadron with Sopwith Snipes and Nieuport Nighthawks intended for tropical testing. After fifteen months in India this unit was now moved to Hinaidi in Iraq. Indeed the whole of this deployment was something of an experiment since it was realised that the terrain over which operations had to be flown was so inhospitable that it was necessary for the two-seaters to carry a spare wheel, survival rations and even water in goatskins slung from the gun-ring!

OTHER FLASHPOINTS

The most serious potential flashpoint of 1922 was the Chanak Crisis which drew from one British newspaper the headline 'War Almost Inevitable' when the armies of Mustafa Kemel had defeated the Greeks at the River Sakarya and seemed poised to march into Europe. Their only way was blocked by 1,200 British troops, supported by the RAF's Sopwith Snipes and Nieuport Nightjars, which were being maintained despite the exceptionally primitive conditions. In the event, it is likely that the presence of this air power caused Kemel to back down. He later overthrew the Sultan and became the first president of modern Turkey.

No. 203 Squadron, which had been formed from the Navy's original C Squadron and later became 1 Squadron of the RNAS in 1916, had supplied the air arm for this miniscule British Army contribution, being equipped with the Nieuport Nightjar biplane, only twenty-three of which were ever delivered to the service. Their power units were Bentley rotary engines similar to those which had powered the late Sopwith Camels in the closing war years. Six of 203 Squadron's latest aircraft were delivered aboard HMS *Argus* to give 'teeth' to the British intervention in the Chanak emergency, a base being set up near Constantinople (later Istanbul).

Also brought to the area of operations was 4 Squadron, equipped with another veteran type that had vindicated itself during the First World War: the F2b, Bristol Fighter (affectionately known at that time as the 'Biff'). The squadron's C Flight had been serving at Stonehenge, with A Flight deployed to the 11th Irish Wing until January 1922, soon after which the whole unit embarked on HMS *Ark Royal*, which delivered the Bristols to Kilia Bay in the Dardanelles. Here they were transferred to HMS *Argus* and on 11 October 1922 they were flown

RFC uniforms were discarded only slowly. Here at Cologne in 1919 Flight Lieutenant Jones wears the new sky blue uniform with gold lace rank insignia and a khaki cap with RAF insignia, while his Observer retains the khaki uniform but with an RAF badge on what looks like a naval cap. (Dr A.G. Wilson MC)

off, despite the fact that for all the pilots, this was their first experience of deck take-offs and none had received any training.

The new area of operations for all the RAF units was to prove exceptionally difficult. At first there were problems with dust-storms and heat, but with the onset of the rainy season airfields swiftly became seas of clinging mud, making take-off, landing and even taxi-ing impossible since the aircraft simply sank axle-deep in the quagmire. An attempt was made to lay artificial runways; these were laid out in wire netting, 10 yards wide and 60 yards length,

RAF strength abroad in 1920 included 56 Squadron flying Sopwith 7F.1 Snipes. Here E7529 of that unit is started up at Aboukir. The wheel covers are red, with a thin white rim; a narrow white band encircles the fuselage aft of the roundel and the fin is doped with unpigmented cellulose. (via Mrs I.W. Austin)

pegged down and covered in canvas – but even these could sink 5 or 6in soon after being laid down. Then, as the final days of October approached, gales sprang up, with winds reaching speeds of 60 or 70mph and in the midst of the extensive flooding, tents and canvas hangars, an older type than the heavier Bessoneau, were blown down and torn asunder.

The Middle East immediately after the end of the First World War featured significantly in the deliberations on the future deployment of the RAF. It was finally decided that almost one-third of the squadron strength

RE8s in the Middle East. 'She was no good!', one veteran told the author, but others liked the type. The trouble lay chiefly in the small fin area. (Author's collection)

*A DH6 in the Middle East.
(Alexander Turnbull Library, New
Zealand)*

should be based in Mesopotamia, chiefly to cooperate with ground forces. This turned out to be an unpopular decision since it was taken in an atmosphere heavy with overt plans to dismember the infant service and restore something of the former structure. This was a common attitude in many quarters and was reflected in a comment from Sir Henry Wilson who, having planned the role of the British Expeditionary Force in France and acted as the principal liaison officer with the French at the beginning of the conflict, wrote early in May 1919, the year after his appointment as Chief of the Imperial General Staff: 'The sooner the Air Force crashes the better. It is a wicked waste of money as run at present.'

POLITICAL STRUGGLES

There were others who sided with this view and advanced such arguments that as a corps of the Army, the flying service had been perfectly adequate, that the greater part of its personnel had signed on only for 'the duration' and that the size of the force, now about 3,500 officers and 29,000 men strong as against the 1919 figures of 17,267 and 108,753 respectively, was insufficient to justify its existence as a separate service, with an estimated 484 aircraft in 1924.

This call was largely supported by the Army, since the Royal Navy had for long gone its own way in matters aeronautical, but even so there were certain factions even here who resented the new situation. A typical example was the comparatively minor issue of opposing all new rank titles that seemed to have a nautical ring when these were proposed (among others) as replacements for those of strictly army origin, which had been in use with effect from 1 April 1918.

Issues such as these continued to be debated well into the succeeding decade while the men of the RAF remained occupied with the less esoteric considerations of a succession of minor wars. These were not confined to military operations in distant lands, although these were to continue, with aerial campaigns in the 1920s including the attack that caused the retreat of Zeidi robbers who had penetrated into Yemen in 1925, and the peaceful life-saving intervention into the discord created by warring factions in Afghanistan in 1928–9, culminating in the evacuation of Kabul. This began on 23 December 1928 and continued until 25 February, and saved the lives of 586 persons of various nationalities. The aircraft involved flew some 57,438 miles in all, over mountains 10,000ft in height, with 28,160 miles being required for the actual evacuation.

But beside such sorties as these, which were among the first to shed a humanitarian light on the view that the public continued to hold towards the new service, there were others, especially those in the Middle East which involved conflict. But it was the conflicts between the bureaucrats and politicians, fought in the corridors of power at home, that threatened to overwhelm the new service. At times it seemed that the only champion of the RAF's continuing existence was the man who had done more than any other to create it, laying down in wise detail almost every aspect of its structure despite the parsimonious, narrow-minded Treasury officials.

This champion was Hugh Trenchard. Known to his men as 'Boom' from his deep and penetrating voice, he had been the commander of the RFC's No. 1 Wing in France, taking charge in August 1915 of the entire

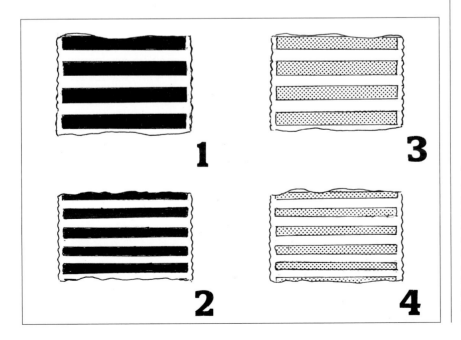

The new flying service called for new decorations. These included (1) Distinguished Flying Cross (violet and white); (2) Distinguished Flying Medal (violet and white); (3) Air Force Cross (scarlet and white); (4) Air Force Medal (scarlet and white). All four were instituted on 3 June 1918, the horizontal lines being exchanged for diagonal ones in the following August. (Author)

Royal Flying Corps. By 1919 he was Chief of Air Staff at the Air Ministry; a post he held for ten years, thus enabling him singlemindedly to forge a new service from the remains of the old. While still a major-general, Trenchard had been charged with the formation of the new service, being assisted by the no less able but now largely forgotten Rear Admiral Mark Kerr. But it was Trenchard that the rank and file remembered. In 1922 T.E. Lawrence, who joined the RAF as 'Aircraftman Shaw' in October that year, wrote '. . . he steers through all the ingenuity and cleverness and hesitations of the little men who help or hinder him'.

Thus in the final analysis it was Trenchard's personal efficiency in producing a formula for the successor of the Royal Flying Corps which finally won the day. Examination found it to be so clear, visionary and all-inclusive that even those of the other services who had sought to dismantle and absorb the RAF after the Armistice were forced to admit that no superior or even comparable options could be presented.

CHAPTER ELEVEN

THE WOMEN'S SERVICES

The women's uniform that never was. A symbolic 'WRAF' imagined by Cadet Milne Mac Michael to celebrate the foundation of the RAF. Entitled 'Two Strings to Her Bow', it appeared in the May 1918 issue of Roosters and Fledglings, *the magazine of the RFC officers' training establishments in Hastings, Sussex. The airfield was at nearby Fairlight. (Author's collection)*

BY CADET MILNE MAC MICHAEL (formerly of No. 2 Wing)

Great Britain and her Allies had been at war with Kaiser Wilhelm's Germany for twenty-three months when the Battle of the Somme opened on a wet and stormy 1 July 1916. Some 66,000 British soldiers were thrown against the enemy along an 18-mile front. The advance began at 7.30a.m. within an hour just under half this force had been cut down by the German defenders. No army could absorb losses on such a scale as this for long, and the attempts to find a solution went a considerable distance towards the creation of a women's force in the British services.

On 4 May 1915 Prime Minister Asquith had said in a speech: 'Let there not be a man or woman among us who, when the war is over, will not be able to say "I was not idle".' Yet it is far from likely that he envisaged a step as significant, revolutionary even, as that which was about to be taken. (His reference was far more likely a gesture in the direction of the Suffragettes who had been prominent in his earlier days of office.) Even so, the position at the end of 1916 was sufficiently grave for Field Marshal Sir Douglas Haig, commanding the British Armies in France, to state on 10 December his

165

A WRAF with friend. The shoulder title and early form of eagle and cap badge are clearly seen, this resembling that of a naval CPO. The strap is black patent leather and the brass buttons plain, with only a crown and eagle design. (IWM Q27528 via Bruce Robertson)

acceptance in principle of women replacing men as clerks at GHQ and on communication duties. Eight days later a lieutenant-colonel commented that more women should be taken on charge than the number of men they were replacing as 'they cannot stand as much strain as men'; he added that they might also perform administrative and disciplinary work, together with cooking and domestic duties. Haig was again vocal on the subject in the new year stating on 15 January that women might also act as telegraphists and as telephone operators in rear areas of the Front. A month later the Army Council was actively issuing instructions laying down conditions of service for women and on 11 March Haig formally accepted the idea of women being employed in France for selected non-combatant duties.

Almost simultaneously, the Navy embarked on a similar path, as illustrated by the publication of a report entitled *Female Labour on Air Stations*. The result at the beginning of the following year was the formation of the WRNS,* the Women's Royal Naval Service. They were employed at shore establishments only, their activities confined at first to domestic and clerical work, but this soon widened to embrace a range of tasks including dispatch riding and depth-charge maintenance for aircraft patrolling coastal waters in search of U-boats. But while internal memos and the deliberations of committees were exchanged and studied in the corridors of power as 1917 dawned, few realised that they were in effect re-inventing an earlier idea of women in the services.

The seed of this idea had been planted by the Marchioness of Londonderry, wife of a future Secretary of State for Air, who suggested to the War Office in July 1915 that a Women's Legion should be formed to assist the Army with cooking, since there was already a shortage of skilled and experienced men for this. Her proposal laid the foundations of the Legion's Military Cookery Section, and when the suggestion was put into

*A forgotten pioneer who did much to establish this service was Sybil, Marchioness of Cholmondeley, wife of the 5th Marquess. She was descended from both the Sassoon and Rothschild families.

practice, at first experimentally in convalescent camps, it was pronounced a success. Some twelve months later the idea was extended to a wider spectrum of military establishments, women later using their skills in a wide variety of duties as clerks, typists, waitresses and domestic staff, store-keepers, checkers, telephone operators postal workers and motor transport drivers. Typists were paid £1 7s 6d per week (those with a knowledge of shorthand received an extra £1 a week). The Women's Legion Motor Drivers (WLMD) Section, which was especially associated with the Royal Flying Corps although they worked for all the services and government departments, provided the transport drivers, although they were not permitted to drive heavy vehicles. A charge of 14s was deducted weekly from every woman's pay, if she was living away from home, for board and lodging.

The RFC chauffeuse of Car 32. The lettering on her shoulder title is larger than that on the men's uniforms. (Author's collection [700])

There also existed the organisation known as Women Civilian Subordinates (WCS), members of which were not issued with uniforms but wore civilian clothing consisting of a white blouse, with a tie, and a dark skirt. Their appearance was later changed by the adoption of a khaki-coloured coat-dress with a pair of patch pockets and turned-back cuffs with buttons. This garment was to clear the ground by no more than 12in and was secured by leather-covered buttons and a cloth belt with two more buttons. It reached to the throat and had a deep shirt-like collar under which was a long and fairly wide tie secured by a clip in the form of an RFC eagle with an integral crown centrally above. (Close scrutiny of photographs reveals that RFC wings, possibly 'sweetheart brooches', and two-bladed propellers were also permitted, perhaps unofficially.) All was topped by a soft 'campaign-style' hat with a brim, in the front of which the headband carried a dull-finish metal RFC badge, identical to that worn by men (as were the embroidered shoulder titles). The ensemble was based on the uniform of the Women's Army Auxiliary Corps (WAACs), which became the Queen Mary's Army Auxiliary Corps (QMAAC) in April 1918. Indeed, the ' new' garb for the Women Civilian Subordinates was nothing more than a modification of the WAACs' surplus garments. Members of this organisation mostly lived at home, and went to work each day at an RFC establishment, drivers no doubt being classed as 'technical women', any four of whom, at least at one Auxiliary Service Corps motor transport centre south-east of London, were officially categorised as the equivalent of three 'technical soldiers'.

In terms of releasing men for combatant duties, the absorption of women into the fighting services was so successful that on 7 July 1917 the

War Office announced the formation of a new corps, the Women's Auxiliary Army Corps (WAAC), a service organised on normal military lines with a rank structure; officers were designated as Controllers (Staff Officers) and Administrators (regimental officers), with Forewomen and Assistant Forewomen (NCOs). This body primarily worked alongside the Army; but in parallel with it was also created the Women's Section, Royal Flying Corps, a service again much engaged in driving duties and for whom a new uniform was created. This was considerably more practical for such work, although the WSRFC was by no means occupied exclusively with driving motor vehicles. It consisted now of a three-quarter length jacket with reveres, patch pockets and shoulder tabs with rank insignia and buttons, RFC sleeve titles and RFC brass buttons, three on the front fastening, two on each cuff and a pair on the cloth belt in the manner of that worn by the Civilian Subordinates. This jacket was worn over a white blouse with a soft khaki tie and a skirt to the same length as previously, although for motor-cyclists, the skirt was exchanged for riding breeches and laced boots terminating just below the knee. For this work, too, the standard 'campaign-style' hat of the Civilian Subordinates was exchanged for a soft-top, peaked cap with a khaki head-band and brass RFC badge. Brown leather gloves with deep gauntlets were worn by drivers and motor-cyclists alike. Female dispatch-riders, unlike their male counterparts (see Chapter Three) did not do night duty.

The wider use of women was not without problems. Volunteers from under-privileged groups, some of whom had endured grinding poverty in civilian life, needed instruction in basics of hygiene and personal care. A list of items they were expected to have before being sent to a unit was issued. It included:

One pair of strong boots or shoes (augmenting those officially issued)
One pair of low-heeled shoes for indoor wear
Two pairs of khaki stockings (augmenting the official issue)
Two pairs (at least) of combinations
Two pairs of dark knickers (with washable linings)
Two pairs of loosely woven wool vests
Two pairs of pyjamas or nightdresses
One dozen handkerchiefs.

The arrival of women into the Armed Forces, which had been a male bastion for hundreds of years, resulted in the novelty of seeing ladies on airfields and other military installations of both the Royal Flying Corps and the Royal Naval Air Service. At the same time, they freed a large number of men for combatant duties, and the size of this fresh phalanx of men may be gathered from the number and diversity of trades undertaken by women in March 1918. These were summarised as: 2,969 clerks; 1,322 store workers; 899 sail-makers; 680 cooks; 436 drivers of motor vehicles; 263 fitters and 153 riggers; while the final group of 1,681 girls was mysteriously categorised as 'miscellaneous trades and trainees'. Fitters and riggers were much admired for their 'hands-on' experience with aeroplanes.

Many former members of the Civilian Subordinates transferred to this new service and there followed a period during which the coat-dress of

An RFC motorcycle combination rider astride an RAF P&M machine. The cylinder on the handle-bars was an acetylene holder to power the headlamp. (IWM Q12291 via Bruce Robertson)

that organisation continued to be worn, although seemingly with the deep shirt collar of the blouse drawn over that of the coat, but with the former tie retained. The Chief Controller of the new Women's Auxiliary Army Corps was Mrs Chalmers Watson MD and the Chief Controller in France was Mrs H.C.I. Gwynne-Vaughan. (The former was the sister of Lieutenant-Colonel Geddes who in December 1916 had been championing the cause of women for administrative and disciplinary posts.) Nineteen days after the announcement of the foundation of the WAAC, a huge conference of women's societies was held in London. Addressed by Mrs Chalmers Watson, this conference attracted representatives of the pioneer Women's Legion, the First Aid Nursing Yeomanry (popularly known as FANY) and the Voluntary Aid Detachment (VADS) among others, the massive success of the meeting being crowned by the publication on 28 March 1918 of Paper FS No. 14 by the Air Council with the title *Constitution and Regulations of the Women's Royal Air Force.*

There now existed a number of women's services, chief among them being the Women's Auxiliary Army Corps, the Women's Legion Motor Drivers (a description necessary to differentiate between drivers of mechanical transport and horse-drawn vehicles) and the Women Civilian

WRAF cloth shoulder badge. Commonly worn at the top of the sleeve in early 1919, a few appeared about 4in below a black cloth crescent bearing the letters WRAF, stitched in white. The cap badge with this uniform resembled that of a CPO in the Royal Navy. In the middle of the year these cap badges began to be replaced by brass RAF badges with the adoption of the final blue clothing, the high-collared tunic of which resembled the men's earlier RFC 'maternity jacket' but with metal buttons. Officers' uniforms were closely based on those of their male counterparts. (Author)

Subordinates, but problems were beginning to arise in the recruitment field. In August 1917 the War Cabinet had decided to amalgamate the Royal Flying Corps and the Royal Naval Air Service; henceforth volunteers for enrolment into the Women's Section of the former, for example, found themselves either drafted into the WAAC or passed over and seemingly ignored. Some resentment was caused, matter, and the predicament was not resolved until 28 December when it was announced that henceforth the RFC would carry out its own recruiting.

Birth-pangs for the new RAF, both the male and female services, were many. Memos and internal communiques proliferated and were exchanged in a frenzy of activity in the corridors of power, with the outcome (at least as far as women were concerned) being made public on 29 January 1918 with the Air Council's announcement that it proposed to found a Women's Auxiliary Air Force Corps (WAAFC), subject to Treasury approval. All women currently working at air establishments were expected to transfer to the new service by 1 April. In the meantime the Admiralty had forestalled the War Office by the issue of Admiralty Publication B.2258 on 4 February promulgating the Women's Royal Naval Service, making the provision that women currently employed at naval air stations were free to transfer to the proposed WAAFC if they wished.

Meanwhile at station level, recruits were at a loss to understand why they had volunteered for service with the RFC only to be issued with WAAC uniforms, although they also received new winged insignia to be sewn on their tunics and hats in due course. In fact the proposed service never existed under the title stated, since on 5 March 1918, twenty-six days before the official formation of the Royal Air Force, King George V had been 'graciously pleased' to agree that the new women's service be known as the Women's Royal Air Force (WRAF), the necessary constitution and regulations being promulgated by FS (Field Service) Publication no. 14, dated 29 March 1918.

Although there had been persistent rumours in the previous weeks that the new uniform would be similar to the 'sky-blue' version proposed for the men, the regulation tunic and skirt turned out to be little different from that formerly worn, even retaining khaki for the 10,168 girls who had transferred to the service from the earlier services by 1 July. At the beginning of August, the figure was 15,433, a total that indicated the intake of some 5,000 recruits from civilian life. For these and others, the old uniform was now enlivened by a set of entirely new insignia. Gone were the old black cloth crescents with their white embroidered lettering from the top of the sleeve, their place being taken by new patches of similar shape with the letters 'W.R.A.F.' Below this, again embroidered in white on a black patch, was a fairly large eagle with outspread wings and lowered head, similar to the one now depicted on the brass buttons below a crown, although it is true that the wings of this bird were more arched than those of the sleeve insignia. Between

these, some girls bore a third badge, which consisted of a rectangle of black cloth bearing the single letter 'I', indicating that the wearer was an 'Immobile'.

In this way the WRAF was divided into two categories, Mobiles and Immobiles. All below NCO rank were Members, who lived at home and reported each day to an air establishment in their vicinity. 'Immobiles' could not be posted to any other area, except for an initial training period of four weeks, and had to be at least eighteen. 'Mobiles' (a category which included all officers) had to have attained their twentieth birthday and for an extra 13s per quarter could be posted anywhere in the United Kingdom or even overseas.

During the early days of the new service for women, badges were the same as those worn on the former RFC uniforms but these were replaced by the very similar WRAF ones, only the headgear showing the change that had taken place. Gone was the old 'campaign style' hat and in its place was universally adopted the soft-topped, peaked cap earlier favoured by women RFC motor-cyclists. The front of this was now adorned with a cloth badge clearly based on that of a Chief Petty Officer in the Royal Navy. This depicted a red eagle with its head to the wearer's left, within a stitched twin circle on a black cloth disc topped with a crown. Use of this was of comparatively short duration, since it was later replaced by a brass RAF badge, officers having this in gilt metal throughout.

The uniforms remained khaki, however, and for cold weather a long gaberdine 'trench coat' could be worn. This was double-breasted, and worn with the lapels buttoned back; it had a buckled belt and arm badges as on the tunic. Greatcoats were also issued although they carried no such badges. A white shirt and black tie was retained as before.

In charge of the new WRAF, with the rank of Chief Superintendent was Lady Gertrude Crawford, but her command lasted no more than a month. She was replaced by the Hon. Violet Douglas-Pennant, the rank now being styled that of Commandant, but in September 1918 a further change of command found Mrs H.C.I. Gwynne-Vaughan in charge. She was able to draw on her great experience gained while acting as Chief Controller of the WAAC in France, where she had been responsible for some 25,000 women, and brought to the post her knowledge of coordinating the work of men and women. She strongly supported the idea of members of the new service being posted abroad; once it was decided that this was acceptable, a new set of regulations had to be drawn up. For example, girls posted to Cologne with the British Army of Occupation were permitted only limited fraternisation with males at official social functions.

At the lower levels of command, the rank structure was simpler than that for the men, officers being known as Senior Leaders, Chief Section Leaders or Section Leaders, while NCOs were described as Chief Leaders (Sergeants) and Sub-Leaders (Corporals, although their rank insignia resembled that of a Lance Corporal). Otherwise the insignia of rank was the same as their male counterparts for officers and NCOs.

Eighteen WRAF members, including two sergeants and two corporals, pictured at Cologne in early 1919. The Nissen huts behind were named after Colonel Nissen who had devised them three years earlier. (IWM Q27254 via Bruce Robertson)

The WRAF in 1919.

Q 27254

There were four categories of work for WAAFs. Identified by letters of the alphabet, these were set out in pamphlet M 105/4 as:

Category 'A' Clerk, Shorthand Writer, Typist
Category 'B' Cleaner, Cook, Waitress, Laundress, Domestic Worker
Category 'C' Chauffeuse, Photographer, Fitter, Tinsmith, Metal Worker, Rigger, Wireless Mechanic, Wireless Operator, Carpenter, Painter
Category 'D' General duties including: Storekeeper, Tailoress, Shoemaker, Sailmaker, Motor-Cyclist.

The envisaged strength of the WRAF had been 90,000 women, but this figure was never achieved. By the end of the war it was officially quoted as no more than 24,400. Although the service did not survive for long after the Armistice of 1918, it had its moments of pride and recognition of a job well done. For many serving in Germany this came on 18 August 1919 when a large number of servicewomen were inspected by the Secretary of State for Air, Winston Churchill, at Lindenthal, Cologne. Their uniforms now presented a slightly different appearance since the WRAF shoulder title had been discarded and the eagle, previously below it, had been raised up to the former position of the lettering.

Most of the girls inspected by Churchill had been part of a total of 1,000 sent overseas, arriving in Cologne in March 1919 from the Maresquel depot in France. These were the first WRAF members to go abroad. (An earlier scheme to send them as clerks, domestics and storewomen to release men from the Independent Force Headquarters in south-east France had failed to materialise.) Cologne was now the Headquarters of the RAF in Germany, and the Sud Park Hotel had been requisitioned as the WRAF's Headquarters, to house the 14 officers and 342 'Members'. They were under the command of Miss K. Curlett OBE, whose jurisdiction embraced the No. 1 Advanced Aircraft Stores Depot at Merheim and No. 1 Aircraft Depot at Dormagen, both employing women.

The 'war to end wars' was now over and the female labour that had made such a massive contribution to the victory was rapidly dispersed. In the munitions factories at home where women – the 'Munitionettes'

An obviously posed picture, but nevertheless representative of the work performed by girls in Category C, which was regarded as the technical branch of the women's service. Its trades included fitters, metal-workers and riggers. All recruits began with a four-week course at Halton Training Depot. (Bruce Robertson collection)

This group photograph was probably taken at Thetford in 1918. The lady on the left is wearing a coat-dress with RFC shoulder titles, while the lady on the right is wearing a later uniform with WRAF shoulder title and an 'Immobile' panel beneath. (This normally appeared below the lettering but above the eagle badge although this seems to be absent here.) Hem lines are a regulation 12in above the ground. The male sergeant in the front row shows the four-blade propeller marking above his rank chevrons and three of the men in the back row carry canes. (Bruce Robertson collection)

– had made up some 73 per cent of the total 24,719-strong workforce, many of them were discharged at short notice, as were their uniformed counterparts in the Women's Police Service, recruited specially to keep order in munitions works. It was all too evident that the gender shift caused by the war was already beginning to revert.

The same was true in the Services, partly because women who felt they had 'done their bit' were restless to return home and their 'traditional' roles. There was also a determination that life must 'get back to normal' and return to the old way of life, its values and ideas. Few people realised then that the clock could never be turned back, and that the world of 1914 had been shot dead by a political fanatic in Sarajevo.

But the women's services proved to have powerful enemies at home, some senior officers (female as well as male) making it quite clear that women were not acceptable in the services in peace-time. By the end of 1919 the WRAF was beginning to disintegrate. The first sign of this was the resignation of the Assistant Commandant, but the last girls had left Germany by November 1919, followed by their sisters from France by March 1920. Six months later the new blue uniforms began to be issued and a recruiting campaign was seemingly begun, a girl featured on posters bearing the declaration 'Serve Your Country by Joining the W.R.A.F.

There is fit work for every Fit Woman', and showing a 'Member' wearing a tunic obviously based on the 'maternity jacket' of the Royal Flying Corps but fastened on the opposite side. Yet despite these measures, by December the WRAF had gone. There was now no women's air service.

The summary dissolution of the short-lived WRAF was a grievous blow to the men and women who, during the greatest war mankind had ever experienced, had laboured long and hard to create it. Thus they welcomed the announcement that Mrs Gwynne-Vaughan and Miss Trefusis-Forbes, assisted by Lady Trenchard, were planning to keep alive the spirit of the WRAF by forming the Women's Emergency Service (WES) to provide officer training in any future war. Eighteen years later, now recognised by both the Army and Air Council, this was one of the foundation stones of the new ATS via No. 20 RAF (County of London) Company, from which was eventually to emerge the Women's Auxiliary Air Force. This was mobilised in August 1939 after authorisation by royal warrant on 28 June. Similarly the dissolution of the WRNS after the Armistice of 1918 saw the foundation of the Association of WRNS. This in its turn was to become the kernel of the refounded service of the Second World War.

THE FOUNDATIONS ARE BUILT UPON

These then were the men and women, machines and tactics that made up the Royal Flying Corps and the Royal Naval Air Service, which amalgamated on 1 April 1918 to produce to the new service on which the vast majority of the world's air arms are modelled. The Armistice of 1918 signalled the hoped-for end of what was sincerely believed in many quarters to have been a 'war to end all wars'. Many of the young men who survived had, in many cases, been trained only to serve as airborne killers so that for some there followed an aimless period before demobilisation, when they roamed the now silent battlefields, looked at the fruits of their work from a fresh viewpoint and toured the countryside seeking the graves of fallen comrades. Some remained in the new service, perhaps to fight in a remote corner of the globe, perhaps to be assigned

After the end of the war RAF duties included flying official mail between Kenley and Versailles. While thus engaged, this DH4, no. F5718, came to grief at Sart in Belgium on 15 April 1918. The pilot was Lieutenant Beaudry and the observer AC2 Harper. (A.E. Jessop)

'Hurrah for the next man . . .'. RFC graves were frequently marked by a four-blade airscrew fashioned into a cross. This particular one was a memorial, originally bearing a plate commemorating Lieutenant Harold Barklay-Winton (1892–1918) and marked 'RR Falcon III'. It survived with no attention except an annual coat of varnish until 1960 when, worm-eaten, and its lamination parting, it was burnt on the orders of the family. The adjacent cross is 'In loving memory of my brother' Lieutenant Philip Michell RFC. (V.J. Garwood via Author)

such duties as aerial newspaper and mail distribution in the autumn railway strike of 1919.

Understandably, some exchanged their uniforms for civilian ones and became aircrew in the speedily developing field of civil flying, which was simultaneously providing work for the hundreds of fitters, riggers and mechanics who had also been suddenly thrown on to the employment market. Similarly, long-distance flying, route surveys and even barnstorming like flying circus performers provided a living for some former RFC and RNAS men, whatever their category.

Others, unaware that a way of life had been shot dead at Sarajevo four years earlier, and obedient to the sorry belief of the time that a return to the atmosphere of the age before August 1914 was best, turned their backs for ever on aviation. In some quarters, especially among older folk, flyers were looked on almost as criminals, one lady summing up this belief in the statement that 'I don't think they ought to be allowed to make them things to go up there prying into the Almighty's private affairs'. They stopped wearing their uniforms, putting them on only for the annual Armistice Day celebrations on 11 November and for re-unions, including those of a new organisation, The Comrades of the Royal Air Force; known to-day as the Royal Air Forces Association (RAFA), of which the first Chairman was Air Commodore Samson (see Chapter 7).

The 54ft tall RAF memorial stands on the Victoria Embankment, London, at the top of Whitehall Stairs. It was unveiled in July 1923 in the presence of the Duke of York (later King George VI), who wore the new RAF uniform for the ceremony. The great bronze eagle was designed by A. Parlanti, the sculptor also responsible for the aluminium 'Victory Bells' said to have been cast from metal melted down from enemy aircraft, and sold to the public in 1945. (Author [66])

There was almost a reunion atmosphere too about an occasional BBC radio series titled 'Flying High'. Described as 'a variety performed by members of the RFC, RNAS and RAF', it was devised and produced by Charles Brewer, and the first episode, broadcast on 25 November 1936, was performed before an RAFA audience. The stars, who had all seen service during the war years, included G.H. Elliott, Hugh Wakefield, Laddie Cliff, Roy Royston, Will Russell, Ralph Coram, Sonny Day and Jack Warman. Men like these and hundreds of other veterans of the air war would talk, tease, reminisce and perhaps tell how they had to explain the old, forgotten board games of the war years to their children. There were games such as 'The War in the Air', a pastime that featured Bleriot Monoplanes and Henry Farmans, 'The Battle in the Skies', described as 'the most fascinating air game for young and old', and 'Bombarding the Zepps', the board game of 1916 which reflected public concern with the likelihood of attacks on the homeland. They all mirrored the public's short-lived awareness of the importance of the RFC and RNAS while hostilities lasted.

Some of these ex-RFC/RAF men were able to carve out new careers for themselves, or perhaps returned to former ones. Some achieved fame in a wide variety of fields: Tom Browne, a bomber pilot of the Independent Air Force, and Goderic Hodges, a balloon observer, both became renowned schoolmasters. Another group included Oswald Mosley, a Member of Parliament and later organiser of the British Union of Facists. Aged just nineteen, and 6ft 2in tall with an upright bearing, he had been commissioned into the 16th Lancers when he volunteered for the new flying service in August 1914. Together with another young officer, who was to die only three weeks later, they were the first cavalry officers to volunteer for the RFC. Before the end of that year, Mosley was flying over the lines as an observer, but in the following year he opted for pilot training. Leg injuries received in a crash landing in 1917 put an end to his flying career. An interesting number of personalities in the arts and entertainment world of the 1920s,

DH9A E9902 at Lympne, Kent. (Author's collection)

Taken in 1923, this photograph shows some of the cast of 'Children's Hour'. In the centre is 'Aunt Sophie', with (left) 'Uncle Rex' and 'Uncle Caractacus'. Rex Palmer served with 111 Squadron RFC while Cecil Lewis served with 56 Squadron and was a pioneer of aviation wireless telegraphy. (Author's collection)

1930s and beyond had served in Britain's first flying service, only a small number having done so before the outbreak of war. They included: Ronald Adam RFC, actor and POW, who also served in the Second World War; Sir Lewis Casson RFC, theatrical producer; Vernon Castle RFC, dancer; Billy Cotton RFC, band leader; Roland Culver RFC cadet, actor; G.H. Elliott RNAS, singer (he was known as 'the chocolate-coloured coon'); Tommy Handley RNAS, comedian; Laurence Irving, actor grandson of Henry Irving; Mervyn Johns RFC, actor; Henry Kendall RNAS, actor/producer, who later worked for the BBC and ITV; Cecil Lewis RFC, one-time 'Uncle Caractacus' of BBC radio's 'Children's Hour'; Robert Loraine RFC, actor; Derek McCulloch,* 'Mac' of BBC

*Lieutenant McCulloch is known to have flown at least once as an observer to Captain E.H. ('Bill') Lawford, who, after the war became an experienced airline pilot with AT&T and later Imperial Airways. He was also known as a writer and broadcaster on the subject of civil aviation in the late 1920s and early 1930s. The flight took place on 4 May 1918, testing BE2e B6151 for 45 minutes to an altitude of 5,000ft, after taking off from Farnborough, Hants. Captain Lawford went on to become a test-pilot. His flying career had begun when he gained pilot's certificate no. 442 in March 1913 before joining 5 Squadron RFC in November 1914. He was graded a First Class Pilot in the RFC on 31 May 1916, afterwards serving with 7 Squadron in France on reconnaissance duties, artillery observation and bombing attacks. He was later awarded the new Air Force Cross. His radio broadcast at 5.15p.m. on 16 July 1934 (there had been at least one previously, in 1929) attracted much interest.

This Bristol F2b belonging to B Flight, 20 Squadron, had earlier served with 31 Squadron and when the picture was taken it was attached to 12 Squadron at Spich. Bessonneau Type H canvas hangars such as the one in the background were widely used by the RFC in all operational theatres. The date is about March 1919. (Dr A.G. Wilson MC)

The RAF badge when first introduced featured an eagle resembling that of the former RNAS against the background of a garter. This is one of the few public representations of it on a war memorial. (Author [249])

radio's 'Children's Hour'; Billy Merrin, musician; Ivor Novello RNAS, composer; Rex Palmer RFC, broadcaster and the first London Station Director of 2L0 and an early 'Children's Hour' character called 'Uncle Rex'; Jack Payne RFC, dance band leader; John Tilley, comedian; Ben Travers RNAS, author of the Whitehall farces; Jack Warner RFC, actor ('Dixon of Dock Green'); Herbert Wilcox RFC, film producer (whose wife Anna Neagle often wore an RFC badge as costume jewellery); and George W. Bransby-Williams RFC, actor. Matrimony brought 25-year-old RFC officer Archibald Christie into another field of the arts when in 1914 he married Agatha Miller – later creator of such fictional characters as Jane Marple and Hercule Periot!

Laurence Irving and Ivor Novello both served on the staff at Chingford at one time, apparently managing to get themselves posted there when news of planned amateur theatricals reached them. Novello was described as 'an RNVR two-striper' at the time.

Archibald Christie served with distinction in France between August 1914 and September 1918, holding the rank of captain when flying with 12 Squadron in 1916. Leaving the RAF after the war as a lieutenant-colonel, he had by then been awarded the CMG, DSO and Order of St Stanislas with Swords, 3rd Class, and had been Mentioned in Dispatches five times. First commissioned in the Royal Field Artillery in 1909 he transferred to the RFC in 1913, having qualified as a pilot (gaining RAeC Certificate no. 245) at Brooklands in a Bristol Boxkite on 16 July 1912. He died on 20 December 1967, aged seventy-three.

Now their generation is fading and soon all its members, famous and forgotten alike, will be gone for ever, leaving the traditions of the RFC and RNAS enshrined in those of the RAF. Theirs was the first war to be fought in the air and it is hard today to realise that these pioneers, flying their flimsy wood-and-fabric, wire-braced machines were laying the foundations on which the complexities and horrors of modern aerial warfare are built.

This memorial in a Kent church records the death of nineteen-year-old Second Lieutenant Francis George Wake Marchant RFC. He and Second Lieutenant C.C. Hann were reported 'missing' by the evening of Sunday 22 October 1916, a day of ferocious fighting on the Somme. They presumably died together in one of 3 Squadron's two-seat Morane LA monoplanes used for low-level attacks. (Author [335])

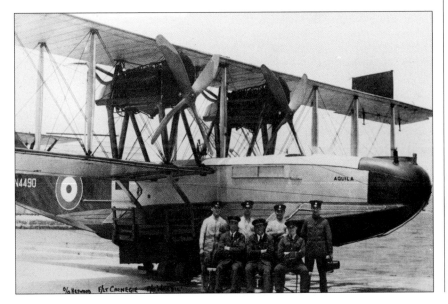

Long-range flights were also the order of the day, including one in Felixstowe F.2A N4490 Aquila between Malta and Gibraltar in 1921. Seated in front are the crew: left to right, Flight Lieutenant Heywood (W/T), Flight Lieutenant Carnegie AFC (pilot) and Flying Officer Waedil (second pilot). (Bruce Robertson collection)

THE SONGS THEY SANG

Although one frequently reads of an overworked wind-up gramophone used in RFC and RNAS messes, the Victorian tradition of 'songs round the piano' still ruled almost supreme, for in spontaneous song the men could express their hopes and fears, and the universal contempt for authority. It helped to maintain morale much more than any commercial gramophone record ever could, although these had their place. Popular records included 'The Londonderry Air', 'The Cobbler's Song' from *Chu-Chin-Chow* (with 2,238 performances clocked up at His Majesty's Theatre, Haymarket, by 1916) or excerpts from 'The Bing Boys'.

Some of the ditties tended to be bawdy or at least have what one veteran termed 'uncensored variations'. Many were based on popular or well-known tunes of the time, making an interesting contrast with the musical backgrounds used by the songs of the rest of the Army, which tended to favour hymn tunes. Well-known examples include 'The Church's One Foundation' which supplied the tune for the PBI's 'We are Fred Karno's Army' (the rag-time infantry) while to the tune of 'While Shepherds Watched' there was 'The Parson Came Home Drunk Last Night (as drunk as he could be!)'. Otherwise a good jingling rhythm was adopted, as for 'The Bells of Hell' (go ting-a-ling a-ling, for you but not for me)'. The singing of mess songs spawned its own traditions, as in 40 Squadron which claimed to have a 'killer piano', said to doom those who played it. One song that was particularly popular with 46 Squadron, since it had been composed by one of their number, Lieutenant Marchant, and chanted to the rhythm of the 23rd Psalm was the mildly profane:

The Pilot's Psalm
The BE2c is my bus; therefore shall I want.
He maketh me to come down in green pastures.
He leadeth me where I wish not to go.
He maketh me to be sick; he leadeth me astray on all cross-country flights.
Yea, though I fly o'er No-man's-land where mine enemies would compass me about, I fear much evil, for thou art with me; thy joystick and thy prop discomfort me.

Thou prepareth a crash for me in the presence of mine enemies;
the RAF anointeth my hair with oil, thy tank leaketh badly.
Surely to goodness thou shalt not follow me all the days of my life,
else I shall dwell in the House of Colney Hatch for ever.

Inevitably the aircraft that were the centre of the pilots' lives featured prominently in songs. A song about the BE2 types was sung to the tune of 'Dixie Land'.

The BE Song
Oh! they found a bit of iron what
Some bloke had thrown away,
And the RAF said, 'This is just the thing
We've sought for many a day.'

They built a weird machine,
The strangest ever seen;
They'd quite forgotten the thing was rotten,
And they shoved it in a flying machine.

Then they ordered simply thousands more,
And sent them out to fight.
When the blokes who had to fly them swore,
The RAF* said 'They're all right;
The 'bus is stable as can be;
We invented every bit ourselves, you see!'
They were so darn' slow, they wouldn't go,
And they called them RAF 2Cs!

Unfortunately the tune of another aircraft song is lost, but its lyrics have survived.

The Ballad of the Bristol Fighter
There are half a dozen buses
On which I've had a whack,
From the RE8 to the two-ton weight
Of the lumbering old Nine Ack.

On the rotary-engined Avro
I've attempted several tricks;
And I'll beat the band on the Clutching Hand,
Better known as the DH6.

And many a first-class joyride
I've had on them last and first,
And many a strut I had go phut
And many a wheel tyre burst.

*RAF = Royal Aircraft Factory.

But few of them know the secret
Of making my heart rejoice,
Like a well-rigged Bristol Fighter
With a two-six-five Rolls-Royce.

She stands at her place on the tarmac,
Like a tiger crouched for the spring,
From the arching spine of her fuselage line
To the ample spread of her wing.

With her wires like sinews tautened,
And her tail-skid's jaunty twist,
Whilst her grey-cowled snout juts grimly out
Like a boxer's tight, clenched fist.

Is there a sweeter music,
Or a more contented sound,
Than the purring clop of her broad, curved prop,
As it gently ticks around?

Then open her up, crescendo
In a deep-toned, swelling roar,
Till she quivers and rocks as she strains at the chocks,
And clamours amain to soar.

Whisk them away my laddies,
Taxy her into the wind,
Then off we skim on a spinning rim
With the tail well up behind.

Hold her down to a hundred,
Then up in a climbing turn
Till we catch our breath in the air, up high.
I wouldn't exchange my seat not I,
For a thousand pounds to burn.

Among the pupils at HMS *Chingford*, an RNAS training school in 1915, was 22-year-old Sub-Lieutenant David Ivor Davies (Ivor Novello*), who had already composed 'Keep the Home Fires Burning', first known as 'till the Boys Come Home', and the tune was quickly adopted by trainees manhandling Maurice Farmans into the sheds at the end of the day:

The Chingford Chant
Keep poor 'B' Class stowing
Though the lorry's going
Though the lorry's due to leave
The aerodrome.

---

*Ivor Novello had been transferred to Chingford from 'HMS Crystal Palace', the popular name for HMS *Victory VI*, the station's official, but little-used name.

There's another Maurice
Waiting out there for us,
We must shove the damned thing in
Or we can't go home.

Only slightly less popular with 110 Bomber-Reconnaissance Squadron was the following, the tune of which has been lost. It ran thus and was entitled:

Return from Essen
I want to go to Essen
To drop my little egg.
The Kaiser, he thinks it's out of reach;
Somebody's pulling his leg.

I want to go to Essen
To call on Fraulein Krupp.
My DH9a will come back
All the way;
And the Kaiser will have
The wind up!

Widely popular and regarded as 'very old' was a song which was still being bellowed in messes in the next war. Sung to the tune of 'The Tarpaulin Jacket', it existed in many forms, the longest having some twelve verses, and was known as:

The Dying Airman
The young aviator lay dying,
And as in the wreckage he lay,
To his comrades gathered around him,
These last parting words did he say:

Chorus:
Take the cylinder out of my kidneys,
The connecting rod out of my brain,
From the small of my back take the camshaft,
And assemble the engine again.

Another aircraft-orientated song, especially popular in 22 Squadron, was rendered to the tune of 'D'ye ken John Peel' and was known as:

'You Haven't a Hope
When you soar into the air on a Sopwith Scout,
And you're scrapping with a Hun and your gun cuts out,
Well you stuff down your nose 'til your plugs fall out,
'Cos we haven't a hope in the morning.

For a batman woke me from my bed,
I'd had a thick night and a very sore head,
And I said to myself, to myself I said,
'Oh we haven't got a hope in the morning.'

So I went to the sheds and examined my gun,
Then my engine I tried to run,
And the revs that it gave were a thousand and one,
'Cos it hadn't got a hope in the morning.

We were escorting '22',
Hadn't a notion what to do,
So we shot down a Hun and an FE too,
'Cos they hadn't a hope in the morning.

We went to Cambrai all in vain,
The FEs said "We must explain
Our camera's broke, we must do it again,
'Cos we haven't got a hope in the morning.

Obviously the following was closely related to this and was also sung to the tune of 'So Early in the Morning'. Widely regarded as the prerogative of 22 Squadron, it was known by the same title.

Early in the Morning
The Orderly Bloke was asleep in bed,
He woke up with an awful head,
The telephone bell began to ring,
More hot air from the 14th Wing.

Chorus:
So early in the morning,
So early in the morning,
So early in the morning, before the break of day.

The Orderly Officer said 'What's that?'
The Wing replied, 'There's a Halberstadt
Over Albert, so they say,
Go and drive the bugger away!'

Six unfortunate sleepy heads,
Known as pilots, left their beds.
And the Flight Commander wiped his eye
As he led the formation into the sky.

And we hadn't been gone five minutes, I'm sure,
When the 14th Wing rang up once more:
'It isn't a Hun – the patrol must stop!
It's only an old two-seater 'Sop!'

Then the mists began to rise
'Till they filled the wintry skies,
The patrol should have been back by nine:
At eleven o'clock there was still no sign.

Then old Jack Russell began to swear.
He said, 'Chaps, oh dear, oh dear!
What has happened I want to know!'
When a message came from our CO:

'Oxo's down by Combles way,
Foster's crashed at Dieppe, they say,
Nobby's on some French aerodrome,
None of the others has yet got home.'

Now at last my song is done,
And as you see there was no Hun.
The moral of it is very clear.
Crescendo – 'We must have much less hot air!'

Narrative songs were clearly popular, and these were sung to the popular tunes of the period, perhaps because they tended to be very long. One of the shorter examples used the tune of 'Alabama Choo-choo' and was known as:

The Dawn Patrol
When the Dawn Patrol sets out to cross the lines,
I'll be there, I'll do my share.
When we see some buses quickly climbing east,
We're far too low, that's von Bulow
And his Albatri.
The beggar's on my tail, I'm turning rather pale,
My bus seems like a snail as down I go, Oh,
Why can't that damned Archie stop?
Gee, I've gone and shot my prop,
Have a heart, have a heart,
'Cos I'm on the Dawn Patrol.

When the Dawn Patrol gets over to Cambrai,
I'm with them still, against my will,
When we see some bright red buses underneath,
We've done it once too often, that's Richtofen
And his Albatri.
He's stalling up at me, he's shooting up at me,
Why can't the leader see those Huns below, Oh,
Only one last thing I ask,
Where's my blasted brandy flask,
Have a heart, have a heart,
For we're on the Dawn Patrol.

In similar style was the following, which not only attempted (successfully) to describe the adrenaline surge felt in battle, albeit in somewhat schoolboy terms, but also touches on what today would be called 'friendly fire'.

Over the Lines
We were flying in formation and contrived to keep our station,
Though the wind was trying hard to sweep the sky.
And we watched the puffs of powder, heard the Archies booming louder
And we didn't need to stop to reason why.
With the German lines below us, and a gale that seemed to throw us
Into nowhere, as it would a schoolboy's kite,
We went skimming through the ether always keeping close together
And we felt the joy of battle grip us tight.

Then from out of the horizon which we kept our eager eyes on
Swept the Fokkers in their deadly fanwise dash.
Soon the Vickers guns were cracking and a couple started backing
Whilst a third was sent down flaming in a flash.
How we blessed our Bristol Fighters as we closed in with the blighters,
And we zoomed and banked and raced them through the air.
We abandoned our formation, but we won the situation,
Won it easily with four machines to spare.
Then Archie burst around us and the beggar nearly found us,
But we dived towards our lines without delay,
And we finished gay and merry from a binge of gin and sherry,
For we knew we lived to see another day.

An aircraft type and unit loyalty combine again with perhaps more than
a hint of 'friendly fire' (or at least misidentification) in the following song,
sung to the tune of 'We've Come Up from Somerset'.

The Song of Forty-six
Oh, we've come up from Forty-six,
We're the Sopwith Pups, you know,
And wherever the beastly Hun may be,
The Sopwith Pups will go.
And if you want a proper scrap,
Don't chase BEs any more,
For we'll come up and do the job,
Because we're Forty-six!

Naturally morale could be kept up by poking fun at the enemy, as in the
tongue-twisting lines bellowed to the tune of 'Sister Susie's Shirts for
Soldiers' and known as:

Heavy Handed Hans
Heavy Handed Hans flies Halberstadters.
In handy Halberstadters for a flight our Hans does Start.
His Oberst says 'Oh dash it!
I fear that he will crash it.'
See how Heavy Handed Hans ham-handles handy Halberstadts.

The enemy was again the butt of the nine lines which, sung to the tune
of 'Hush-a-Bye, Baby', were known as:

Hans vos my name
Hans vos my name, und a pilot vos I.
Out mit von Karl I vent for a fly.
Pilots of Kultur ve vos, dere's no doubt,
Each of us flew in an Albatros scouts.
Ve looked for BEs for to strafe mit our guns.
Ven last I saw Karl, I knew he vos dones,
For right on his tail vere two little Sops.
Oh, hush-a-bye, baby, on the tree tops!

The enemy also featured in the many verses of another popular and distinctly indelicate piece with a nonsense chorus, the verse running:

Two German officers crossed the Rhine, skiboo, skiboo.
To love the women and taste the wine, skiboo, skiboo.
Oh, landlord, you've a daughter fair,
With lily-white arms and golden hair.
Skiboo, skiboo, skiboolby boo, skidam, dam, dam.

Pilots figured in the majority of RFC mess songs, but just occasionally others were remembered. The following was dedicated to observers. It was rendered to the tune 'A Bachelor Gay' from the hit show at Daly's Theatre in Cranbourn Street. By 1917 'The Maid of the Mountains' had run to 1,325 performances. It was regarded as belonging exclusively to 22 Squadron RFC and was called: 'You're only a PBO' ('Poor Bloody Observer'):

When you get in the old machine to start on a damned OP
You cover yourself with tons of clothes and they're all of them NBG,
The pilot sits near the engine's warmth, his body with heat aglow
While you must stand in the back and cuss
Till the ice on your whiskers stalls the bus –
You're only a PBO, yes only a PBO.

Chorus:
At seventeen he's shooting rather badly at a Pfalz of tender blue,
At fifteen thou. point out sadly some Huns of a different hue,
At ten or twelve he's shooting rather madly at six or eight or more.
When he fancies he is past hope
Fires a long burst as a last hope,
And the Hun spins down on fire to the floor!

When you're doing an escort stunt and the Huns get on your tail,
You fire and aim till you see 'em flame and down they go like hail.
Alas, the pilot's jealous scorn is a thing we learn to know.
You may get twenty Huns in flames,
Don't think they'll believe your claims,
For you're only a PBO, yes only a PBO.

Chorus:
We all of us know the case when the pilot came home alone,
No doubt it was only a slight mistake, but the altitude's clearly shown,
He suddenly shoved his joystick down as far as it would go.
'Hello, you seem to have gone,' he said.
'I fear you must be somewhat dead,
But you're only a PBO, yes only a PBO.'

Chorus:
When you're flying an old Nine A on a bumpy, windy day,
And your engine begins to splutter out and you think you have lost
your way,
Be careful to keep your head to wind if you want to reduce your glide,
And sideslip over a downwind fence,
If you want to remain inside your field,
If you want to remain inside, if you want to remain inside.

Chorus:
At eighty-five you head he in so nicely, a glide you should not exceed;
At seventy-five you flatten out precisely, and still you've got lots of
speed.
But at fifty you'll be stalling,
And you realise that you're falling,
And you crash her as she's never crashed before!

An alternative first verse existed which from the third line onwards ran
as follows:

The pilot, HE sits in the engine sump
His body with 'eat aglow!
But YOU must sit in the back and cuss
'Till the ice on your whiskers stalls the bus-
You're only a PBO!
A miserable PBO.

The original of a parody which was popular throughout the Corps but
chiefly with 46 Squadron was this piece, which retained its nursery-rhyme
name. There were many verses, only the first being quoted here:

Cock Robin
Who killed Cock Robin?
'I', said the Hun,
With my Spandau gun,
I killed Cock Robin.'

Chorus:
All the planes in the air,
Went a-dipping and a-throbbing,
When they heard of the death of poor Cock Robin,
When they heard of the death of poor Cock Robin.

Sung to the tune of 'Asleep in the Deep' was another narrative song:

Stormy the Night
Stormy the night and lowering the sky,
Proudly the 'plane doth ride.
Hark how the passenger's startled cry
Rings as he clutches the side.
These in the cockpit the pilot lays,
Cursing his ballast, who weakly prays.
Tho' death be near, he knows no fear,
For at his side are a dozen beer.

Chorus:
Brightly the flares from the landing ground blaze,
Bidding us list to the hint it conveys.
Pilot take care, pilot take care.
Hundreds have crashed, so beware, beware.
Many brave hearts have neglected their charts,
So beware, beware.
What of the tempest the following morn?
There is no trace or sign.
Save where the wreckage bestrews the corn,
Peacefully the sun doth shine.
But ere the wild, raging storm did stop
Two gallant airmen were caught on the hop,
No more to roam, afar from home,
No more forced landings because of the Gnome.

A ditty that must have proved difficult to sing with a few jugs of beer on board, was the piece using both the tune and the title of: 'In Other Words':

I was fighting a Hun in the heyday of youth,
Or perhaps 'twas a Nieuport or Spad.
I put in a burst at a moderate range
And it didn't seem too bad.
For he put down his nose in a curious way,
And as I watched, I am happy to say:

Chorus:
He descended with unparalleled rapidity,
His velocity 't'would beat me to compute.
I speak with unimpeachable veracity,
With evidence complete and absolute.
He suffered from spontaneous combustion
As towards terrestrial sanctuary he dashed,
In other words – he crashed!

I was telling the tale when a message came through
To say 'twas a poor RE8.

The news somewhat dashed me, I rather supposed
I was in for a bit of hate.
The CO approached me. I felt rather weak,
For his face was all mottled, and when he did speak

Chorus:
He strafed me with unmitigated violence,
With wholly reprehensible abuse.
His language in its blasphemous simplicity
Was rather more exotic than abstruse.
He mentioned that the height of his ambition
Was to see your humble servant duly hung.
I returned to Home Establishment next morning,
In other words – I was strung!

As a pilot in France I flew over the lines
And there met an Albatros scout.
It seemed that he saw me, or so I presumed;
His manoeuvres left small room for doubt.
For he sat on my tail without further delay
Of my subsequent actions I think I may say:

Chorus:
My turns approximated to the vertical,
I deemed it most judicious to proceed.
I frequently gyrated on my axis
And attained colossal atmospheric speed,
I descended with unparalleled momentum,
My propeller's point of rupture I surpassed,
And performed the most astonishing evolutions,
In other words – * *** ****!

I was testing a Camel on last Friday week
For the purpose of passing her out.
And before fifteen seconds of flight had elapsed
I was filled with a horrible doubt,
As to whether intact I should land from my flight.
I half thought I'd crash – and half thought quite right!

Chorus:
The machine seemed to lack coagulation,
The struts and sockets didn't rendezvous,
The wings had lost their super-imposition,
Their stagger and their incidental, too!
The fuselage developed undulations
The circumjacent fabric came unstitched
Instanter was reduction to components,
In other words – she's pitched!

Some RFC songs were extremely long, the following being an example.
It had clearly been based on 'The Wreck of the Hesperus', a poem that

described the loss of a schooner of that name in the previous century. The parody was appropriately entitled 'The Wreck of the Old FE.'

It was an old FE2b,
That flew the wintry sky;
The pilot had taken a second AM*
To bear him company.

Red were his eyes as the crimson rose,
His nose like the dawn of day;
His feet as cold as a mess-room stove
As they ploughed their chilly way.

The skipper he sat in the pilot's seat,
His heart was in his mouth,
As he watched how the veering wind did blow
The clouds now west, now south.

Then up spake the observer bold,
With a gesture of his hand,
'I'm hanged if I know where the hell we are,
So hurry up and land.'

'Last week the sky was full of planes,
Today no planes I see.'
But the pilot spat on his aneroid,
And a scornful laugh laughed he.

Higher and higher he climbed the bus,
And looked for his escort bold;
But they were down in the mess-room hut
(If you wish the truth to be told).

Down came the storm and smote amain
The FE in her strength;
She shuddered and stalled, like a frightened steed,
Then dropped a cable's length.

'Lie down, lie down, my little AM,
And do not tremble so;
For I can weather the toughest gale
That ever wind did blow.'

'Oh Captain! I hear a pop-pop-pop;
Oh say, what may that be?'
'It's a blasted Hun on my blinking tail',
And he turned around to see.

*Air Mechanic.

'Oh Captain! I see two crosses black;
Oh say, what may it be?'
'Grab hold of the Lewis and shoot, you fool,
And don't stand talking to me.'

'Oh Captain! I don't understand the gun,
Oh say, what shall I do?'
But the Captain's words were wafted back,
And broke the prop in two.

Then down through the fleecy clouds below,
The FE drifted fast;
The observer thought of his future,
And the pilot thought of his past.

And ever the fitful gusts between
A sound – what can it be?
'Twas Archie paying his last respects
To the wreck of the old FE.

The trenches were right below her bows,
She drifted a dreary wreck,
And the Captain swore if he DID get down,
He'd break the blighter's neck.

She struck where the verdant, waving grass
Looked soft as a downy bed;
But a couple of cows got in her way,
So she quietly stood on her head.

Full twenty yards across the ground
The luckless pair were cast.
'I think I'll go,' said the luckless AM
'The danger is not past.'

At daybreak in a barren field,
He still was running round;
Whilst close behind the pilot came,
Forever gaining ground.

The oil was frozen on his face,
His mouth was full of sand,
But nearer came the avenger grim
With joystick in his hand.

Such was the wreck of the old FE
In the land of rain and mud.
Lord, save us all from such an AM,
And make the weather dud.

But popular songs remained the sources of tunes such as that from 'Tonight's the Night' which retained the same name as its original:

The Only, Only Way
If by some delightful chance,
When you're flying out in France,
Some old Boche machine you meet,
Very slow and obsolete,
Don't turn round and watch your tail,
Tricks like that are getting stale;
Just put down your bally nose,
And murmur, 'Chaps, here goes!'

Chorus:
It's the only, only way,
It's the only trick to play;
He's the only Hun, you're the only Pup,
And he's only getting the wind right up;
So go on and do not stop
'Till his tail's damn near your prop.
If he only crashes this side in flames,
Well, you'll only know they'll believe your claims.
So keep him right
In the Aldis sight.
It's the o-o-o-only way!

Occasionally someone would be inspired to compose a musical piece that was both topical and original, but once again they were based around well-known tunes. A case of this was to be found in the parody 'Chingford a la Chu Chin Chow' where for the Christmas Entertainment in 1917 the Robbers' Chorus from the West End production was presented as:

We are the party of the ground,
We spend our lifetime swinging props.
Through mud we grope for oil and dope
Until the flying stops.
And after that we clean machines
With cotton waste and paraffin;
Then clean the shed and off to bed,
Of course we never clean ourselves.

But Chingford was equipped with Avro 504s and Alcolom's 'Any Time's Kissing Time' from the same show reappeared as:

People have slandered our 80 Gnomes,
Laughed at our inlet valve springs;
Though they have conked with us far from home,
Broken exhaust valves and springs,
Many a bloke crashed by a choke
Going to civil life sings:

Youth is the time for flying
So the prospectuses say.
Why do they keep on supplying
Gnomes with their treacherous ways?
If I'd been taught on DHs
I'd not have committed this crime.
But still it's so, we have to go
E'er we've finished our flying time.

Of course authentically worded popular songs were also in vogue, among them being 'She's got a hole in her stocking', 'Some girl has got to darn his socks', 'Sister Susie', 'Hello my Dearie', 'I'm Lonesome for You' and 'Another Little Drink'. But inevitably the fact that a flyer's operational time on the Western Front averaged only three weeks, the thought of sudden death occasionally broke in with the aid of such songs as 'When I Die'.

And when I die,
Don't bury me at all;
Just pickle my bones
In alcohol.
Put a bottle of booze
At my head and my feet,
And then I know,
My bones will keep.

Perhaps the grimmest of all the songs in the RFC's repertoire was handed down from a regiment billeted in a cholera-stricken camp in India, long before the days of flying:

Who dreads to the dust returning?
Who shrinks from the sable shore?
Where the high and haughty yearning
Of the soul shall be no more.

Ho, stand to your glasses, steady,
This world is a world of lies;
A cup to the dead already,
'Hurrah for the next man that dies!'

Despite the brave face these men wore in company, death was never far from their thoughts, and it is small wonder that at some time every RFC mess echoed to the plaintive strains of 'When This Ruddy War is Over'.

FACTS AND FIGURES

COMFORTS ORGANISATIONS AND MEDICAL CARE

Royal Flying Corps Hospital: 37 Bryanston Square, London W1, and 82 Eaton Square, London SW1. (Hon. Treasurer: Mr Walter Field)

Royal Flying Corps Aid Committee: Surrey House, Marble Arch, London W1. (Hon. Treasurer: Lady Henderson)

Royal Naval Air Service Comforts Fund Committee: London and Midland Bank, 129 Bond Street, London W1. (Parcels to Mrs Henry Balfour, Headington, Oxford.)

Royal Flying Corps Club: 13 Bruton Street, London W1. (Founded by Lieutenant-Colonel W.C. Bersey in January 1917.)

GOVERNMENT OFFICES

The Air Board: Room 242, The War Office, Whitehall, London SW1.

Royal Flying Corps Despatch Office: Masons Yard, Duke Street, St James, London SW1.

The Central Ferry Pilots' Pool: Portman Square, Baker Street, London W1.

Headquarters, No. 18 Home Defence Wing RFC: 15 Albemarle Street, London W1. (This Wing was formed on 25 March 1916 and was commanded by Lieutenant-Colonel Fenton.

SELECTED ABBREVIATIONS

AAP	Aircraft Acceptance Park
AM	Air Mechanic
AP	Aircraft Park
ARS	Aeroplane Repair Section
ASD	Aeroplane Supply Depot
ATA	Air Transport Auxiliary (Second World War)
AT&T	Air Transport & Travel Company
BE	Bleriot Experimental
CFS	Central Flying School
CMG	Companion of the Order of St Michael and St George

Flt/Sgt	Flight Sergeant
GHQ	General Headquarters
GOC	General Officer Commanding
GS	General Service (Wagon)
HD	Home Defence
HMA	His Majesty's Airship
KB	Kite Balloon
MW	Military Wing (of the RFC)
PC10	A khaki-green dope for upper surfaces of aircraft
PC12	A similar dope to the above but of a redder hue; used on aircraft based in the Middle East
PFO	Probationary Flying Officer (RNAS)
QMAAC	Queen Mary's Army Auxiliary Corps
QM	Quarter-Master
RAMC	Royal Army Medical Corps
RAS	Reserve Aeroplane Squadron. Two aircraft from these units were supplied to bases near London for night defence work in October 1916
RAE	Royal Aircraft Establishment
RAF	Royal Aircraft Factory (until 31 March 1918)
RAF	Royal Air Force (used from 1 April 1918)
RE	Royal Engineers
RFA	Royal Field Artillery
RFC	Royal Flying Corps
RNAS	Royal Naval Air Service
SD	Stores Depot
SOC	Struck Off Charge
TDS	Training Depot Station
TS	Training Squadron
u/t	Under training
WAAC	Women's Army Auxiliary Corps
WAAFC	Women's Auxiliary Air Force Corps
WCS	Women Civilian Subordinates
WES	Women's Emergency Service
WLMD	Women's Legion Motor Drivers
WRAF	Women's Royal Air Force
WS	Wireless School

COMPARATIVE COMMISSIONED RANKS

RFC/RAF	RNAS	RAF (Current)
Field Marshal	–	Marshal of the RAF
General	–	Air Chief Marshal
Lieutenant-General	–	Air Marshal
Major General	–	Air Vice Marshal
Brigadier-General	–	Air Commodore
Colonel	–	Group Captain
Lieutenant-Colonel	Wing Commander	Wing Commander

RFC/RAF	RNAS	RAF (Current)
Major	Squadron Commander	Squadron Leader
Captain	Flight Commander	Flight Lieutenant
Lieutenant	Flight Lieutenant	Flying Officer
Second Lieutenant	Flight Sub-Lieutenant*	Pilot Officer

(Flight Sub-Lieutenant was a Warrant rank.)

RNAS ranks were abolished in favour of Army ones with effect from 1 April 1918 and these continued in use until they were replaced by the RAF ranks still in current use on 27 August 1919. The designation of the Army rank of Brigadier-General was replaced by the term 'Colonel-Commandant' soon after 1918. The original title was restored in 1928, but now abbreviated to 'Brigadier'.

EQUIVALENT RNAS/ROYAL NAVY RANKS

RNAS	RN
Wing Commander	Commander
Squadron Commander	Lieutenant Commander
Flight Commander	Lieutenant
Flight Lieutenant	Sub-Lieutenant
Flight Sub-Lieutenant	Acting Sub-Lieutenant

THE SIZE OF THE AIR BATTALION, ROYAL ENGINEERS

Strength on formation, 1 April 1911: 160 (including 14 officers)
Aircraft: 5 (1 Bleriot XII, 1 Farman III, 1 Paulhan, 1 de Havilland SE1, 1 Howard Wright)

THE SIZE OF THE RFC (PERSONNEL)

Date	Strength
January 1915	2,559 (including 223 officers)
July	6,526 (including 605 officers)
January 1916	16,229 (including 1,341 officers)
July	35,819 (including 3,107 officers)
January 1917	55,931 (including 6,739 officers)
July	85,163 (including 8,955 officers)
January 1918	121,518 (including 13,741 officers)
March	144,078 (including 18,286 officers)

GENERAL FLYING CASUALTIES AT UNIT LEVEL, 1914–1918

Wounded or injured:	7,245 (including 5,369 officers)
Missing or captured:	3,212 (including 2,839 officers)
Killed:	6,166 (including 4,579 officers)

Not all of those lost died in action, but official figures give no indication of wastage through accidents. For flyers, the following narrative will suffice as typical of the latter incidents.

Arthur James Maitland had been newly commissioned as a second lieutenant in 1917 and after completing his flying training, September found him proudly putting up his pilot's wings. He had volunteered to join the Royal Flying Corps in the previous May at eighteen years of age and on Friday the 21st, he telephoned his father John at Enfield with the glad news that he had been posted to Beddington Aerodrome in Surrey, a station that was even then known as Croydon after the nearest town of any size.

On the following day Arthur reported to Captain George Taylor who took the younger man on a flight in an Avro 504 to assess his ability. Finding Arthur a competent pilot, Taylor authorised the new officer to take up a Sopwith Pup, a type on which he had already had some experience. After the two had tested the engine together, Taylor lingered on the little aerodrome to watch his new pilot. Maitland made a normal take-off and climbed into the early evening sky to an altitude of some 2,500ft. Those on the ground noted that the pilot seemed determined to impress his casual audience on the ground, showing his confidence by rolling the machine four or five times before beginning a 'spinning dive' which was seemingly intended to end in a spectacular zoom from zero feet.

Among those watching his performance were Sergeant Harold Wood of the RFC and Lance Corporal Springate RAMC. Although the latter knew nothing about flying, he was uneasy at the low altitude from which the dive had begun, and on his own initiative he ordered the station's ambulance crew to stand by.

The inevitable crash took place in a field beside the lane that ran south beyond the eastern limits of the aerodrome. The impact broke Maitland's neck and fractured his skull: Captain H. Manners Holt RAMC, after examining the body, announced that death must have been instantaneous, a finding that the civil coroner had no hesitation in confirming.

The hazards of military flying began to concern many soon after the outbreak of war. Even Rudyard Kipling touched on the subject in his savage short story *Mary Postgate*, which appeared in the collection *A Diversity of Creatures*, published in 1915.

THE CENTRAL FLYING SCHOOL

Foundation authorisation: Army Order dated 23 April 1912
Funding: Shared by War Office and Admiralty
Administration: War Office
Area of site: 2,400 acres
Cost of temporary buildings: £25,000
Opened: 12 June 1912

First course: Commenced 17 August 1912
Second course: Commenced January 1913
First fatal crash: October 1913 (Major Merrick DSO)
Serviceable aircraft on charge, January 1913: 12
Additional aircraft received during period: 8

AIRCRAFT MARKINGS – AN OUTLINE

From the creation of the RFC/RNAS until their earliest appearance in France, British military aircraft had flown in a clear dope finish, innocent of all markings except a number on the rudder according to the differing Army or Royal Navy allocations. Since it soon became clear that some form of national marking was required under war conditions (Lieutenant Joubert de la Ferte was later to recall the roar of musketry from friend and foe alike which greeted the appearance of an aeroplane over the trenches), an Army Order dated 2 October 1914 gave details of the 'form most suitable' for the Union Flags to be borne under the wing-tips and on the rudders of aircraft, adding 'the colours to be very bright'.

To these were added, with effect from 11 December, roundels similar to those already in use by France but with the order of the colours reversed; these were also carried on each side of the rudder and often on the upper surface of tailplanes and elevators. Here, as on the wings, their diameter occupied the full cord. Union Flags were subsequently discarded.

Meanwhile RNAS aircraft were marked with a red ring under the wings between 8 December 1914 and (at least officially) 1 November 1915. Sometimes the ring had a narrow white outline, the centre being a white disc, although the near-white of the clear-doped fabric was sometimes regarded as sufficient here. These markings gave way to three-colour roundels although there was nothing to stop the temporary addition of a blue disc in the centre of a red naval ring, making them in effect French markings! Both the RFC and RNAS adopted vertical rudder stripes with effect from June 1915. These were identical to those of the French, with the red area aft also being frequently carried across the elevators of some naval aircraft, a fashion which continued infrequently until 1918.

From 8 May 1916 khaki-green PC10 or PC12 dope (a redder shade for protection in areas outside Europe) was adopted for upper surfaces and since the blue outer ring of the roundels tended to merge with this at a distance, a 1in wide white border was added with effect from 15 July. Night-flying aircraft were doped over all in dull black until the introduction of 'Nivo', a dark grey-green shade, late in 1918. National markings on the 'black' doped planes consisted of a plain white ring, but most later aircraft had red and blue only, although there were discrepancies.

Both the red and blue shades tended to be unsatisfactory at first, the Oxford blue in particular being prone to fade. In due course they were replaced by vermilion and Post Office red. Roundel proportions were officially 1:3:5, which they still remain on the RAF ensign.

RAF SCHOOLS IN NOVEMBER 1918

The training programme was systematised by Brigadier-General E.R. Ludlow-Hewitt.

Schools of Aeronautics: Bath, Bristol, Cheltenham, Denham, Oxford, Reading.

Schools of Aerial Fighting: East Fortune, Freiston, Marske-by-Sea, Sedgeford, Turnberry.

Schools of Navigation and Bomb Dropping: Andover, Stonehenge, Thetford.

Observers' Schools: Eastchurch, Hythe, Manston, New Romney.

Marine Operations School: Dover.

Ground Armament School: Uxbridge.

Wireless School: Chattis Hill.

School of Army Co-operation: Worthy Down (Winchester).

School of Photography, Map Reading and Reconnaissance: Farnborough.

Marine Observers' School: Andeburgh, Eastchurch.

Balloon Training Depots: Richmond Park, Roehampton.

Training Base and Schools: Lydd, Salisbury, Sheerness.

Flying Instructors' Schools: Ayr, Curragh, Gosport, Lilbourne, Redcar, Shoreham.

The RAF College at Cranwell was opened by Commodore Godfrey M. Paine in April 1916 and had been the RNAS Training Headquarters, also responsible for Calshot, Chingford, Eastbourne, Eastchurch, Redcar, Vendome (France) and Windermere, with disciplinary instruction at Crystal Palace (although earlier the Admiralty had relied on civilian schools for preliminary training).

THE RAF EAGLE

One only has to look at an RAF officer's uniform to find evidence that the Royal Air Force's roots lay in both the Royal Flying Corps and the Royal Naval Air Service; in addition, brown gloves are an echo of Army tradition, while rings indicating rank on cuffs are reminders of the Royal Navy. Cap badges, too, have a distinctly nautical look and it is still asked whether the bird in the centre represents an eagle or albatross. That it is the former was made clear by Admiralty Order No. 2, dated June 1914, which states that for the centre piece replacing the anchor on officers' caps 'The badge of an eagle will be worn by members of the RNAS'.

FROM RNAS TO RAF

However, although the bird on the RAF badge today resembles the original, the line of the wings is now more arched than before. When it was adopted in August 1918 it was superimposed on a circlet made up of a garter with a buckle bearing the motto of the former Royal Flying Corps; this design was discarded on the advice of the College of Arms in 1922 as 'heraldically incorrect' and it was replaced by a plain circlet with a sprig of laurel before its registration in the following year.

Responsibility for the RAF badge has long been a subject for debate, there being general agreement that it was designed by 'an anonymous clerk employed by Gieves Ltd, the tailors', and only now is it recognised to be the work of Mr George Lines, an embroidery draughtsman employed by Starkey Ltd of Beak Street, London W1. This company, described as 'Gold Lace Men and Embroiderers' was a subsidiary of 'Gieves of Old Bond Street', as the famous outfitters were known at the time, which had been set up to handle gold wire work (2½% gold, 7½% silver, polished with potassium cyanide), Gieves not having the facilities for specialist embroidery.

It was common knowledge among the staff that Mr Lines, who had seen service during the First World War as an army cook, was responsible for the RAF eagle badge. In fact he had prepared a number of designs which had been submitted to the authorities via Gieves as a result of a wide appeal for ideas. There were also several submissions from Waterlow Brothers and Leyton, the engravers and printers who, according to an old file in the Ministry of Defence archives, were paid 20 guineas for their trouble. Among four designs put forward by the firm of Langford Jones, two strongly resembled the final choice.

Members of the armed forces were also asked to suggest designs, and as a result Warrant Officer Charles Pepper RN, then employed at the Navy's seaplane drawing office in the Strand, submitted one that was seemingly inspired by the RNAS cap badge but took the form of an albatross. Mr Pepper explained 'I wanted to symbolise mastery of the air. The enemy was already using the eagle and the fact that I was in the Navy led me to think of the albatross.' The final sketch was based on a stuffed bird exhibited in the British Museum. The letter from Sir William Weir,* secretary to the RAF, acknowledging receipt of Pepper's design, has long been cherished and preserved by his family.

The final Royal Air Force crest was described in Air Ministry Order A666 as 'In front of a circle inscribed with the motto *Per Ardua Ad Astra*, and ensigned with the Imperial Crown, an eagle volant and effronte, the head lowered and to the sinister.'

The RAF badge is therefore entirely appropriate, since it was designed by a former soldier and 'seconded' by a member of the Royal Navy, so that it may be said to fairly represent the illustrious twin sources from which the Royal Air Force sprang: the Royal Flying Corps and the Royal Naval Air Service.

---

*William Douglas Weir (1877–1959) had earlier been Scottish Director of Munitions (1915–16), Controller of Aeronautical Supplies (1917–18), Director-General of Aircraft Production (1918) and Secretary of State for Air (1918–19). He was knighted in 1917, received a baronetcy in 1918 and became Viscount Weir in 1938.

VALEDICTION

'This is the tale of the young men who went up and fought and died on just such a summer's afternoon as this.'

Major Joycelyn Bradford, June 1955

BIBLIOGRAPHY

Anon. *The Work and Training of the Royal Flying Corps*, Illustrated London News, 1917

Anon. *The Work and Training of the Royal Naval Air Service*, Illustrated London News, 1917

Bickel, L.E. *Flying, Banking & Music*, Bournemouth Local Studies Publications, 1986

Bruce, J.M. *The Aeroplanes of the Royal Flying Corps (Military Wing)*, Putnam, 1982

Butcher, P.E. *Skill and Devotion*, Radio Modeller Book Division, 1971

Chamier, Air Commodore J.A. *The Birth of the Royal Air Force*, Pitman, 1943

Cole, C. and Cheesman, E.F. *The Air Defence of Britain 1914–1918*, Putnam, 1984

Congdon, Squadron Leader Philip S.M. *Per Ardua Ad Astra*, Airlife, 1987

Coppens, Major W. *Days on the Wing*, Aviation Book Club, 1938

Ege, Lennant, *Balloons and Airships*, Blandford, 1973

Escott, Squadron Leader Beryl E. *Women in Air Force Blue*, PSL, 1989

Hammerson, Sir John (ed.) *ABC of the RAF*, Amalgamated Press, 1943

Hering, Squadron Leader Peter G. *Customs and Traditions of the Royal Air Force*, Gale & Polden, 1961

Johns, W.E. (ed.) *Popular Flying*, John Hamilton, 1932–39

McCudden, Major J.B. *Five Years in the Royal Flying Corps*, John Hamilton, 1918/1930

Robertson, Bruce. *The Army and Aviation*, Robert Hale, 1981

Tredrey, F.D. *Pioneer Pilot*, Peter Davies, 1976

Wilson, H.W. *The Great War*, Amalgamated Press, 1914–1919

INDEX

Military Aeroplane Competition, 13
Military Trials, 13
Millar, Miss Gertie, 59
Moore-Brabazon, J.T.C., 140
Moseley, O., 178
Motor vehicles,
 Clement-Talbot tenders, 60
 Crossley tenders, 24, 60
 Daimler tenders, 60
 Douglas motor-cycles, 60
 Leyland 3-ton lorries, 60
 Mercedes tenders, 60
 mobile darkrooms, 139
 mobile telephone exchanges, 60
 Phelan & Moore motor-cycles 60
 Rolls-Royce armoured cars, 122
 Triumph motor-cycles, 60

Naval air stations, 106
Neagle, Miss Anna, 180
Neuve Chapelle, battle of, 124
Novello, I., 180

Palmer, R., 180
Park, K.R., 115
Payne, J., 180
Personnel wastage, 202
Photography, 139
 cameras, 140–2
 Photography Experimental Section
  140
 stereoscopy, 141–3
Portal, C.F.A., 115–16
Puttees, 36

RAF Association, 177
RAF Schools, 31–2
Ranken darts, 11
RFC,
 Army distribution, 19
 distribution (1916–17), 22–3
 Experimental Branch, 13–14
 first victory, 121–2
 Military Wing, 10
 Naval Wing, 34, 39
 pay structure, 32
 School of Navigation, 25
Roehampton Park, 54–5
Rollestone Camp, 55
Royal Aero Club, 8
Royal Engineers, 9

Royston, R., 178
Russell, W.,
Russian Expedition, 150–7

Samson, C.R., 8, 24–5, 122
School of Ballooning, 2, 5, 55
School of Engineering, 2
Ships,
 HMS *Africa*, 10
 HMS *Birmingham*, 62
 HMS *Caledon*, 62
 HMS *Calliope*, 62
 HMS *Canning*, 62
 HMS *Daedalus*, 40
 HMS *Egandine*, 123–4
 HMS *Empress*, 124
 HMS *Furious*, 152
 HMS *Hermes*, 12
 HMS *Hibernia*, 10
 HMS *London*, 10
 HMS *Pegasus*, 152
 HMS *Pembroke II*, 24
 HMS *Penstemon*, 4
 HMS *Riviera*, 123–4, 155
 HMS *Vernon*, 10
 HMS *Vindictive*, 152
 RMS *Kildonan Castle*, 157
Smith-Barry, R.R., 27–9
Somme, battle of, 126–7, 134, 165

Tedder, A.W., 116
Tilley, J., 180
Travers, B., 180
Trefusis-Forbes, Miss, 179
Trenchard, Lady, 175

Uniforms, 32–50

Wakefield, H., 178
Wireless, 143–6
Women Civilian Subordinates, 167–8
Women's Army Auxiliary Corps,
 167–70
Women's Auxiliary Air Force Corps,
 167, 170
Women's Legion, 166–7
Women's Royal Air Force, 170–4
 'Mobiles'/'Immobiles', 171
Women's Royal Naval Service, 166, 175

Yarmouth, 13